Blake Edwards

Contemporary Film Directors in America

Series Editors: Peter Lehman (Arizona State University, USA) and
William Luhr (Saint Peter's University, USA)

The *Contemporary Film Directors in America* series focuses on recent and current film directors within the contexts of globalization and the convergence of the entertainment and technology industries. The definition of "American" includes film directors who have worked in America and with American production companies, regardless of citizenship, and the series considers hyphenate directors who are also writers and producers working in multiple media forms including radio, television, and film.

Blake Edwards: Film Director as Multitalented Auteur
William Luhr and Peter Lehman

Blake Edwards

Film Director as Multitalented Auteur

William Luhr and Peter Lehman

WILEY Blackwell

Contents

List of Figures

Preface

We met Blake Edwards for the first time in 1979 to interview him in his suite at the Sherry Netherland Hotel in New York. It was the beginning of a relationship that would last 30 years. We last saw him at the invitational opening of what would be his final one-man art show in 2009. During those three decades, we visited his film and theater sets as well as his art exhibitions and did a number of interviews with him in his company offices in Hollywood as well as in his New York townhouse and his home in Brentwood. We also published our books *Blake Edwards* and *Returning to the Scene: Blake Edwards, Volume 2*. Both of those books were written while he was in mid-career and focused entirely on films that he directed. This book is our third and final one about that remarkable career. We did not draw upon our set visits in our first two books, saving them for this final volume, which covers his entire career. Like our previous books, this one is a critical analysis of his films, but we have also expanded it to cover films he wrote but didn't direct and to include radio, television, theater, and art exhibitions. We use the interviews and our observations from watching him work only insofar as they shed light on his creative methods and mindset. This is not a biography, and we did not ask Blake or others about his personal life, though on a few occasions Blake brought up some issues he felt were relevant.

Since we quote from many unpublished conversations and interviews during our set visits, we have added an Appendix listing many of those we interviewed with the dates of the interviews. The interviews have all been transcribed and quotations from them are edited and accurate. When we have relied upon conversations that were not taped we summarize the point rather than quote it directly. Unless we were both present, we only use conversations that we documented with each other at the time.

A word about our publications. Everything we have each done throughout our long collaboration on this project and all our projects has been part of an equal co-author relationship. In that spirit, we have always rotated the order of our names between each article and also between each book. For example, our previous book, *Thinking About Movies: Watching,*

Questioning and Enjoying had Peter's name first, so this book has Bill's name first. The position of our names in no way implies that one of us was the "lead" author or did more than the other. In that spirit, whenever possible we have published our interviews without attributing who asked which questions.

It has been a great privilege for us as film scholars to get to know Blake and watch him work, as we hope this book demonstrates.

Acknowledgments

This book draws heavily on research on Blake Edwards's films conducted for over three decades. We acknowledge all the many industry and creative contributors who granted us interviews and gave generously of their time and expertise for the book, but we want to give special thanks to the following who gave so much support to us: Tony Adams, Gene Schwam, Ken Wales, Dick Gallup, and James Hirsch.

We are also deeply indebted to our two research assistants who worked with us throughout the process. Elana Shearer organized and scanned many screenplays and interviews and transcribed several. We were new to using Google Docs as collaborators, and whenever we had problems, she quickly solved them for us with good cheer. Jessica Conn did the screen grabs and researched the copyright credits for them. She also was in charge of submitting the manuscript and the screen grabs to Wiley throughout the production process and she continued to guide our use of Google Docs with good cheer. Without Elana and Jessica we'd still be scratching our heads and looking for stuff. Thanks also to Eric Monder.

Finally, this book would not have been possible without more than three decades of support and cooperation from Blake Edwards. He granted us countless interviews, gave us a standing invitation to visit any of his sets, arranged for us to interview many of his business and creative associates, including Julie Andrews, who was always generous, gracious, and complimentary about the importance of our work on Blake's films. We cannot imagine a greater compliment.

From William Luhr

I would like to thank the New York University Faculty Resource Network, along with Chris Straayer of NYU's Department of Cinema Studies, who have provided valuable research help and facilities, as has the staff of the Film Study Center of the Museum of Modern Art. Generous assistance has also come from the members of the Columbia University Seminar on Cinema and Interdisciplinary Interpretation, particularly my co-chair, Cynthia Lucia, as well as

Krin Gabbard, David Sterritt, Pamela Grace, Martha Nochimson, Robert T. Eberwein, and Christopher Sharrett. Our fruitful and intellectually stimulating seminar has received constant support from Alice Newton, Pamela Guardia, Gessenia Alvarez-Lazauskas, and Summer Hart of the University Seminars Office. At Saint Peter's University, gratitude goes to the President Eugene Cornacchia, Academic Vice President Frederick Bonato, Academic Dean WeiDong Zhu, English Department Chair Scott Stoddart, Robert Adelson and the Office of Information Technology, the members of the Committee for the Professional Development of the Faculty, John M. Walsh, Rachel Wifall, Jonathan Brantley, Daisy DeCoster, Barbara Kuzminski, Deborah Kearney, David Surrey, Jon Boshart, Leonor I. Lega, and Joseph McLaughlin for generous support, technical assistance, and research help. Keith Ditkowsky and Joseph Mannion have been of valuable help. As always, I am deeply indebted to my parents, Eilleen and Walter; my aunts, Helen and Grace; my brothers, Walter and Richie; as well as Bob, Carole, Jim, Judy, and David.

From Peter Lehman

I would like to thank the Arizona State University deans who supported and encouraged my research and administrative work: College of Liberal Arts and Sciences Deans David Young and Quentin Wheeler and associate and area deans Len Gordon, Deborah Losse, and Neal Lester. Special thanks to President Michael Crow for his support for granting Blake Edwards an honorary Doctor of Humane Letters degree and for participating in a special hooding ceremony with the ASU Symphony Orchestra celebrating Blake's films and the music from them. Special thanks also to Timothy Russell for working with me in planning the concert and for his superlative conducting. I still hear the opening and closing performances of Henry Mancini's theme from *Peter Gunn* pulsating in my memory of that very special evening. Finally, Joseph Buenker, Associate Librarian, Humanities, went above and beyond the call of duty researching reviews of Edwards's films in *Variety*.

As always, I owe my wife Melanie Magisos more than I can ever acknowledge. I'm very lucky to be part of a family of movie lovers, including my brother Steve, my daughter Eleanor and her husband Jason, and my grandchildren Jonah and Lila. I grew up in a home with parents and a grandpa who were regular moviegoers. When my parents who were refugees from Nazi Germany first arrived in New York someone took them to Radio City Music Hall, where they saw their first Mickey Mouse cartoon, after which my mother with great affection nicknamed my father Mickey. And my father never tired of fondly recalling Charlie Chaplin eating his shoe in *The Gold Rush*, which he saw as a young man in Germany. Movies are powerful.

CHAPTER 1

Introduction: "Call Me Blake."

Today, Blake Edwards at best is primarily known to the public for ten films he directed at three points in his career beginning with *Breakfast at Tiffany's* and *The Days of Wine and Roses* in the early 1960s; followed by five mid-1960s to mid-1970s Pink Panther films; and culminating with *"10," S.O.B.,* and *Victor/Victoria* between 1979 and 1982. But this is only the tip of the proverbial iceberg. Edwards is rightly often considered the most important filmmaker of his generation. Yet even this overlooks the importance of his successful work in radio, television, and theater. It also excludes his extensive work in addition to directing as a writer, producer, and actor as well as his work as a studio artist. In this book we expand and refocus our understanding of this ceaselessly creative multimedia, multi-hyphenate artist, including major screenplays of films that were unproduced, a stage play script that has also not yet been produced, and a survey of his public one-man shows and retrospectives of his work as a studio artist featuring paintings and sculpture.

Although it is not widely known, Blake Edwards began his postwar filmmaking career in 1948 with a B Western, *Panhandle*, which he cowrote and coproduced and in which he acted. He followed that with another B Western,

Blake Edwards: Film Director as Multitalented Auteur, First Edition.
William Luhr and Peter Lehman.
© 2023 John Wiley & Sons Ltd. Published 2023 by John Wiley & Sons Ltd.

which he once again cowrote and coproduced. These were very low-budget films for minor studios, Monogram and Allied Artists. Edwards did not rise to sustained public prominence as a film director until over a decade later, as mentioned above, when he made *Breakfast at Tiffany's* (1961), *Days of Wine and Roses* (1962), and *The Pink Panther* (1963), all of which were released by prestigious, high-visibility studios (Paramount, Warner Brothers, and United Artists respectively). Yet, between 1948 and the early 1960s, Blake Edwards burst upon the scene as a writer-producer-director-actor in radio, television, and film. He was everywhere doing virtually everything.

We will tell that story in Chapter 2, but we begin here for several reasons. We want to briefly situate Edwards within the historical context of profound changes within the film and television industries between 1948, when he began his career, and 1993, when he directed his last theatrical film; we want to survey the current state of scholarship on Edwards; and we want to outline our goals for this book, where we will minimize repetition from our earlier two books and the work of others since then.

Blake Edwards grew up in Hollywood and often referred to himself as a third-generation filmmaker since his step-grandfather, J. Gordon Edwards, was a silent film director most known for his popular films with Theda Bara. His stepfather, Jack McEdward, was an assistant director as well as a theater director. Distinguished film historian Kevin Brownlow told us a remarkable anecdote about this aspect of Edwards's family history during a Pordenone Silent Film Festival. Film archivists and historians had long presumed that all of J. Gordon Edwards's Theda Bara films had been destroyed in a fire. Tragically none had survived even in any international film archives. Remarkably, Brownlow was involved in the discovery and restoration of one of the lost films. Knowing of Edwards's pride in his family's place in film history, Brownlow invited Blake Edwards and Julie Andrews to a private screening. Edwards had never seen one of his step-grandfather's films, and he was deeply appreciative of the screening Brownlow had set up. Brownlow also sent us documents about that private screening. Clearly, the history of film, including the silent era, meant a great deal to Blake Edwards and became a significant influence on him as a filmmaker.

Although Edwards is nearly always thought of as a comedy filmmaker, we will focus attention on the many serious films he made, many of which are forgotten, overlooked, or marginalized. Careful analysis of these films foregrounds the complex and creative way he approached genre conventions in all his films, sometimes mixing genres, sometimes interrogating them, sometimes overwhelming convention with invention, and sometimes satirizing them. We will draw upon decades of research, including visiting the sets of four of his films and two of his plays, watching him work and talking with and interviewing him and many of his creative and business collaborators. We have also conducted formal interviews with dozens of actors, editors, set designers, producers and publicists, and so on.

Blake Edwards has been recognized as an auteur since the 1960s, a status that was highlighted in 1968 with the publication of Andrew Sarris's groundbreaking book, *The American Cinema: Directors and Directions 1929–1968*. Sarris had placed Edwards in the category "The Far Side of Paradise," meaning directors immediately below the giants in the Pantheon, even though much of Edwards's best work would come in the following decades.[1] That recognition began in France when Jean-Luc Godard praised *Mister Cory* (1957) as a serious artistic accomplishment in *Cahiers du Cinéma*.[2] Sarris perceptively summarized aspects of Edwards's worldview and film style. It was important at the time to make the case for directors as serious artists who could develop their unique visions within the Hollywood studio system, despite its emphasis on box office, stars, and genre entertainment. It was not uncommon in academia at that time for many to consider such directors as Ingmar Bergman and Federico Fellini as serious artists in contrast to the presumed mere Hollywood entertainers with their eye on the box office.

It is within this context that we published two books on Edwards's films: the first, simply titled *Blake Edwards* (1982), and the second, *Returning to the Scene: Blake Edwards, Volume 2* (1989).[3] In those volumes, we tried to expand Edwards's auteur standing in two ways. We based our readings of his films on detailed close formal analyses which stressed how such aspects of film style as composition, editing, screen space, and visual motifs all shape and form the story they tell. Secondly, we helped introduce and apply important work in contemporary film theory such as feminist and psychoanalytic theory to expand upon previous auteur criticism of Edwards's films.

Since the publication of our first two books on Edwards, another major critical study has appeared in 2009: Sam Wasson's excellent *A Splurch in the Kisser: The Movies of Blake Edwards*. He chronologically analyzes the films Edwards has directed. As the title suggests, he emphasizes how Edwards used visual style to build such central features of the films as gag structures. This strategy foregrounds how Edwards worked creatively as a filmmaker, minimizing abstract discussions of character, theme, plot, and worldview which could just as well be summarizing novels instead of films. Rather than attempt to footnote every possible reference to his book, we will simply acknowledge its general importance to our work. We published our second book on Edwards on January 1, 1989, and Wasson's book came 20 years later, and the year before Edwards died. As such Wasson covers all the late-period films released after we finished writing our second book in 1989. At this point in time, we recommend that readers seeking an introduction to the films of Blake Edwards begin with *A Splurch in the Kisser*. If some of our points seem similar at times, it does not mean there is a direct influence. We have been working on this book for several decades, and much of our research and the directions of our argument took place prior to reading Wasson's book. For example, we have analyzed Edwards's gag structure in relation to what Edwards called "topping the topper topper," a style he credited to Leo McCarey and his work with Laurel and Hardy. There are connections between "topping the topper topper" and the "splurch." Another shared assumption with Wasson relates to genre: As we reviewed Edwards's entire career for this book, we were struck by the fact that all of his genre films, radio shows, and television series were unusual departures from the genre norms of the time, so much so that many of them could more accurately be described as genre mixes. Wasson, although focused on the films Edwards directed, makes the same point. Wasson generously credits us with influencing him, and we want to credit him with influencing us. It is due to Wasson's work that we decided we did not need to focus in detail on all the films that Edwards had made since our previous work, nor did we need to update our previous analyses. That has had a profound impact on the structure of this book, freeing us up to focus on different things.

In addition to Wasson's book, we are indebted to Richard Brody's brief, but profound, reevaluation of Edwards's career in his article "What to Stream: Blake Edwards's Masterwork Documentary of His Wife, Julie Andrews" in *The New Yorker Magazine*, March 26, 2020.[4] We were not even aware of the 1972 documentary *Julie* prior to reading this article, and now we have an entire chapter on it in this book. But Brody goes on to reassess Edwards's entire career, granting that "Edwards (who died in 2010) was a comedic genius, the most skilled and inspired director of physical comedy working in Hollywood in his time," but then, noting his dissatisfaction with various scenes within those films, he claims, "Yet Edwards has also made some of the best movies of modern times, including 'Experiment in Terror,' 'Days of Wine and Roses,' 'Wild Rovers,' and even 'Sunset,' which has been much, and wrongly, maligned, including by Edwards himself." The argument about these dramas, or "serious" films as they are, regrettably, often labeled since comedies can be just as serious as dramas, along with the documentary *Julie*, inspired us to devote an entire section of this book to chapter-length analyses of each of the nine non-comic films, including the four Brody singles out. We held these four films in very high regard long before reading Brody's article, and we had written about three of them, but his spirit of reevaluating the Edwards oeuvre in this fashion inspired us to be the first book to focus an entire section on

Edwards's non-comic films, which we will call "dramas" for short. Those are the *only* films directed by Edwards that we analyze in such a manner, devoting an entire chapter to each film. Our goal is not just to help change the limited notion of Blake Edwards as "a comic director" but to further explore the relationship between his comedies and these dramas. We were surprised by some of the discoveries we made.

In this book we emphasize three different areas of Edwards's work: In Chapter 2 we will look at his immensely productive early period in which he burst upon the scene in radio (*Richard Diamond, Private Detective*), television (*Peter Gunn*), and film (*Operation Petticoat*), to hint at what lies beneath the tip of the iceberg. We were fortunate to interview some key figures from that period, including writer-director Richard Quine; composer Henry Mancini; choreographer Miriam Nelson; actor Craig Stevens; and writer-producer-director Owen Crump, since Edwards worked in so many different capacities, beginning primarily as a writer for radio and cowriting a series of screenplays with Richard Quine. He moved up to directing when Quine moved from B films to A films and from Columbia to Universal. Edwards worked extensively with two major figures in this early period: Dick Powell in radio and television, and Richard Quine in film. Interestingly, Edwards only ever mentioned Powell to interviewers including us within one specific context – his abrupt transition from singing and dancing in musicals to being a tough *Film Noir* detective in *Murder, My Sweet* (1944). Yet Powell was also a model of a multimedia, multi-hyphenate creator working as an actor and producer in radio, television, and film and may have influenced Edwards to develop his career in that direction. And although both Powell and Quine worked repeatedly with Edwards when they were established figures and he was an up and coming figure, he never called either of them a mentor. Throughout most of his career, he saved that praise for Leo McCarey with whom he never worked but whom he knew well and with whom he had many discussions about filmmaking. McCarey was yet another writer-director-producer. Yet once again, Edwards repeats the same point every time: McCarey's style of developing visual gags in such a manner that, just when the spectator laughs and thinks it is over (the topper), he extends it in a new direction for another laugh (topping the topper) and the spectator laughs again at what they think is the surprising end to the gag only to have it extended yet again (topping the topper topper). And he always recounted the same example from a McCarey film. Not surprisingly, Edwards called this "topping the topper topper" and it would be the central model for much of the comedy which made him famous and won him critical acclaim. Powell, Quine, and McCarey, three writer-producer-directors, seem to be the most prominent formative figures in Edwards's early work. By the end of his career, however, as Sam Wasson reminds us, during a distinguished awards ceremony which we attended with Billy Wilder present, Edwards said, "Whether you know it or not, Billy, you have always been my mentor."[5]

As we situate Edwards historically as a writer-producer-director, it is important to remember that a long tradition of such hyphenates existed in Hollywood and that several of them also worked in various media and theatrical forms. This began during the silent era before the elaborate compartmentalization of later times emerged. A look at Charles Chaplin's credits in most of his films gives an indication of this. Chaplin was often the director, producer, star, writer, and at times composed the music and did the choreography. Our argument for the importance of Edwards as a multi-hyphenate, multimedia creator was not that he was an original (far from it) but, rather, that he became the most prominent such creator at a crucial moment in film history defining the post–World War II years up to the contemporary convergence of the entertainment and technology industries when such multi-hyphenate, multimedia creators became a new norm within a totally reorganized entertainment industry. Thus, he not only pointed to the past, but he also became an extraordinary link to the future. During his career both the nature of the film industry and the studio system, and their relationship with television, changed dramatically.

Under the Hollywood studio system when Edwards began, studios had actors and directors under contract and Edwards's relationship with Columbia Pictures' founder and president, Harry Cohn, as well as with director Richard Quine and star Frankie Laine was in that sense typical. Quine had a multipicture deal with Columbia to direct a series of films starring Mickey Rooney, and then the popular singer Frankie Laine. These were B films, meaning they had a smaller budget, shorter running times, and were intended as the second half of double features. In addition to their A features, studios such as Columbia frequently also produced such B features. When Quine was elevated to the status of directing larger-budget A features with established film stars, Edwards was assigned to direct the two films in the contracted Frankie Laine series. Edwards's start at Columbia thus epitomized many aspects of the studio system.

Edwards told us an anecdote about working with Cohn at Columbia. While he and Quine were in production on a film, Cohn called them into his office and complained about the film, saying it needed a scene with a moving speech. When Quine asked if he wanted something like Hamlet's soliloquy, Cohn replied, "No, something like 'To be or not to be'." Edwards lost it and doubled over with laughter. Cohn asked Quine, "What's the matter with your boy?" Edwards replied, "To be or not to be *is* Hamlet's soliloquy." Cohn then said, "You're fired." The studio heads had such power under that system.

When Edwards went to Universal to direct Tony Curtis in the first film that he had written by himself and, outside of the Frankie Laine B series, he was able to do so because of another feature of the studio system: studios often loaned a star or director to another studio. They loaned Richard Quine to Universal in 1954, where he directed Tony Curtis in *So This Is Paris*, a musical. Edwards was no longer under contract to Columbia, and undoubtedly it was Quine's presence at Universal along with his having directed Tony Curtis that paved the way for Edwards's first drama, *Mister Cory* (1957), which also starred Curtis. When Edwards returned to Columbia Pictures in 1962 to direct *Experiment in Terror*, the poster boldly announced, "Columbia Pictures Presents a Blake Edwards Production." His status within the industry had clearly changed. He was no longer a B director or under contract to direct films with stars that were assigned to him.

Edwards had two major transitionary periods in his career. With *Breakfast at Tiffany's* (1961), *Experiment in Terror* (1962), and *Days of Wine and Roses* (1962), he transitioned from his early period into his middle period beginning with *The Pink Panther* in 1963. It was only after *The Pink Panther* and the box-office success of the five-film series he did with Peter Sellers playing Inspector Clouseau from 1963 to 1978, as well as the many other comedies he made during that time, that he became known as a comic director. In 1962, he was poised as a talented filmmaker in many genres and the diversity of these three transitionary films illustrates this: romantic comedy, a *Film Noir*–type crime procedural, and a grim social problem drama about alcoholism. Furthermore, two top stars, Audrey Hepburn and Jack Lemmon, had each chosen Edwards to direct their films; he did not originate the projects. Nor did he write the screenplays in any of the three transitional films; it seemed that he wanted to prove that he could tackle any genre and work with top actors. It is then ironic that he became known as a "physical comedy" director from the very beginning of his middle period when, at the last minute, he cast Peter Sellers in a production which he initiated and for which he cowrote the screenplay. Right after proving he could do anything, he zeroed in on slapstick comedy, a form that had languished and which enjoyed little or no critical prestige. This set the stage for the manner in which his non-comic and dramatic films were largely overlooked and underrated. It is startling how quickly the man who directed *Experiment in Terror* and *Days of Wine and Roses*, two black-and-white, serious dramas, would be forgotten in the wave of widescreen color slapstick comedies which quickly followed: *The Pink Panther* (1963), *A Shot in the Dark* (1964), *The Great Race* (1965), *What Did You Do in the War, Daddy?* (1966), *The Party* (1968), and *Darling Lili* (1970). And his prominence in such genres as tough guy private eyes in radio and television did not stick to him, not even when, as in 1969, he made *Gunn*, a feature film adaptation of his late 1950s television hit, *Peter Gunn*.

Edwards's second transitionary period from his middle period into his late period was again formed by three films: *"10"* (1979), *S.O.B* (1981), and *Victor/Victoria* (1982). With these films Edwards transitioned from making films with elaborate sexual subtexts, including all five of the Pink Panther films which were widely viewed as just family films. Indeed, leading up to *"10,"* Edwards had made three Pink Panther films in a row. *"10"* is a sexually explicit comedy about a man with a midlife crisis; *S.O.B.* is a sexually explicit comedy about a film producer who transforms a G-rated family picture into an adult film with nudity; and *Victor/Victoria* is a comedy about a woman pretending to be a man pretending to be a woman. Following the transitionary films, many of Edwards's late-period films would be sex comedies: *The Man Who Loved Women* (1983); *Micki & Maude* (1984); *That's Life!* (1986); *Blind Date* (1987); *Skin Deep* (1989); and *Switch* (1991), nearly all of which deal with men having midlife crises (*Blind Date* is the exception).

Edwards had another type of transition during this middle period that was related to the end of the old studio system and the production and distribution systems in the new Hollywood. Edwards's trials and tribulations dealing with the collapse of the old studio system and the rise of the new Hollywood conglomerates coincided very closely with his middle period. Edwards, however, felt alienated from the new Hollywood and the conglomerate model. He had bad experiences at Paramount, which had become a Gulf and Western Company headed by Robert Evans, and with James Aubrey at MGM. The manner in which the new breed of CEOs interfered with production and postproduction frequently led to clashes. Edwards told us that at least the old Hollywood moguls knew and cared about movies, whereas the new ones cared only about business. He described the situation as follows: He said he would never presume to tell Gulf and Western where to drill for oil and that they in turn should not tell him how to make movies. He compared the way the new moguls reedited finished films to taking a chair with four legs and cutting one of the legs off. Edwards's clashes with the new conglomerates began after Gulf and Western acquired Paramount Pictures in 1966, and he made *Darling Lili*, which was released in 1970. Paramount insisted on changes in the script, making it a more traditional musical which would capitalize on Julie Andrews's image. The only songs Edwards originally wanted in the film were ones performed by Lili Smith played by Julie Andrews. In other words, the songs were all about performance within the film's narrative context. In most musicals the characters break into song while interacting with one another. Edwards compromised to make the film but was unhappy with it. In 1992, however, he was honored at the Cannes Film Festival with the Legion of Honor, and his restored director's cut received its premiere screening. Whereas most directors add scenes to their new versions of their films, Edwards did the opposite, cutting about 30 minutes, including a musical number of children singing in the countryside. Edwards told us that he could not restore the film to his original vision since scenes he wanted had never been shot. This version, however, approximated his vision for the film and is now available on DVD.

Investor Kirk Kerkorian, with holdings in an airline and Las Vegas casinos, bought a controlling interest in MGM in 1969 and appointed James Aubrey as president and CEO. *The Hollywood Reporter* called Kerkorian "the most hated man in Hollywood," claiming, "In 1969, the MGM owner needed someone to run his company. He found James T. Aubrey, a former CBS executive who was widely known as the Smiling Cobra. He knew nothing about film, having spent much of his career in television, most notably at CBS."[6] Edwards's account of his experience with Aubrey when he made *Wild Rovers* at MGM definitely fits the description. Edwards's cut told the story within a complex plot structure including sophisticated shifts in time and use of voice-over narration. Aubrey drastically recut it by shortening the film by 30 minutes, making it a straightforward narrative with entire scenes and characters missing. Luckily, once again many years later, a director's cut appeared on DVD, and this time, the missing footage was restored.

Edwards was devastated by the experience and wanted his next film to be an adaptation of a Kingsley Amis novel, *The Green Man*, but Aubrey wanted Edwards to direct another MGM property, *The Carey Treatment*. Edwards agreed to do so only if Aubrey would commit to letting Edwards make *The Green Man* next. Once again everything went wrong and, due to studio interference, Edwards quit immediately after the completion of principal photography and sued unsuccessfully to have his name removed from the film. In despair, he decided to leave Hollywood and go to England, where Julie Andrews had a television and film deal with Sir Lew Grade's ITC. This led to the other transition in his creative career, which was short-lived but important. He made an extremely interesting documentary, *Julie* (1972), about his life with Julie Andrews while she was preparing for a television special, and a feature film, *The Tamarind Seed* (1974), a serious international spy drama starring Omar Sharif and Julie Andrews. That film is about such complex life transitions with a Russian spy defecting from Russia to England and eventually Canada. But the next project, *The Return of the Pink Panther* (1975), marked the return of his collaboration with Peter Sellers. The film was a big success and led to Edwards's successful return to Hollywood, where he quickly followed with *The Pink Panther Strikes Again* (1976) and *Revenge of the Pink Panther* (1978). These successes were then followed by the transition to his late period with *"10," S.O.B., and Victor/Victoria*, discussed above. When Edwards returned he managed to fit in with the new Hollywood.

All of Edwards's Pink Panther films with Sellers as Clouseau as well as the later ones with Ted Wass and Roberto Benigni in a similar role were made with United Artists, but this gives a false sense of continuity. Much like Columbia, MGM, and Paramount, United Artists underwent major changes over the years, including in 1967, when TransAmerica purchased the company, and then in 1981, when MGM purchased it from TransAmerica. In short, the United Artists that Edwards worked with in 1963 and 1964 was not the same company to which he returned in the mid-to-late 1970s. And when he returned for the remaining films in the series in 1982 and 1983 and for the last time in 1993, it was once again part of a different conglomerate. Of special interest in this UA history is the fact that, after TransAmerica took over, several leading executives left and formed a new company, Orion Films. Edwards had been so pleased working with them that he made *"10,"* his first non–Pink Panther film after returning from England, with Orion and he had a wonderful experience, including good box office and good reviews. He made his next film, *S.O.B.*, with Lorimar. Ironically, given all these changes in the new Hollywood, Paramount acquired the distribution rights to Lorimar films after Edwards made it. So, *S.O.B.*, which included a vicious satire of a studio head, David Blackman, based on Robert Evans and played by Robert Vaughan, was released by Paramount while Evans was the CEO! But this caused no problems since Paramount only had distribution rights and no cuts were made.

Between 1983 and 1988 Edwards made six films for Columbia: *The Man Who Loved Women* (1983), *Micki & Maude* (1984), *A Fine Mess* (1986), *That's Life!* (1986), *Blind Date* (1987), and *Sunset* (1988). Once again, the studio was far different from that where he made *Experiment in Terror* in 1962. In fact, it was a prime example of what happened in the wake of the demise of the old studio system. The Coca-Cola Company purchased Columbia Pictures in 1982 and was a founding partner in starting a new studio, Tri-Star (for which Edwards made *Blind Date* and *Sunset*), forming yet another conglomerate, Columbia Pictures Entertainment, in 1987. Richard Gallop, who had a background in financial law, joined Columbia as a senior vice-president and general counsel in 1981 and led the team negotiating the merger with Coca-Cola. He then became the president and CFO of Columbia Pictures from 1983 to 1986.

Gallop came to Tucson, Arizona, in 1984 for a test audience screening of Blake Edwards's *Micki & Maude*. While in Tucson he gave a guest lecture at the University of Arizona film program. Gallop took an interest in us and our first book on Edwards, assisting our research and talking with us about working with Blake. Although Gallop told us that Edwards called him regularly from the set of his current film as he had the night before to talk about ordinary production concerns and they had a follow-up call scheduled, they did not have an antagonistic or difficult relationship. Edwards had a good experience with Columbia and, later, Tri-Star. Edwards told us that he used to think of his battles with Hollywood as sitting by a river waiting for the bodies of his enemy to come floating by until he realized that there were such people downstream waiting for his body to come floating past. Edwards had developed the reputation of being an extremely difficult director for studios to work with after his high-visibility battles and even lawsuits with Evans and Aubrey, but, after returning to Hollywood in 1976, Edwards had no such further battles.

A problem, for example, arose with *A Fine Mess*, which was originally titled *The Music Box*. Edwards planned the film as a remake of a Laurel and Hardy short, *The Music Box*. The central scene showed Laurel and Hardy moving a grand piano up a steep flight of stairs, only to discover that they had the wrong address. After viewing the footage, the studio asked Edwards to cut his version of that scene from his film, which he did, retitling it after the duo's iconic phrase where Hardy repeatedly berates Laurel by declaring he has gotten them into "a fine mess." But Edwards did not harbor anger toward studio executives, telling us that he was struggling with serious depression and chronic fatigue syndrome when he made the film. He would even tell us later that he had no memory of even making *A Fine Mess* and Henry Mancini told us, "That one got away from us" (more on that below).

Edwards followed that bad experience by making the low-budget, non-union independent film, *That's Life!*, which Columbia acquired for distribution. Although the film ultimately failed at the box office, the studio was so enthusiastic about the film, which got the highest scores from preview audiences that they had ever seen, they decided to change the planned slow rollout in major cities to a big national opening. Despite the failure, producer Tony Adams told us that neither he nor Blake held bad feelings, adding that the more experience he (Tony) had, the more he concluded that he never knew how any film would do before opening. *Skin Deep* (1989) and *Switch* (1991) were Edwards's last two sex comedies; the former was released by Twentieth Century Fox where he had made *High Time* in 1960, and the latter by Warner Brothers, where he had made *Days of Wine and Roses*. Blake Edwards's production Company, BECO, was involved in both and, once again, there were no bitter battles with the studios.

This brief account of Edwards's changing relationships with studios and of the changes within the studio system is central to understanding his career trajectory. He was a writer-director at heart seeking maximum control from the very beginning of his career, and he had the usual tensions with the studios at times, but he had no reputation as a difficult director until the 1970s. All of that changed dramatically with three films in a row with widely publicized bitter battles: *Darling Lili*, *Wild Rovers*, and *The Carey Treatment*. Paramount accused Edwards of going well over budget with *Darling Lili*, a film that failed badly at the box office. Edwards felt that that experience unjustly gave him the bad reputation that he carried for many years. The following battles with MGM over cuts in *Wild Rovers* and production interference during *The Carey Treatment* threatened to end his career in Hollywood but, after his brief period in England, he returned to Hollywood and worked for two decades that were free of such extreme turbulence. His late-period films had modest budgets, and he completed them without delays and without going over budget. He had successfully transitioned from the old to the new Hollywood.

In order to fully understand Edwards's career achievements, we also need to briefly look at the television industry during this time period. Edwards was an important figure in television in the late 1950s, achieving his greatest success with *Peter Gunn* (1958–1961), a half-hour black-and-white private eye series. At that time television was seen as a starting point for those with ambitions to become film directors. The same was true for actors. Successful film directors seldom moved to television, and movie stars seldom acted on television. Most of the exceptions were actors and directors whose careers had peaked and who could no longer find work in film. There was at this time a strict hierarchy between film and television with film at the top. As always, there were a few exceptions such as *Alfred Hitchcock Presents* (1955–1962).

Once again, Edwards's career does not conform to the norm. After working as an actor in mostly small roles from 1942, he began his behind-the-camera work in film as a writer-producer of two B Westerns, *Stampede* and *Panhandle*, in 1948–1949. In 1949 he created and wrote most of the episodes for *Richard Diamond, Private Detective*. By 1952 he was already writing screenplays with director Richard Quine: *Sound Off* and *Rainbow Round My*

Shoulder. Edwards would write four more screenplays with Quine between 1952 and 1954. During those years he also wrote nine episodes for *Four Star Playhouse* on television and created *The Mickey Rooney Show* for television with Quine. He directed five of the nine episodes on *Four Star Playhouse*, and, in 1954, he also wrote and directed an unsold television pilot: *Mickey Spillane's "Mike Hammer!"*. In the following year, 1955, Edwards began his career as a film director. And these are just the highlights from those years! Edwards launched his career simultaneously in radio, television, and film as a writer, producer, and director. In other words, he began as a multimedia, multi-hyphenate figure, and he would continue as one to the end of his life.

By the time he created and produced as well as wrote and directed a number of episodes of *Peter Gunn*, Edwards had directed six feature films. He had also written the screenplay for the highly successful Quine film, *Operation Mad Ball*. In a sense, he was going from film to television rather than television to film. And he would continue that complex interrelationship: in 1967, six years after the end of the television series, he adapted it for the feature film *Gunn*. In 1989 he attempted to reboot the series with a pilot made-for-TV movie, *Peter Gunn*. He also expanded his television work as a director by collaborating with Julie Andrews, beginning with his made-for-television documentary *Julie* (1972) and several Julie Andrews television specials – *Julie and Dick at Covent Garden* (1974) and *Julie: My Favorite Things* (1975) – and he directed all seven episodes of the series *Julie* (1992), which he did not write or produce. He also cowrote the screenplay for *The Ferret*, a made-for-TV movie (1984), and wrote and directed a made-for-TV movie pilot, *Justin Case* (1988), which aired as an episode of *The Magical World of Disney*. The pilot starred George Carlin but was not picked up as a series. Edwards was at work on yet another reboot of the Peter Gunn television series at the time of his death.

From these film and television industry perspectives, Blake Edwards may well be the most important and influential film director of his generation, essentially starting in the old studio system and successfully transitioning into the new Hollywood era of conglomerates, combined with a television career beginning in the heyday of the 30-minute TV shows made for small screen low-definition analogue TV and ending in 1992, exactly when the convergence of the film and technology industries would totally redefine both film and television and the interrelationship between them. Edwards began his behind-the-camera career full force in 1948 and directed his last TV series in 1992 and his last film in 1993.

The early 1990s were precisely when new digital technology along with the premium cable companies such as HBO began to transform television, followed by new streaming companies such as Amazon (2005) and Netflix (2007). Initially they streamed older film and television shows and then expanded to create new shows and movies. Digital technology quickly changed television and home movies, first by replacing low-definition VHS tapes with high-definition DVDs, which also letterboxed movies in their correct aspect ratio and added sound, including 5.1 Dolby Surround Sound. Old analogue televisions were quickly replaced with digital large TV screens with stereo sound and then with even larger flat-screen TVs. Soon, the concept of "home theaters" with large screens and complete surround sound speakers became a new norm. And similar changes were taking place in filmmaking, most importantly beginning with replacing shooting on 35 mm film with digital film cameras and projecting digital video rather than 35 mm in movie theaters. The old distinctions between film and television began to disappear, affecting not just production, distribution, and exhibition but also creativity. Suddenly, film directors creating and executive producing television shows became a new norm, and made-for-TV movies produced by such companies as Amazon and Netflix acquired new levels of prestige and recognition. Similarly, actors in their prime went back and forth between television series and theatrical filmmaking.

Blake Edwards became the last major director to come out of the old Hollywood studio system and to work extensively in television throughout his career. As such he is an important link between the old Hollywood multi-hyphenate multimedia film directors and the next generation of new Hollywood film multi-hyphenates such as J. J. Abrams. And there is one more important distinction to note. Beginning in the late 1960s, critics and scholars began to refer to a new Hollywood Golden Era. Most of the prominent new filmmakers were either young counterculture figures such as Bob Rafelson and Dennis Hopper or, like Steven Spielberg, George Lucas, and Martin Scorsese, they were film school graduates from such prestigious universities as UCLA, USC, and NYU. The film curriculum also included film history, theory, and criticism. Blake Edwards, on the other hand, didn't even go to college, let alone film school. He began to go to community college but that was interrupted by his joining the Coast Guard. He had no formal film training, and this may account for how he was overlooked for so long in American academic film scholarship. He was unfortunately perceived as being part of the old Hollywood entertainment film genre establishment at a time when new, rebellious younger filmmakers were being lionized for redefining that entertainment tradition. But now, decades later, Blake Edwards's films appear to stand out over many lesser films that were overrated at the time. He did not easily fit in anywhere. His career is riddled with paradox. To many he appears to be mainstream Hollywood or even Mr. Julie Andrews, as Radley Metzger once called him, but to others, he appears to be a highly innovative, sometimes even experimental, filmmaker.

We also want to add a word of caution about approaching both the issues of multimedia and the issues of multi-hyphenate creativity. The two are inextricably bound together. Edwards was frequently asked whether he preferred writing, directing, or producing. He wisely once answered that his answers were different at different times. A key point for us is that all these functions are entirely different in each medium: In radio for example, writing was primary, and directors were of minor importance, whereas in film, directing was of primary importance and writing was preliminary to actually creating the film which told the story visually. One area in which Edwards's career trajectory conformed to the norm was that, after becoming a film director, his primary role in television was as a creator-producer, not as a writer or director, although he did both from time to time. Significantly, he wrote and directed the pilot episode of *Peter Gunn*, which establishes the premise, the characters, and the visual style for the series. In conformity with television norms, the opening credits boldly declare, "Created and Produced by Blake Edwards." The closing credits then identify who wrote and who directed each episode, which are a variety of different writers and directors, but the writers did not direct the episodes they wrote and the directors did not write the episodes they directed. Only Blake Edwards at times fulfilled both the writer-director roles.

As a producer Edwards had total control of the production, enabling Henry Mancini for example to have an unprecedented role. Mancini told us that, in addition to creating the opening credit theme music, which in accordance with standard practice was used for each episode, he was able to compose new music to fit each episode on a weekly basis, which was not standard practice. Edwards guaranteed that Mancini would have the final cut ready by a certain day of the week, enabling Mancini to create the score in time for broadcast. The norm at the time was "canned music" put over the scenes. Edwards even went to bat for Mancini to retain the rights to his music to receive royalties from records and concerts. Edwards controlled all the major creative decisions. When he wanted to expand the series from 30 minutes to a full hour and to go from black and white to color and the studio refused, Edwards simply cancelled the series, even though it was a top-rated show at the time.

We use this as a simple example of the need to always understand writing, directing, and producing in careful relationship to radio, television, or film at the time. In feature filmmaking, for example, as was a norm at the time, Edwards always talked of the importance of screenplays in creating a story worth telling to begin the process of filmmaking. But, as his career trajectory shows, this was not a view of writing as the "primary" thing, however much he enjoyed it; if it were, why would he also nearly always direct the films based on his own scripts? And his style of film directing was notoriously tied to carefully working out the action, camera positions, and compositions on the set each day. He knew that films were *made*, not *written*. And he even made several highly improvised films with short screenplays that mostly established the premise and the characters. For all practical purposes, the story was not written at all. And, having been influenced by his love of silent film, he frequently had major scenes without the primacy of dialogue and at times even without any dialogue in his films, and, being influenced by radio, he frequently gave primary importance to diegetic sounds.

Edwards was a profoundly complex creative man and generalizations about his love of writing, producing, or directing offer no insight into how he worked creatively. He quite rightly said different things to different people on different days. When speaking to the Writer's Guild, he spoke about the primacy of the screenplay, but that does not mean he always identified primarily as a writer. On the other hand, when we asked him whether he most enjoyed working in radio, television, or film, he answered radio, with a profound insight as to why. As a writer he loved how the story was told almost entirely through the spoken word and the listeners had to use their imaginations to fill in what the characters and their interactions looked like. In other words, he understood the primacy of the written-spoken word in *radio* and that appealed to his love of language and the imagination. His films, as we will see, would also frequently revel in both of those, including Clouseau's never-ending mangling of the English language and word pronunciation and scenes of his characters arguing over language and even asking one another to define exactly what a word they are using means. Since Edwards was successful in radio, television, and film, it is not surprising that he would have such a media-specific understanding of our question and offer insight with his profound answer.

We have designed this book to emphasize aspects of Edwards's work which have received little or no attention. Despite his extraordinary burst of creativity simultaneously as a writer, producer, director, and even actor inventively working in many different genres in radio, television, and film from 1948 to 1962, traditional auteur critics and scholars have always made the case for serious artistic achievement as being solely the province of film directors. In the case of Blake Edwards that means little more than occasionally acknowledging some of his radio and television work such as *Peter Gunn* and *Richard Diamond, Private Detective* or acknowledging that he wrote screenplays for films he did not direct that included such gems as *Operation Mad Ball*. The main assumptions are that these are early works of a struggling media artist on his way to becoming a film director and that his importance lies there.

We will challenge that in Chapter 2 on Edwards's early period. Given the startling number of movies he wrote, or directed or acted in, and the number of television and radio shows he created and produced and sometimes directed and wrote for, totaling hundreds of episodes, this is a preliminary, and not a definitive, study of that period, and more scholarship on the early period is needed. We take his work in radio and television seriously and pose a number of questions. First and foremost, we hope to discover how Edwards creates as a multi-hyphenate, multimedia artist. Our goal is not to make a case for an identifiable worldview with recognizable themes, plots, and characters. That was done decades ago. We want to explore how Edwards worked creatively as a multi-hyphenate multimedia artist wearing his various hats as he engages quite different media.

For example, one of Edwards's great strengths as a filmmaker is his use of highly structured screen space and its relationship to off-screen space. How, if at all, does that relate to his work in radio, a form of media entirely reliant on sound? Does Edwards hear soundscapes in relationship to the space where the action is centered and surrounding spaces from which other sounds emanate? The *Richard Diamond, Private Detective* episode "Satire of Radio Detectives" (1949) is based upon an irate neighbor in Diamond's apartment building who pounds on the wall to get Diamond to stop singing. We hear his pounding from the sound perspective in Diamond's apartment, and we also hear the singing from the perspective of the irate neighbor. How, for example, does the manner in which sound effects accompany radio dialogue relate to Edwards's use of film sound? We consider a sequence with dialogue which is structured around the sights and sounds of running water in *The Party* below.

How does his interest in film screen space apply to analogue, low-definition television screen space at the time that people watched TV with the light on in distractive environments as opposed to high-definition films projected on large screens in the dark? Does Edwards's lifelong love of silent film relate to sound film, radio, and television? Logic would seem to dictate that nothing could be further from silent film than radio, but such is not the case with Blake Edwards. We will see, for example, in the next chapter that a sequence of four successive episodes of Season One of *Peter Gunn* literally have short silent films for their pre-credit sequences, using editing to empathize that we do not hear a spoken word. Similarly, in *The Party* Edwards has two silent films in the middle of his sound film. But radio explains much about Edwards's use of silent films. The term "silent film" has always been something of a misnomer since nearly all films of the silent era included musical accompaniment. Film scholars have replaced the term "silent film" with "early cinema." Interestingly, another common term for sound film at the time it arrived was "talkies." What Edwards does in his inclusion of silent film in some of his work is to think of sound film as talkies and he eliminates the talking. But, as in radio, he foregrounds sounds emanating from the diegetic space. For example, *The Party* includes two seemingly silent film sequences. The first is a dinner scene in which we hear the constant din of conversation without hearing the words or following anything that anyone says. And that conversational din is augmented by off-screen sound such as a crash coming from the kitchen after a waiter enters with a full tray of dirty dishes. The second silent film sequence involves a character singing a song, but the action builds in relationship to the main character, who desperately has to urinate while the sound of running water coming from multiple sources builds on the soundtrack – a water fountain with a nude male urinating, water coming from a toilet being flushed and then overflowing, and culminating with the main character trapped on the lawn when the sprinkler system turns on. All of this without a spoken word. Similarly, in the four pre-credit episodes of *Peter Gunn* discussed above, although we never hear a word, we hear all kinds of sounds from cars to guns.

Another important question about how working in radio and television might have affected his filmmaking comes from the fact that his most important work in both came in the form of episodic series storytelling within a 30-minute format, which, minus commercials and station breaks, was about 27 minutes. Even *Panhandle*, the first film he wrote, produced, and acted in, was 85 minutes long. By contrast his last Western, *Wild Rovers*, was released in a studio cut of 106 minutes but was later restored to 136 minutes in a director's cut. But in addition to the experience of telling a story in a 30-minute format, Edwards learned how to tell stories in a series format, with familiar characters and settings. How did this affect his film work? Edwards was the first Hollywood "A" film director of his generation to begin making feature film series starting in 1963 with his Pink Panther-Inspector Clouseau films, a series which would end with eight films thirty years later in 1993! The other major film series of that time were the James Bond films, which had many directors, and Sergio Leone's *Man with No Name* Western series starring Clint Eastwood. But Leone was working in Italy in the "Spaghetti Western" genre, which was perceived in the United States as a foreign B film.

Edwards also continued his *Peter Gunn* television series in films, first with his feature-length theatrical film *Gunn* (1967), and then with a made-for-TV movie *Peter Gunn* (1988), which was also a pilot for a proposed new television series. And he was working on a new Peter Gunn television series reboot late in his career. As we shall see in the final chapter, he had also completed two screenplays of a potential *"10"* series to include *10 (Again)* and *10½*. So even when working in film, he was thinking of various forms of series, sequels, and reboots. And he also adapted several of his films as plays, a form of remaking them in yet another art form.

Nearly all of Edwards's films belong to the category of Hollywood "entertainment" genres: Westerns, detective films, comedies, and musicals – but the way he creatively approaches those genres undermines their unity and definition. The mixing of various genres, the jarring disruptions of genre tones, and the satirizing of genre elements are present from the very beginning of his career in radio, television, and film. Richard Diamond, for example, may appear to be just another tough-guy noir-type private eye, but of course those private eyes were not known for their singing. But nearly every episode of *Richard Diamond, Private Detective* includes his singing to his girlfriend, and, as the title of the episode "Satire of Radio Detectives" indicates, Edwards would even foreground satiric comedy in that episode.

In Chapter 2, we will survey Edwards's early work in radio, television, and film as a writer, producer, director, and actor. We follow that not with the predictable survey of the middle period with the well-known comedies but, rather, with focused attention to his non-comic, "serious," dramatic films from his early, middle, and late periods. We do that not to denigrate his accomplishments as a director of comedies, which we think rank him not only as the foremost director of comedies in his generation, but also as one of the foremost in film history. Like Edwards, we think comedy is just as serious as drama, but we also think that Richard Brody is right that Edwards also made some of the best films of modern times that were not comedies, and we hope that focusing on these will bring renewed attention to his achievements in other genres. Although Brody acknowledges that Edwards was "a comedic genius, the most skilled and inspired director of physical comedy working in Hollywood in his time," with the use of the word "also" he categorizes those films as separate from what he calls the "best movies of our time." But he is right in bringing attention to the fact that the recognition of the comedies has, with the exception of *Days of Wine and Roses*, all but obliterated awareness of the many other films in Edwards's career. In Chapters 3–11, we will carefully analyze those other films (*Mister Cory*, *Experiment in Terror*, *Days of Wine and Roses*, *Gunn*, *Wild Rovers*, *The Carey Treatment*, *Julie*, *The Tamarind Seed*, and *Sunset*, respectively), focusing on how Edwards worked creatively in those genres and exploring how these disparate works relate to one another.

In Chapter 12, we will survey his theater work, *Victor/Victoria: The Musical* and *Big Rosemary* (an adaptation of the second film he wrote and directed); his studio art exhibitions; and his finished screenplays for films which he wrote by himself but which he did not live to make: *10 (Again)*, *10½*, *It Never Rains*, and *Alter Ego* as well as theater plays which he also wrote that are unproduced at this time: *The Pink Panther Musical*, *A Shot in the Dark*, and *Scapegoat*. He remained active until the end of his life, and his interest in series, sequels, reboots, and theater adaptations of his own films was prominent. The chapter will also survey two tributes to Edwards which we can report upon since we were directly involved: the prestigious Preston Sturges Lifetime Achievement Award in Hollywood and the honorary PhD awarded to him by Arizona State University, Tempe.

We conclude this chapter with an account of our experiences on visiting Edwards's sets to watch him work since, in our previous books, we did not use those research visits to his sets nor the many conversations with him and formal interviews and casual conversations with many of the actors and creative collaborators as well as the business people in his office and production company. We will try to give a sense of how he worked as a director and what it was like to have ongoing interviews and conversations with him about his film and creative work. We first interviewed Edwards in his suite at the Sherry Netherland Hotel in Manhattan in 1979. He was in New York to testify in a trial against a company using the Pink Panther in an unauthorized television commercial.

We were dressed in suits and ties, to which we will return later. While we were sitting in the lobby waiting to begin the interview, we saw Dudley Moore walk by, who at the time we did not know was staying in the same hotel. Edwards greeted us at the door to his suite. He had no staff or assistant with him during the interview. He was gracious and forthright in answering our questions. He was interested in what we had to say, and he was never defensive. Nor did he adopt a false persona to hide behind. Sometimes he would comment upon an insight we had. When we observed that the physical gags in the Pink Panther films shifted away from Clouseau and onto other characters such as Cato as the series developed, he said that that was a smart observation. He said that Peter Sellers was increasingly unable to do the slapstick gags due to his deteriorating physical condition and that he had to totally restructure them on the set. That was the only off-the-record comment he ever made to us, asking that we not use that part of the interview while Peter Sellers was alive. When at the end of the interview we asked him whether he was aware of how much of the humor in the Pink Panther films was about Clouseau not living up to the cultural norms of masculinity, he remarked, "increasingly so," and said we'd be interested in his next film, *"10,"* and in *Victor/Victoria*, the plot of which he then described to us. His comment about being increasingly aware of the masculinity issues in the Pink Panther films is profoundly revealing about Blake's introspective, creative mindset. He acknowledged that he did not have total awareness of and insight into every aspect of his creative work, and that of course explains his respect for the interview process. He enjoyed hearing the questions, and he did not think he had the answers to them all and certainly not the only answers. But his comment also reveals how he grew as an artist, moving from his middle period to his late period through introspective reevaluation. He always simply tried his best to answer our questions, and this would continue throughout our long-term relationship with him. With a minor exception about his play *Big Rosemary*, which we discuss in Chapter 12, he never asked us to not say something, nor did he ever criticize anything we had published. He set a tone of implicit mutual respect for one another and what we each did. He respected our critical distance from him.

When we arrived for the first day of our visit to the set of *A Fine Mess*, a slapstick comedy starring Ted Danson and Howie Mandel, we were dressed in ties and jackets. Katie Morgan, a production assistant, told us everyone thought we were "suits" working for the studio. We quickly learned that Edwards's sets were informal. We stayed near the rear of the set watching everything from a distance. We did not approach Blake. The next day we passed him as we were going to lunch, and he stopped to say hi and ask us how we were. When we exchanged greetings, he told us in detail about his struggle with chronic fatigue syndrome and depression, which had developed since our 1979 interview with him. He was very candid and told us of his Clouseau-like comic failed attempt to commit suicide with everything going wrong, but the grim underlying message about his health was clear; it was no laughing matter.

We were quickly welcomed and integrated with the crew and actors. On the Dinkie's set, he motioned for us to join him and listen in on the conversation he was having with Harry Stradling, Jr., director of photography, and Tony

FIGURE 1.1   *A Fine Mess,* © 1986 Columbia Pictures Industries, Inc.

Adams, producer. Dinkie's was a hamburger drive-in restaurant with servers roller-skating to the cars laden with trays of food they were delivering or clearing away (Figure 1.1). He had started working on the set early in the day, and it was our introduction to the manner in which he carefully worked out his camera placements, movements, and compositions on the set. They were not scripted in advance, and, with the exception of *The Great Race*, he never used story boards. He spent most of the day in quiet, solitary contemplation of the complex moving parts of the scene, determining how to shoot it. For long periods of time he spoke to no one. On a few occasions, Tony Adams approached him for a word and quickly left. It was our introduction to a key aspect of his working style. We asked him when he worked out the camera placement and movements, and he said he began as he was driving to the set every day. For him the creative act of filmmaking included a great deal of improvisation, not just with the actors but also with cinematography and a vision of the editing. We would see this on every visit to every set. What stuck out to us was how much of that time was spent in solitary contemplation as his director of photography and actors all stood waiting. When he knew what he wanted, he spoke with the director of photography and the actors.

This working style caused Ted Danson to approach us at one point and say that Edwards had given him no feedback and that he was so quiet and spent so much time watching and contemplating that Danson was insecure about what Edwards thought of his performance. He asked if we knew, but Blake had not said a word to us either about the actors' performances. His working style often had a brooding, enigmatic quality. When, later in the shoot, we told Danson that Edwards had mentioned that his performance was fine, he exhaled dramatically and said, "Whew, what a relief!"

The Dinkie's scene also included a choreographer and, for the entire day, we heard Fats Domino singing "I'm Going to be a Wheel Someday" as the skating choreography was being rehearsed. We were surprised when the completed film had a different song on the soundtrack.

Another aspect of Blake's working style included having family and close associates on the set for key scenes. Blake's elderly parents, Julie Andrews, and Milton Wexler, his therapist, who sat next to Blake, were all seated together when they shot the Dinkie's scene in the evening. And Blake pointed out to us that Richard Quine was standing at the rear edge of the set, which enabled us to meet him, have an informal conversation about his work with Blake, and schedule a follow-up formal interview.

After a productive week watching Edwards work and meeting and talking with many of the cast and crew, we approached him to say goodbye after the completion of work on Friday afternoon. As always, we called him "Mr. Edwards," to which he responded, "After that interview and a week of this, it's still Mr. Edwards? Call me Blake." And he warmly extended an open invitation to visit any of his future sets.

A Fine Mess received poor reviews and was a box-office failure. Jonathan Baumbach's video review of it in *The New York Times*, however, strikes us as insightful not only about that film, but also about much of Edwards's work in general:

> Blake Edwards's farces, often deplored on first appearance, have a way of becoming classics a few years later. "A Fine Mess," which was mildly abhorred in its recent brief theatrical release, gets better on re-seeing. The film's nonstop silliness – there are three chase sequences in the first 10 minutes – is wonderfully choreographed. The jokes may be old, but they are reconceived with considerable energy and wit... The plot has something to do with a doped race horse that wins two races on the same day on different courses. I counted 23 laughs, when I was able to stop laughing long enough to count.[7]

Although even Edwards dismissed it due to his health issues, which seemed to us to be minimal while watching him work, much of the film is hilarious. It belongs to a subgroup of his comedies including *Blind Date* in which the plot simply sets a number of things in motion. Character development is minimal since the films are structured around their gags as we see the characters dash around in a crazy world. And Baumbach is correct that with the passage of time Edwards's farces frequently gain a good and sometimes even cult status reputation.

In 1988, we visited the set of *Sunset*, a film to which we devote an entire chapter. We interviewed Bruce Willis in his trailer during a break in the shooting schedule, and several aspects of the interview were of great interest to us. His first film with Edwards had been *Blind Date*, which was also directed by Edwards. Willis was thrilled to be working with Edwards because he admired him and wanted to learn about filmmaking from him. He mentioned *The Great Race* as having had a big impact upon him, which, as we discuss in the final chapter, was the same film J. J. Abrams mentioned as critical to his love of learning about films. Such unexpected connections between figures as diverse as Willis and Abrams are revealing. Every generation of Edwards's admirers identifies a different film as crucial in the impact it had upon them. For us it was *The Pink Panther* and *A Shot in the Dark*.

Once again, our visit coincided with another major location shoot, this one set in a train station where Tom Mix (Bruce Willis) goes to greet Wyatt Earp (James Garner) upon his arrival in Hollywood (see Figure 11.5 in Chapter 11). Edwards enjoyed a cordial working relationship with both Garner, with whom he had worked on *Victor/Victoria*, and Willis, with whom he had worked on *Blind Date*. Between shots the three of them sat around engaged in casual conversation. Edwards had a closeness with them which we did not see with Danson and Mandel in *A Fine Mess*. The next day Edwards invited us to watch the dailies with him and Julie Andrews. It was fascinating to see the filmed version immediately after having been on location witnessing the scene being shot. We had watched them shoot a close-up of Earp's boots as he steps off the train, and that shot even in the dailies already had a strong impact within the context of long shots (Figure 1.2). We also had a charming casual conversation with James Garner on the set between takes. He had nothing but praise for working with Edwards. Despite

FIGURE 1.2   *Sunset*, © 1988 Tri-Star Pictures.

Edwards's industry reputation as being a difficult director, we have been struck by how often the stars in his films love working with him and often return to star again in another.

Our next visit was to the set of *Switch* (1991), a gender comedy starring Ellen Barkin and Jimmy Smits. The premise of the film in which Steve Brooks (Perry King), a womanizer, is killed by avenging women only to come back to life as Amanda Brooks (Ellen Barkin), a man in a woman's body, clearly recalls *Victor/Victoria* in which Julie Andrews played Victoria, a female performer who pretended to be a man pretending to be a woman. For much of the film, Andrews dressed and behaved as a man. But whereas Andrews played all three parts herself in a demanding role portraying a woman who then transforms herself into a man who as a performer then pretends to reveal himself onstage as a man masquerading as a woman, *Switch* simply replaces Perry, the male character, with Barkin, the version of the male character trapped within a woman's body. Thus, two actors play different incarnations of the same character.

The tone on the set was closer than that on *A Fine Mess*. During days when she was filming, Barkin used to regularly sit directly next to Edwards between takes and they enjoyed talking together. We never, for example, saw either Danson or Mandel sitting next to Edwards and chatting with him. And his mood throughout our visit was upbeat without him speaking about bouts of depression or chronic fatigue syndrome. There were three highlights for us on this visit. We did an extensive interview with Jimmy Smits, who told us that Edwards was the first director to cast him in a role that had nothing to do with his being Hispanic. This was profoundly important to him. He felt freed of the burden of his character always representing a fixed racial ethnic background. He was entirely right of course, and it conflicts with any simple characterization of Edwards as racist given his use of Mickey Rooney as an offensive, stereotypical Asian male in *Breakfast at Tiffany's*, which we discuss later. This is a reverse form of color-blind casting. There is absolutely nothing in the film, not one moment, that suggests that Smits's character, Walter Stone, is Hispanic, nor is there a moment that invokes Hispanic stereotypes.[8] Like many younger actors who worked with Edwards, Smits was also thrilled to be working with a great master of physical comedy. He even told us to be sure not to miss a major barroom brawl the next day which would involve elaborate choreography, with Edwards using four cameras covering the action from every part of the room. Although he was not a character in that scene, Smits eagerly looked forward to joining us as observers of how Edwards staged and shot such sequences.

Smits was right and watching the rehearsals and filming of that scene was another highlight of our visit to the set of that film. The scene was in some ways parallel to the Dinkie's scene in *A Fine Mess* where suddenly everything in the film is set into extreme motion. In the next chapter we will explore how Edwards's use of extreme violence in his *Peter Gunn* television series was structurally similar to his use of slapstick in his comedies and dance numbers in his musicals. But the barroom brawl in *Switch* involved another highlight for us. Edwards surprised us by telling us to report to the costuming department since he wanted us to be extras at the bar in the first part of the scene preceding the outbreak of the fight. Off we went to the costume department where we were fitted as he wanted us to appear. The costume people knew what he wanted but we didn't, nor did it matter. Nor did he give us any direction on what to do or how to behave as two guys having a drink when action began between the main characters. So, we had fun reacting as we wished. But instead of getting an Academy Award for best supporting actors, we ended up on the cutting room floor. Edwards cut that part of the action from the film.

Sunset was the next set we visited but, since we devote an entire chapter to that film, we will end this section about our film set visits with an account of Edwards's last film, *Son of the Pink Panther* (1993). The film was shot at the Pinewood Studios outside London, and there were many highpoints for us, including interviews with Julie Andrews, Roberto Benigni, Graham Stark, Burt Kwouk, Herbert Lom, and Jennifer Edwards, as well as lunch with Blake and Jennifer at the Pinewood Studios private restaurant. Blake's mood was generally upbeat. After learning that Peter was a cigar aficionado, he invited us into his trailer to offer us Cuban cigars, and he invited us to listen in on a conversation planning the title credit sequence. He was, however, in a dark mood on one of the days, which foreshadowed what we would often see in our Minneapolis visit to *Victor/Victoria: The Musical*, his next project.

Roberto Benigni told us, "It was important to not imitate and not do Peter Sellers again." He was particularly enthusiastic about this role because he wanted to learn as much as possible about comedy from watching Edwards work. When we asked Graham Stark how the set of *Son of the Pink Panther* compared to that on the earlier films in the series, he said, "Actually, very good. It's funny, this picture revived a lot. I don't know why but I have a theory on this and I think it's a lot to do with Roberto. Now Roberto, whom I'd never met before, but funnily enough, I'm a great admirer of because I've seen him before and I thought he was amazing." Herbert Lom, on the other hand, was distressed by how distant Edwards was interacting with the cast in comparison to the earlier films where Blake socialized with the actors on the set. Oddly, Benigni told us that he had virtually no interaction with Edwards before or even during the production and that he valued that distance.

Burt Kwouk, who plays Cato in the series, offered an insightful analysis of his character: "I've been asked, 'Well, how do you feel about playing a stereotype?' And I say, 'What, you mean Cato's a stereotype? Well, do you know what the word stereotype means?' It means an exact copy. Now, who the hell behaves like Cato anywhere in the world? So, what is he a stereotype of? You tell me. I can't think of anything like it." Jennifer Edwards gave us insight into her being cast against type in *Sunset*:

> I think for *Sunset* he [Blake] knew that I wanted that kind of a challenge because I'd been talking about for quite a while that it's very difficult for me to be recognized by casting people or directors as playing a villainous sort of role. I mean, I was constantly hearing from people, you know, that if I wanted to go up for a bad-girl role, "Oh no, no. She's too lithe. She's too vulnerable. She's too willowy. She's too..." It made me so angry because the frustrating thing is when you're dealing with real life murderers or bad girls there's no stereotype. They all look differently and they are who they are.

Julie Andrews gave us great insight into how Blake works creatively. For example, she described the extraordinarily complex long take at the beginning of *Darling Lili* which she called

> The best exercise to date that I've ever had in filmmaking ... I had to hit marks and lip-sync perfectly. The camera had to move and dance with me and pull focus perfectly and men had to pull cables out of the way. We shot it originally in Ireland in the theater and it didn't work. And Blake said, "I want to go back to the United States and shoot it on a soundstage so I can control it"... It took a whole day. I don't know how many takes we did. Oh God, six or seven. But that's after monstrous rehearsals and making sure everything was alright.

Chapter 2 lays the groundwork for understanding how Edwards achieved this creative level in his career.

NOTES

1. Andrew Sarris, *The American Cinema: Directors and Directions 1929–1968* (New York: Dutton, 1968).
2. *Godard on Godard*, translated and edited by Tom Milne (New York: Da Capo, 1972), p. 147.

3. Peter Lehman and William Luhr, *Blake Edwards* (Athens: Ohio University Press, 1981) and William Luhr and Peter Lehman, *Returning to the Scene: Blake Edwards, Volume 2* (Athens: Ohio University Press, 1989).

4. Richard Brody, "What to Stream: Blake Edwards's Masterwork Documentary of His Wife, Julie Andrews," *The New Yorker Magazine*, March 26, 2020 (newyorker.com).

5. Sam Wasson, *A Splurch in the Kisser: The Movies of Blake Edwards* (Middletown, CT: Wesleyan University Press, 2009), p. 308.

6. Stephen Galloway, "When Kirk Kerkorian Hired the Most Hated Man in Hollywood," *The Hollywood Reporter*, June 16, 2015 (hollywoodreporter.com).

7. Jonathan Baumbach, Video Review of *A Fine Mess*, *The New York Times*, May 17, 1987, Section 2, p. 30 (nytimes.com).

8. Edwards was also criticized for casting Mickey Rooney as Yunioshi, a Japanese photographer in *Breakfast at Tiffany's*, and Peter Sellers as Hrundi V. Bakshi, an Indian actor in *The Party*, but that criticism misses some essential aspects of the latter film. Although Bakshi, unlike Yunioshi in *Breakfast at Tiffany's*, is a sympathetic figure of identification throughout the film and "gets the girl" at the end, that does not address the casting issue since, from that perspective, an Indian actor could portray the character in the same way. The manner in which Edwards works creatively gets at the deep, underlying issue. *The Party* was conceived as an experimental film using improvisational silent filmmaking styles and techniques; it had no traditional screenplay. To work in that manner Edwards had to work with an actor with whom he had a close working relationship including a history of improvising complexly structured and timed slapstick comedy. Furthermore, the whole idea for the film had been developed with Sellers in mind since he had a strong interest in technology and gadgets which form the basis of the entire structure of the comedy, from retracting floors to high-tech sound amplification systems. The main set in the film is a mansion which disguises a slapstick nightmare in the making. Edwards could not have made that film with a talented Indian actor with whom he had never worked. Certain styles of filmmaking hinge on a close connection between an actor and a director. It is not just a Blake Edwards film, it is a Peter Sellers film too and is now frequently listed as one of the best comedies ever made. Some of course may still argue that it is racist and should not have been made.

The Early Period (1948–1962)

When Blake Edwards's media career began in the late 1940s, his ambition was limitless. This was a lifelong inclination of his. In 1987 his uncle, Owen Crump, told us that as an adolescent he had been "urgently inventive," adding,

> You absolutely could not keep him from going in nineteen differ-ent directions. He always had some tremendous instinct for doing something, making something, and not like children do. He was into all kinds of odd things. His mind was just clickety-clack, even when he was growing up. When he was still a very young, young teenager, he and a friend out here in California decided they would go into the cartoon business and they drew a whole series of strips with cartoon characters that were really quite wonderful. They were just excellent and looked very professional and he was just absolutely out of his mind about being a cartoonist. Well, he was always into some kind of thing like that and he has such a restless mind, which is the same today. He just can't sit still. He has to be writing another script or get-ting involved in some kind of a work that today is theatrical. But, he absolutely has a possessiveness about doing something all the time

Blake Edwards: Film Director as Multitalented Auteur, First Edition.
William Luhr and Peter Lehman.
© 2023 John Wiley & Sons Ltd. Published 2023 by John Wiley & Sons Ltd.

and not for just being busy, but for creating something. With Blake it's just a complete restlessness that he has to this day.

Edwards's creative urgency moved him to engage many modes of expression. Aside from his adolescent cartoon strips, his friend, the popular singer Mel Tormé, has written that in the 1940s Edwards was constantly creating comedy performances.[1] However, as Edwards entered his twenties he focused first on movies, then on radio, then on television, at times overlapping with each other. He adapted with these media forms at a time during which they were changing in fundamental ways and as he accrued more power in them. Edwards's adaptability echoes a line in *Darling Lili* in which Colonel von Ruger talks about the necessity of adapting to constantly changing circumstances and the need to "shift and accommodate on a day-to-day basis."

Edwards told us that when he learned that Dick Powell was interested in developing a radio show, he told Powell that he had a script that capitalized on the two central elements of Powell's media image: his recent films as a hard-boiled detective in the *Film Noir* mode and his earlier image as a popular tenor. In fact, he had no such script at the time, but when Powell expressed interest Edwards returned home, worked throughout the night, and wrote a *Richard Diamond, Private Detective* script. When he showed it to Powell the next day, Powell agreed to produce and star in it. The series was highly successful and lasted from 1949 to 1953, and Edwards wrote the majority of its scripts.

In addition to *Richard Diamond, Private Detective*, Edwards wrote for a number of radio and television series during the 1950s, including *The Lineup* and *Yours Truly, Johnny Dollar*, and directed a 1954 episode of *City Detective*. He also wrote for Powell's television anthology series, *Four Star Playhouse*, where he did his earliest directing on television in five episodes during 1953–1954, prior to any film directing.

Edwards built his major radio and television series at this time around distinctive masculine characters – Richard Diamond as a tough private detective who sings; Peter Gunn as a dapper, yet tough, private detective; and Mr. Lucky as a gambler and frequent amateur private detective who runs an offshore gambling boat and has a colorful sidekick. All of the series involved humor, much of it played off challenges to the main character's masculinity, a gender pattern that would continue throughout Edwards's career. With *Mr. Lucky*, the dapper Mr. Lucky (John Vivyan) was contrasted with his often-comic sidekick, Andamo (Ross Martin).

Edwards's main television series featured central characters reflecting the unflappable image of masculinity that Cary Grant had developed in films. Craig Stevens told us that, after Edwards signed him to star in the *Peter Gunn* series, he redesigned Stevens's image. Edwards had him dress in well-tailored, fashionable suits, wear a close-cut, Ivy League–style haircut, and indicated that he wanted Stevens to project a sophisticated manner, one that provided a bold contrast with his often-brutal underworld environment. *Mr. Lucky* (very loosely based on the premise of a floating, offshore casino in a 1943 Cary Grant film with the same title) also projects a sense of style in a tough world. These differed from the dominant private detective image of the time, that of a rugged working-class tough guy who mixed easily with and was often indistinguishable from underworld characters. That had been the model of Powell's Philip Marlowe in his career-changing role in *Murder, My Sweet*, one upon which Powell drew in a number of his *Films Noir* of the late 1940s, and partially informed the character of Richard Diamond. Intriguingly, Edwards wrote and directed a 1954 television pilot, *Mickey Spillane's "Mike Hammer!"*, that precisely fit that semi-thuggish pattern, but the pilot never sold and Edwards never returned to that model.

Much of the energy behind the relatively new *Film Noir* genre (which was never called by that name in the United States until the 1970s) shifted to television in the 1950s so that, by the early 1960s, *Film Noir* was considered an outdated form. The black-and-white cinematography associated with it became considered passé as the movie industry shifted to predominantly color cinematography. The kinds of story structures traditionally associated with *Film Noir*, particularly police and private detective crime stories, flooded prime-time network television with shows like *Dragnet* and *77 Sunset Strip*, including ones in which Edwards was involved such as *The Adventures of Dante*, which he created and for which he wrote and directed several episodes; *The Adventures of McGraw*, for which he wrote one episode; and *Mr. Lucky* and *Peter Gunn*, which he created, produced, and for which he wrote and directed episodes. *Richard Diamond, Private Detective* was also a popular show from 1957 to 1960. It was produced by Powell's Four Star Television and based on the radio series that Edwards had created, although he had nothing to do with it beyond being credited for creating the character. Edwards told us, however, that when he learned that it was going into production, he went over to Dick Powell's house to complain since he had originated the concept for radio a decade earlier. Eventually, Powell gave him a percentage of the show. The fact that Edwards would ask for a percentage, and Powell would give it to him, is one indication that his profile within the industry had risen by the late 1950s. He also wrote the story for *The Boston Terrier* that appeared on *The Dick Powell Show* in 1962, and in 1963 he wrote the teleplay for a pilot episode of a series for it which was not picked up for development.

Edwards's career-long pattern of creative and production partnerships is evident from this time. He cowrote both *Panhandle* and *Stampede* with John C. Champion. Richard Quine had codirected *Leather Gloves* in which

Edwards acted, and, beginning in 1952 with *Sound Off*, Quine and Edwards embarked on a series of six film collaborations, with Quine as director and Edwards as writer. This extended from movies into television with *The Mickey Rooney Show* (1954–1955). Quine told us:

> I met Blake on the first picture I ever directed, which I codirected with William Asher. It was a very small budget film called *Leather Gloves*. We were looking for a young actor to play a prize fighter, and a stunt man friend of mine, Dick Crockett, brought Blake Edwards in, so we hired Blake to play the fighter. So, our first meeting was as director and actor. It was 1948. Then, after directing a couple more films, I was given the task of coming up with a story for Mickey Rooney. Columbia made a three-picture deal with Mickey. Blake and I had become very good friends on the making of the prizefight film. He was also a friend of Mickey's, which I had been through all my life. I also knew that Blake had written a picture called *Panhandle* (1948) prior to appearing in our film. I recommended that we hire Blake and that Blake and I would work together on the screenplay for the Mickey Rooney film, which indeed we did, and it turned out to be *Sound Off* (1952). In its genre, it was successful, and we then did several films.

Nearly all of Blake Edwards's work in radio was part of the hardboiled detective and crime genre. This is all the more striking in that none of the widely diverse genre films that he made during that period were detective films. What might account for this, and why is it significant? As we've seen, during his early period Edwards was the junior partner in two major collaborations. In film, he worked extensively with Richard Quine who had no interest in detective films and never made one. His primary genres were musicals and comedies. And this also explains Edwards's work on *The Mickey Rooney Show*, which was a comedy that he cocreated with Richard Quine, and for which they cowrote the pilot teleplay. As usual Quine directed the episode (1954). Edwards also wrote one other episode. Neither of them was involved as a producer. Edwards's main collaborator in radio and later television was Dick Powell, who had a major interest in the hardboiled detective genre that revived his musical career after starring as Phillip Marlowe in *Murder, My Sweet* (1944). It is noteworthy that neither Powell nor Quine had any interest in Westerns, which may explain why, after *Panhandle* and *Stampede*, Edwards made no other Westerns in his early period, but he would return to them in his middle and late periods.

The most profound aspect of how Edwards worked in these diverse media forms wearing his multi-hyphenate hats occurs in how he drew creatively on this genre divide as he began his middle period. With Inspector

Clouseau in *The Pink Panther* and *A Shot in the Dark*, Edwards created one of the most – probably *the* most – famous comic detective in the history of film. In so doing he erased the line between the hardboiled detectives in his radio and television work and the comedies that were so prevalent in his films at the time. In one of the boldest moves of genre blending in his career, he in effect unified two seemingly unrelated genres. And he continued in some of his major later comedies to blend the detective genre with films that were not even about crime. *"10"* is always rightly identified as one of Edwards's midlife crisis sex comedies. But in fact, a central thread of the film has the main character, George Webber (Dudley Moore), become an amateur detective when he becomes obsessed with a woman he sees on her way to her wedding. First, he follows her to the church where he hides behind a flower trellis to secretly spy on her. Then he goes to the church where he engages the minister who officiated the wedding in a police-like interrogation, asking who the bride is and where she went for her honeymoon. Then, like all good private detectives, he secretly follows her to the honeymoon resort where he spies on her and her husband.

Victor/Victoria goes even further with a literal Clouseau-like detective who spies on "Victor," and a central macho male Chicago gangster who, having been aroused by "Victoria" thinking she is a woman, obsessively investigates Victor out of homophobic anxiety. To do so, he sneaks into her hotel suite to spy on her in her private bathroom. To the best of our knowledge no one has ever called either *"10"* or *Victor/Victoria* detective films, but in both films the central male characters become amateur detectives investigating their sexual dilemmas. *Victor/Victoria* even contains a scene with the detective which directly parallels one in *"10."* The detective played by Sherlock Tanney (a joke on the actor's real name, Herb Tanney, Edwards's physician in real life) is spying on Victoria through a window during a thunderstorm when he gets hit by lightning and charred black like a cartoon character. Similarly, in *"10"* George Webber gets stung on the nose by a bee while spying at the wedding, causing a commotion when he knocks over the flower trellis and flees.

In these films Edwards is essentially blending the detective genre with the dominant comedy genre, whereas in *The Pink Panther* and *A Shot in the Dark* he was blending the comic detective with the serious crime genre. The creative manner in which Edwards would return to his early work throughout his career was complex and, as we shall see in Chapter 12, continued into his extreme late-period work.

In series TV and radio, the central characters and relationships in each episode remained largely constant, so there was no closure for them since they would reappear in the next episode, although each episode had a different narrative line that was largely resolved by the end. As he developed his major series, Edwards also established grounding spaces, musical themes, and relationships for the main characters. With *Richard Diamond, Private Detective*, the space was Diamond's office and often the Park Avenue penthouse apartment of his girlfriend, Helen Asher, and the central characters were Diamond, Asher, and Police Lieutenant Levinson; with *Peter Gunn*, the space was Mother's jazz club and the central characters were Gunn, his girlfriend Edie, and Police Lieutenant Jacoby; and with *Mr. Lucky*, the space was Mr. Lucky's offshore gambling yacht and the central characters were Mr. Lucky, his sidekick Andamo, and Police Lieutenant Rovaks.

Radio of necessity engaged the audience aurally so Diamond's voice, his singing and whistling were central presences, and individual scenes generally began and ended with dramatic musical cues to orient and later re-orient the listener. Minor characters often had distinctive accents or vocal characteristics, and minor locations did the same, with echoing sounds in a huge warehouse or background noise and music in a nightclub.

Edwards had an extensive film output during his early period and we turn now to brief analyses of six films and one radio program from Edwards's early period which he did not direct but which he wrote, produced, and/or acted in: *Panhandle* (1948), which he cowrote and coproduced and in which he played an important secondary role; *Strangler of the Swamp* (1946), his first major acting role; *Leather Gloves* (1948), coproduced and codirected by Richard Quine, his last important acting role; *Drive a Crooked Road* (1954), for which he wrote the screenplay; *The Atomic Kid* (1954), for which he wrote the story; *My Sister Eileen*, for which he cowrote the screenplay with Richard Quine; and *The Couch* (1962), for which he wrote the story, adapting an episode of Richard Diamond, "The Eight O'Clock Killer" (1950). We've selected these films, most of which are comparatively obscure, to highlight various creative aspects of his roles in them: genre diversity, actors he worked with, and films in which he had a significant acting part even when he was not a writer. We also show a range of creative roles he played in the productions from writing the screenplays or the stories on which the screenplays are based and films which he produced.

PANHANDLE

The opening scene in *Panhandle*, Edwards's first film, deals explicitly with a woman with a rifle threatening a man, patriarchy, and The Law. She stands in a doorway with her rifle pointed at the man, who backs away (Figures 2.1 and 2.2). Under any circumstances it is a bold, creative beginning to a film in 1948 and it literally lays out Edwards's single most profound and dominating preoccupation throughout his career: the unequal power dynamics between men and women within patriarchy. A man looks on

FIGURE 2.1 *Panhandle,* © 1948 Monogram Pictures.

FIGURE 2.2 *Panhandle,* © 1948 Monogram Pictures.

while we see the action unfold and then disarms the woman by whipping the rifle from her. A new power dynamic then surfaces immediately between the two of them since the man, John Sands (Rod Cameron), is the owner of the saddle shop from which she, June O'Carroll (Anne Gwynne), emerges with her rifle. And there is a sexual/romantic tension that immediately develops between them. She then disappears without him knowing who she is or even her name.

Before dark-haired June reappears, John encounters Jean "Dusty" Stewart (Cathy Downs), a blonde woman with whom there is once again an instant sexual-romantic attraction. She works for one of the villains, Matt Garson (Reed Hadley), who "owns the town and territory" and who has proposed to her over twenty times. We will later learn that the dark-haired woman was in fact engaged to John's brother who was murdered and whose death John seeks to avenge. Dusty is also feisty, and it is her actions that save John from being killed during the climactic shootout (Figure 2.3).

John is the perfect incarnation of the Edwards womanizer. Both of the young women he encounters are immediately attracted to him and he to them as if it were "natural." Womanizing, however, is just another gender performance, and one to which Edwards will return repeatedly throughout his career. Rod Cameron is certainly handsome within the norms of the time, but that explains nothing about how the character is developed and used. His womanizing has a brutal, inappropriate aggression when he forces himself

FIGURE 2.3   *Panhandle,* © 1948 Monogram Pictures.

on a woman seemingly justified by the cliché of the time that when a woman says "no," she really means "yes."

Mr. Lucky, the star of the television series with the same name, treats women similarly, from hitting them to throwing them over his shoulder and carrying them out of a room. From the beginning of his career Edwards is already conflicted about simply accepting womanizing as a simple, healthy form of "natural" sexual expression between charismatic men and beautiful women, as if that explains such sexual behavior. To further complicate this, Jean describes John, the man she loves, to Matt Garson saying, "He's beautiful." A strange moment in 1948 when men were not usually called beautiful.

To further complicate the representation of men in the film, Blake Edwards plays the part of Floyd Scofield, a villainous gunslinger, an important secondary male character. Scofield is always somewhat slimy or repulsive. His dressing is too ornate with feminine overtones (Figure 2.4), and he strives to prove his masculinity, which he clearly lacks and about which he is insecure. Such men mistake "striving" for "proving," which literally kills Floyd Scofield in the end. Before he shoots him, John calls him "little man."

Panhandle shows Edwards's preoccupation with race and ethnicity which often involve stereotypes in, for example, *Peter Gunn* and *Mr. Lucky*. The very first scene not only introduces a threatening woman with a rifle but also a meek, submissive Mexican backing away from her (Figure 2.2). It turns out that he, out of respect for the quality of the saddle she had purchased, placed it in the front of the buckboard to protect it. She thought she had been cheated because she didn't know where he had put it. Since John owns the shop, the nameless Mexican points to the submissive servant stereotype, where people of color are happy just to make white people happy and serve them (i.e., both John and June in this single scene).

If the first scene of the film is bold, the last scene leaves the central romantic relationship unresolved with the hero John Sands walking away alone down a dark street (Figure 2.5). After setting up a narrative structure which depicts a dichotomy between dark-haired and blonde women as to who will win John's affections, it is noticeable that the ambiguous ending involves neither of them. This is yet another early example of Edwards ending the romantic plots of his films without the clear formation of a strong heterosexual couple.

STRANGLER OF THE SWAMP

Aside from about thirty roles as an extra or roles with a very minor speaking part, Blake Edwards played three significant supporting roles around this time in his career. The other two were *Strangler of the Swamp* (1946) and

FIGURE 2.4   *Panhandle,* © 1948 Monogram Pictures.

FIGURE 2.5   *Panhandle,* © 1948 Monogram Pictures.

Leather Gloves (1948). In addition to being Edwards's first prominent film acting role – he is listed as the third of the three leads – *Strangler of the Swamp* is his only significant acting role where he worked with someone who was not part of his inner circle or where he was not involved as a writer and producer. He was simply cast in the film to play a role and he never worked with any of the creative principals in the film again. Nevertheless, other aspects of the production intersect with Edwards's later work. The film is a remake. The first version was made in Germany and the second in the United States, and both versions were directed by Frank Wisbar. We have no evidence to suggest this film had any direct impact on Edwards's career, but it certainly demonstrates that remakes were in the air even if they were made in different countries and directed by the same man.

The poster for the film shows a monster attacking a blonde woman in a swamp with red print above declaring, "He was hanged for a crime he didn't commit, and now he's the STRANGLER OF THE SWAMP." The monster has been killing men who participated in the hanging. Christian "Chris" Sanders Jr. (Blake Edwards) returns home to the swamp where he falls in love with Maria Hart (Rosemary La Planche), the daughter of one of the participants in the hanging. Chris is a highly likable, attractive, and affable young man as opposed to the sleazy, threatening, unattractive gunslinger he plays in *Panhandle* (Figure 2.6), but there is a significant similarity. Although Chris is the romantic lead in the film in every traditional way (handsome, courageous, and protective of the woman he loves), his masculinity is called into question: he is saved two times in the film, once by his girlfriend who is about to be his fiancée, and once by his father. In both cases he is near unconsciousness

FIGURE 2.6 *Strangler of the Swamp*, © 1946 Producers Releasing Corporation (PRC).

and has to be assisted and carried away (Figures 2.7 and 2.8). Nor does he get to vanquish the villain/antagonist; remarkably, his girlfriend does so while he lies near death. Chris fails to protect her, which he talks about and sets out to do repeatedly, and he fails to even confront the villain in the climax. She both saves him and assumes the active role of confronting and defeating the Strangler. Although Frank Wisbar cast Edwards as the romantic lead, he may also have seen something in his appearance that suggested a lack of some aspect of traditional masculinity. In *Panhandle* this was striving to prove masculinity and power that he didn't really possess. Chris does not strive. On the contrary, he seems comfortable with his masculinity while simultaneously overestimating his strength and power. Although it may be mere coincidence, Edwards would make such themes and characters central to his own oeuvre as a writer-producer-director rather than as an actor.

LEATHER GLOVES

Leather Gloves was coproduced and codirected by Richard Quine and released November 11, 1948, the same year that Edwards cowrote and coproduced *Panhandle*, which was released on February 22, 1948.

Leather Gloves tells the story of Dave Collins (Cameron Mitchell), a former highly ranked prizefighter who is bribed to lose a fight with Vince

FIGURE 2.7   *Strangler of the Swamp*, © 1946 Producers Releasing Corporation (PRC).

FIGURE 2.8 *Strangler of the Swamp*, © 1946 Producers Releasing Corporation (PRC).

Reedy (Blake Edwards), himself a top-ranked local and regional boxer. Collins immediately falls in love with café waitress Cathy (Jane Nigh) before discovering that she is Vince's girlfriend. That romantic subplot is further complicated by another when Dave also falls in love with Jane Gilbert (Virginia Grey), a rich woman from New York who has a summer home in the West.

Outwardly, Vince Reedy is both an attractive man succeeding with women (Cathy, his attractive girlfriend, wants to become his fiancée) and a strong, powerful man succeeding in the boxing ring where he has never lost a fight (Figure 2.9). Furthermore, when he has the opportunity to fight Collins, a former boxing champ from New York City, he relishes the opportunity to test his masculinity by defeating a much more accomplished opponent than any he has faced before. Though not a braggart like his character in *Panhandle*, he voices with confidence his desire to prove his power in the ring. But once again, weaknesses lie beneath the outward shell of that masculinity. Most obviously, Reedy's left punch is so weak and ineffectual that Collins says, "He must have developed that left for washing windows" and sees instantly that no one so weak in that regard could ever survive the big time. Reedy is also ethically conflicted, first wanting to prove his masculinity in the fight, then agreeing to fix the fight, then wanting to take it back, and finally settling for a bizarre mixture where the first three rounds will be a true test of his power before Collins throws the fight in the

FIGURE 2.9   *Leather Gloves,* © 1948 Columbia Pictures Industries, Inc.

fourth. This ethical waffling undermines Reedy's stature as both a fighter and a lover since the two are mixed and the outcome of the fight is tied to his ability to win "the girl." Cathy wants him to stay and settle down in their small town, threatening that if he wins she will not go with him so he can pursue his dream of fighting in the big time. Vince decides he'll do whatever he needs to do to get what he wants without regard to anything or anyone else. Dave agrees to throw the fight for a marriage with Jane, who is also motivated by knowing Cathy is a rival for Dave's affections since after Vince defeats Dave, Vince will leave town with Cathy who is now fully committed to him.

During the fight Dave has a change of heart and redeems his integrity by not taking the fall in the fourth round as agreed. He does this not for himself, but rather to save the relationship between Vince and Cathy, a young couple whose lives will be ruined if Vince pursues his bigtime dream which Dave knows is certain to end in defeat. In one sense, the fight at the climax of the film ends as Dave predicted, when he graphically destroys Reedy in the fifth round. After taking a horrible beating, Reedy lies unconscious on the floor (recalling Edwards's character at the end of *The Strangler of the Swamp*) (Figure 2.10). In the last shots of him a couple of handlers drag his body away from the ring (Figure 2.11), and then revive him. We never see Reedy again nor hear him utter another word. His masculinity is doubly undercut by the public beating he takes and by the fact that Dave made the decision for him

FIGURE 2.10 *Leather Gloves,* © 1948 Columbia Pictures Industries, Inc.

FIGURE 2.11 *Leather Gloves,* © 1948 Columbia Pictures Industries, Inc.

that he will be spared professional failure so that he and Cathy will now be together in a happy, secure relationship.

It is indeed remarkable that all of Edwards's important roles deal so centrally with issues of masculinity and power, and that in all three roles his masculinity, whether playing a "good guy," a "bad guy," or someone in between, is deeply flawed, leading to death, near death, or total collapse.

DRIVE A CROOKED ROAD

Drive a Crooked Road (1954) tells the story of Eddie Shannon (Mickey Rooney), a race car driver who is lured by a gang of bank robbers comprised of Steve Norris (Kevin McCarthy), Harold Baker (Jack Kelly), and Barbara Mathews (Dianne Foster) into driving the getaway car following the robbery. The plan fails, with tragic consequences. Mickey Rooney's failed masculinity, linked to his small size, lies at the center of his character.

The film has an unusual dramatic structure where we do not see many of the most important things, and an ambiguous ending where the fate of the central characters is unknown. The beginning of the film shows Eddie with a childlike look of joy driving in a car race. After the race we hear Steve and Harold discuss possible candidates for their getaway driver. Steve chooses Eddie, a "little guy" who is lonely and lives in a rented room. When we first see Eddie at work as a car mechanic his coworkers make fun of "the little guy," who never has dates (Figure 2.12). One of the bullies even asks Eddie if he has ever "been alone" with a woman, which within the censorship codes of the time refers to having sex. Thus, from the very beginning Eddie's character is marked as lacking sexually with women and his obsession with cars and racing

FIGURE 2.12   *Drive a Crooked Road*, © 1954 Columbia Pictures Industries, Inc.

are marked as a form of symbolic overcompensation. Cars replace women in his life. Throughout the film he is repeatedly called by his nicknames "little guy" and "shorty," and near the end of the film he is even called a "midget."

Eddie immediately falls in love with Barbara, who brings her car in for service and quickly flirts with him, asking him after a couple days to meet her at the beach. He arrives to find her with Steve, who she says is just a "friend," and she begins to seduce Eddie, who is soon introduced to her social circle which centers on Steve and his housemate Harold. When Steve tells Eddie about their plan to rob the bank and asks him to join as the driver, Eddie initially refuses but succumbs when Barbara implies that he should do it for her. Eddie has a schoolboy-like naivete in his susceptibility to Barbara and his inability to see what others around him are really like.

The unusual narrative structure of the film starts at the very beginning where we join the race in progress. We know nothing about the racers or the drivers and the action is very brief and does not cut between competing cars we can identify, all of which undercuts building suspense as to who will win. This is a film about a bank robbery that we don't see. Eddie and Steve wait in the car as Harold goes in (Figure 2.13) and later emerges with the money (Figure 2.14). Much of the film is about Eddie's skill as a race car driver and his training for the daring robbery, but we only see him begin the escape with a few shots of him on the road which fade away before he completes the drive. There are no thrilling arrival shots. Although we heard talk about danger on

FIGURE 2.13 *Drive a Crooked Road*, © 1954 Columbia Pictures Industries, Inc.

FIGURE 2.14 *Drive a Crooked Road*, © 1954 Columbia Pictures Industries, Inc.

the drive from Highway Patrol roadblocks, we never see them during the drive, only one shot of a patrolman at the beginning when nothing happens. Once again, we see no action. In the scene following the drive, we simply see Eddie back to his routine life and his assumed relationship with Barbara.

When Eddie discovers that Barbara has disappeared from her apartment he goes to Steve's home, assuming he will find her there. This leads to an extraordinary climax in the film. After Barbara brutally confronts Eddie with the fact that she never loved him and that she was just the bait in the trap to get him to be the driver, Steve decides that Eddie has to be killed now that he knows the truth. Steve orders Harold to take Eddie to a location to be shot. Eddie drives while Harold holds a pistol on him, but Eddie suddenly veers off the road and the car rolls down a steep incline, overturning and crashing. Harold is killed in the accident and Eddie escapes, taking the gun and walking back to Steve's house (Figure 2.15).

He arrives to find Barbara, who has fallen down on the beach while fleeing Steve, who she now fears and loathes for having ordered Eddie murdered. Eddie approaches with a gun in his hand as Steve brutalizes Barbara (Figures 2.16 and 2.17). As Eddie attends to Barbara, Steve suddenly kicks Eddie's gun hand trying to disarm him. As Eddie falls backward, the gun goes off, killing Steve. Eddie hears Barbara crying on the beach as she lies in the sand. Eddie approaches and embraces and comforts her, saying, "Everything is gonna be alright. Don't cry. Don't worry. Everything will be alright. Please, please don't cry."

The visuals, however, tell an entirely different story as three police officers surround them and the camera pulls up and back into an extreme high angle long shot as the film ends (Figure 2.18). It is bizarre that Eddie, with childlike devotion, still loves Barbara as if nothing has happened, recalling that when she is asked if Eddie really loves her, she replies that he is devoted

FIGURE 2.15 *Drive a Crooked Road*, © 1954 Columbia Pictures Industries, Inc.

FIGURE 2.16 *Drive a Crooked Road*, © 1954 Columbia Pictures Industries, Inc.

FIGURE 2.17   *Drive a Crooked Road*, © 1954 Columbia Pictures Industries, Inc.

FIGURE 2.18   *Drive a Crooked Road*, © 1954 Columbia Pictures Industries, Inc.

to her but not in love with her, implying he is so inexperienced that he does not know the difference. The scene is also full of unresolved plot issues. Who will the police arrest and why? What will be the consequences? Both Eddie and Barbara are accomplices in the bank robbery. Eddie has also just killed two men, although both were in self-defense. But to the police the first looks like he abandoned the scene of a crash, leaving Harold dead or dying. Then

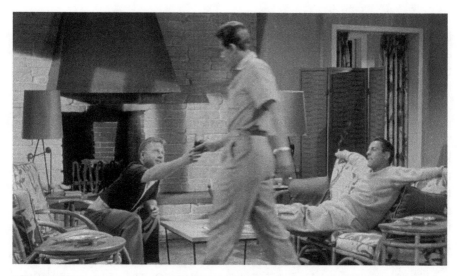

FIGURE 2.19   *Drive a Crooked Road*, © 1954 Columbia Pictures Industries, Inc.

as he embraces Barbara it looks like he killed her fiancé so he could have her for himself. Both of them could be arrested and charged with various serious crimes. Such unresolved endings involving potential heterosexual couples will become hallmarks of Edwards's later films, as will the strangely repressed homoerotic relationship between Steve and Harold. Steve orders Harold around the house to take care of their domestic arrangements and Harold acts like a beleaguered housewife (Figure 2.19).

THE ATOMIC KID

The title of *The Atomic Kid* identifies the main character, Barnaby "Blix" Waterberry (Mickey Rooney), as a "kid" and the film represents him precisely that way. This is a striking contrast to such other Blake Edwards films, radio shows, and television series with the main characters' names and titles: *Mister Cory* and *Mr. Lucky* both emphasize their formal title rather than their first names. *Peter Gunn* and *Richard Diamond* both have names with strong connotations: the former, which is pronounced the same way as the deadly weapon he wields, and the latter with the hard-cutting edge of the jewel with the same name. These names sound not like a kid, but like successful men, not to be messed with.

The Atomic Kid tells the story of Blix and his friend Stan Cooper (Robert Strauss), who accidentally wander into a model home at the center of a nuclear bomb test site. Blix is in the house when the bomb is detonated and inexplicably survives, although he is highly radioactive. IMDb lists the genres as comedy and sci-fi, which are both certainly aspects of the film, but so are the serious social problem film and the espionage genres. The comic style of the film is frequently reminiscent of The Three Stooges.

On the set of *A Fine Mess*, while watching Blake set up a shot that reminded us of The Three Stooges, we asked him if he was a fan of theirs. "Of course," he responded immediately. The Stooges behaved more like kids than adults, were thrown into circumstances and contexts they did not understand, could not control their bodies, and frequently their films end with them madly dashing off from the chaos they have created, all of which are true for Blix in *The Atomic Kid*. Some of the gag scenes in *Mr. Lucky* are also more reminiscent of The Three Stooges than of the Pink Panther films.

The Atomic Kid comes ten years before Stanley Kubrick's comedy also named after the main character: *Dr. Strangelove: Or How I Learned to Stop Worrying and Love the Bomb* (1964). In addition to the dangers that the atomic bomb poses to our existence, *The Atomic Kid* film also critiques military competence and postwar American consumerism centered on the white middle-class nuclear family represented by the mannequin family in the model home at ground zero. This genre mix highlights a feature of Edwards's early work that will continue throughout his career. *Richard Diamond, Private Detective*, for example, mixes Dick Powell's background as a singer in musicals with his later *Film Noir* persona to create a singing tough guy detective.

Blix is virtually a child under adult supervision throughout this film, from his partner, to the doctors and nurse, to the FBI. In the opening scene he looks like a cub scout walking with the scout master, loaded down, clanging and stumbling along, and needing a rest and a snack. It sets the tone for the entire film. He loses control of his body repeatedly, as in the scenes where he crashes into the stove in the kitchen of the target home with head protruding from one of the heating circles (Figure 2.20), falls out of the window while trying to get out of his room (Figures 2.21 and 2.22), which is repeated at the end (Figure 2.23), manages to get stuck on a hanger in his closet with an emphasis on his legs being too short for his feet to touch the ground (Figure 2.24), and most interestingly glows in the dark with radioactivity which he cannot control (Figure 2.25). This film reverses the usual "superman" genre as regards superpowers. Blix is a childlike man granted superpowers, but in this film the powers control him instead of him controlling the powers. This paradox lies at the center of the film.

Blix is constantly referred to as a "little" person by others (a wacko guest on a TV news show even tells the anchorman that the Kid is a Martian, all of

FIGURE 2.20   *The Atomic Kid*, © 1954 Republic Productions, Inc.

FIGURE 2.21   *The Atomic Kid*, © 1954 Republic Productions, Inc.

whom are very little people). Scientists control his every body movement with an electrical device as he lies in a sealed-off room. At the beginning of the film Blix describes his own masculine failure, saying he is a "nobody" who wants to be a "somebody." And even the scientist who studies his

FIGURE 2.22   *The Atomic Kid*, © 1954 Republic Productions, Inc.

FIGURE 2.23   *The Atomic Kid*, © 1954 Republic Productions, Inc.

radiation declares him a failure, saying he is of "zero" interest or value. The nurse who loves him (Elaine Devry, Rooney's wife at the time) calls him "cute" to defend his masculinity, a term which traditionally at that time was used to describe men lacking in conventional masculine strength and power.

FIGURE 2.24 *The Atomic Kid*, © 1954 Republic Productions, Inc.

FIGURE 2.25 *The Atomic Kid*, © 1954 Republic Productions, Inc.

The doctor in charge of the Kid works with two FBI agents who act as "chaperones" and even assist his date-night escape and adventure. The doctor looks upon him as a teenager sneaking out the house thinking he's fooling his parents, and the FBI agents watch and assist with amused disbelief.

For once the male lead who lacks masculinity actually marries the woman he desires, but it means little in the zany comedy of his childlike behavior as Blix gets lost driving through the desert on his honeymoon. His wife points out to him that she thinks he's lost when he thinks he's near San Francisco. Of course, she is right; he is not only lost but has stumbled onto the atomic testing range again. They go to a house only to discover that it has a mannequin family in it. Realizing his error, they rush back to the car and flee in fast motion like The Three Stooges.

MY SISTER EILEEN

My Sister Eileen (1955), directed by Richard Quine, is a rich film in regards to understanding Blake Edwards's early-period work as a screenwriter. The screenplay credited to Blake Edwards and Richard Quine is based upon a layered set of previous texts including books, plays, Broadway productions, and films. The 1955 film is based upon an original 1940 stage play by Joseph Fields and Jerome Chodorov, which in turn was based upon stories by Ruth McKenney. As if this isn't enough, Richard Quine had a major role in the 1942 film production of *My Sister Eileen*. And to top the topper topper, Leonard Bernstein composed the score for the 1953 Broadway production *Wonderful Town*, a new musical version of the Fields and Chodorov play.

One might think that a co-screenwriter would simply be lost in the midst of all this but Edwards negotiates it in creative ways, both by learning from the earlier works and by incorporating aspects of them into his middle- and late-period work and by adding to and making significant changes from the previous versions. The basic story of all these versions centers on the adventures of two sisters from Ohio who come to New York City to make their careers. Ruth Sherwood (Betty Garrett), a writer, is plain looking and Eileen Sherwood (Janet Leigh), a performer, is the "beautiful" sister. Edwards and Quine structure the film around the premise of a gender and sexuality-based masquerade. In order to impress Bob Baker (Jack Lemmon), a publisher, Ruth pretends to be Eileen since Bob is aroused by the mistaken assumption that the romantic and risqué stories are autobiographical whereas Ruth actually writes about her sister Eileen. Thus, Bob's entire infatuation is based upon his erotic imagination; he falls for the masquerade and sees Ruth as an attractive, boldly provocative, and highly sexual woman. Bob only learns the truth at the end of the film.

In the 1942 film, however, there is no masquerade and no sexual confusion. Bob Baker knows from the very beginning who Ruth is. Such masquerades become a major narrative and thematic structure in Edwards's middle and late periods. The most famous is the Julie Andrews character in *Victor/Victoria* who pretends to be a man pretending to be a woman, and Daisy Jane, the madam of a floating bordello who is a man disguised as a woman in *Gunn*.

There is yet another minor, gender-based masquerade added to the 1955 film. In the 1942 film, "The Wreck" Loomis and his wife live in the apartment above that in which Ruth and Eileen live. In the Edwards and Quine version, however, Loomis and his girlfriend are living together but are not married. When the wife's mother comes to visit, the couple disguise the fact that they share the same apartment and Loomis temporarily moves into a spare space in Ruth and Eileen's apartment.

All versions of the set design in *My Sister Eileen* are centered on the basement apartment that Ruth and Eileen rent in Greenwich Village. Both the design and the artists' colony setting are formally important in the film and will reappear throughout Edwards's career. The set design is really about two things: the basement below street level with a window opening up to the outside sidewalk and the fact that the building is directly above an elaborate underground subway tunnel system where construction is taking place. At totally unexpected moments throughout the day and evening, underground blasting rocks and shakes the apartment, totally disrupting those within. Edwards had already used a similar below-the-street-level garage bay for servicing cars with a high window offering a view of the street above in the 1954 film *Drive a Crooked Road*. Such windows open opportunities to bring Edwards's love of off-screen space into play. Many scenes in *My Sister Eileen* play on sets of legs coming and going as passersby walk past the window (Figure 2.26). In one scene, some drunk male voyeurs leer in at the sisters (Figure 2.27). At times minor characters such as a policeman or the visiting mother will crouch down and interact with Ruth and Eileen (Figure 2.28). Edwards fully develops these set design elements in *What Did*

FIGURE 2.26   *My Sister Eileen*, © 1955 Columbia Pictures Industries, Inc.

FIGURE 2.27 *My Sister Eileen*, © 1955 Columbia Pictures Industries, Inc.

FIGURE 2.28 *My Sister Eileen*, © 1955 Columbia Pictures Industries, Inc.

You Do in the War, Daddy? when one of the main characters gets lost in an elaborate underground tunnel system. Occasionally, he will surface by lifting a manhole cover, peering around utterly confused, and then disappear into the tunnels. A very funny minor variation occurs in *Return of the Pink Panther* when Clouseau checks into a hotel that only has a basement room available. This is particularly funny since the entire set is totally off-screen. We never see Clouseau in it and are left to imagine it, much like we are left to imagine a scene we never see after Clouseau announces he's off to the ski slopes.

In *My Sister Eileen*, we regularly see "Papa" Appopolous (Kurt Kasznar), the lovable but tricky artist landlord who humorously hides all the problems with the apartment he rents to Ruth and Eileen, sitting and painting by the apartment house front stoop (Figure 2.29). The artists' colony setting recurs

FIGURE 2.29   *My Sister Eileen,* © 1955 Columbia Pictures Industries, Inc.

in Edwards's career, notably in the *Peter Gunn* television series set in California far from Greenwich Village. Edwards is drawn to the potential of colorful, eccentric counterculture characters such as the landlord associated with bars, coffee houses, and artists' studios in such neighborhoods.

The structure of the music and dance numbers in the film also points to defining formal aspects of Edwards's work not only in musicals but also in such genres as Westerns, *Film Noir*, and slapstick comedy. Bob Fosse's excellent choreography appears throughout *My Sister Eileen*. Near the beginning of the film, Frank (Bob Fosse) and Chick (Tommy Rall) both attempt a romantic relationship with Eileen. As they await her leaving an audition, they break into a remarkable song and dance sequence beautifully directed by Quine with long shots and long takes (Figure 2.30). They competitively sing and dance as they express their desire for Eileen and attempt to outperform the other suitor. Long sections of the number involve nothing but

FIGURE 2.30   *My Sister Eileen,* © 1955 Columbia Pictures Industries, Inc.

elaborately choreographed dance with no lyrics. The dance disrupts the dialogue between the two men and they acknowledge each other as they dance in a manner different from that in their conversations.

Edwards's films, as we will see, frequently involve highly creative conversation scenes not only in terms of how the characters are shot and edited, but also in regard to their often witty dialogue. Yet, Edwards always suddenly shifts into extreme physical action, for example, dances in *Victor/Victoria*, violent and brutal fights in the *Peter Gunn* series, brutal physical slapstick with out-of-control bodies in the Pink Panther films, and sudden fatal shootouts in *Wild Rovers*. These moments frequently disrupt the dominant tones of those films and television shows but in musicals they are part of highly unified genre conventions.

THE COUCH AND "THE EIGHT O'CLOCK KILLER"

The Couch (1962), with a story written by Blake Edwards, was produced and directed by Owen Crump, Edwards's uncle. Crump was himself a writer-producer-director, though he did very little work directing theatrical features. His most prominent feature film was this collaboration with Blake Edwards and everything about the collaboration sheds light on the astonishing range of Edwards's creativity. Edwards's original story is based upon the premise of his radio script "The Eight O'Clock Killer" (1950), one of the best episodes in the *Richard Diamond, Private Detective* radio series.

The episode title refers to a baffling murder case with the killer calling police headquarters in advance to let them know that he will strike at eight o'clock that evening, murdering his victim by stabbing him to death with an icepick. The murders seem to be totally random with no motive until Diamond figures out that one of the relatives of the third victim is an heir to a rich fortune, which misleads the police into thinking they have solved the case. But the killer again notifies them that he will once again strike that night at 8:00pm. This makes no sense to Lt. Levinson, since if the police were right he would stop after killing number three, his rich uncle. But Diamond says that the planned fourth killing is just a ploy to mislead them and that Levinson is falling for it. The episode ends when the fourth killing is prevented at the last second.

The climax occurs as Diamond and Levinson are following the suspect as eight o'clock nears. As they catch up with him and his intended random victim, they lunge to stop him. We hear church bells begin to toll the hour and then a scream followed by a police whistle, all virtually at the same moment, the scream and the whistle further connected by the tolling bells. This is a stunning use of radio sound. The fact that the killer disguises his voice electronically every time he calls the police is another use of sound particularly well suited to radio.

The odd role of psychology is also relevant in this story. Levinson asks Diamond to help him with the case since Diamond is interested in the "psychology" of crime. Diamond says of course he is because that leads to understanding the motive for committing the crime. Then nothing in the episode follows through with that idea. We learn nothing about the nephew's psychology; his simple motive is murdering for wealth as the heir to the estate. The motive not only is much older than psychology itself but has nothing to do with it. The role of psychology would be to understand what drives this young man to murder for such a banal motive. Most people waiting to become wealthy heirs do not murder their relatives to get the money.

In a brilliant stroke of taking the same story in a totally new direction, the film *The Couch* shifts the primary focus to the psychology of the murderer and understanding him through what in fact is psychoanalysis, hence the film's title. Crump describes the evolution of the project as follows: "Blake had an outline of a story called 'The Panic.' I think that was the title. Anyway, it was about a killer who was turned loose in a city and everyone panics because they can't catch the killer. I thought it was kind of an interesting idea. And he said, 'Well, take it, Owen. See what you can do with it.' So, I wrote a treatment and I changed it, I must say, quite a bit. I included a psychiatrist that the killer was going to and who he finally tried to kill, and I called it *The Couch*. I took it to Warner Brothers and by then Blake was in the midst of some other thing, I don't remember what, he was all tied up with something, he always was. And anyway, Warner's liked it, and so we got Robert Bloch, who wrote *Psycho*, to do the screenplay."

Crump ended up directing and producing the film, sharing a credit for cowriting the story with Edwards. The premise remains the same: a killer calls the police to announce ahead of time that he will stab a seemingly random victim at eight o'clock, but the film tells the story from nearly the opposite point of view of that in the radio program. Now the killer becomes the central character and the police detectives are minor. In the film the murders are integrated. The killer strikes victims he knows and who are close to him, including his psychiatrist. The motive of getting an inheritance is totally gone. This movie is centered on a killer's motives deeply rooted in and uncovered by psychoanalysis. This film is *not* about money.

The end of the film involves complex use of a couple visual motifs in contrast to the complex sound montage at the end of the radio program. One of the climatic scenes in the film occurs at a football stadium (Figure 2.31), which parallels the use of the baseball stadium at the end of *Experiment in Terror*, produced and directed by Blake Edwards and also released in 1962. In both, the scenes occur near or at the end of the film and feature big crowds coming into and/or leaving the stadium while the game is in action. As such they create a stunning contrast between the public aspect of the sport and the horrific private drama playing out in that setting with others totally oblivious to what is happening, even when someone in the crowd is stabbed and nearly dies.

The other formal strategy at the film's climax involves the use of mirrors, which points to the split personality of the killer and his mild-mannered, polite persona as others, including his girlfriend, see him (Figure 2.32). And this points simultaneously to how Edwards will use mirrors in such films as *Gunn* and to how Hitchcock may have influenced him with his use of mirrors in *Psycho* two years earlier. The fascinating relationship between *The Couch* and *Psycho* also includes the extraordinary ending of *The Couch* with the main male character, recalling Norman Bates, descending into an utter psychotic breakdown, transforming into a totally submissive child in front of our eyes (Figure 2.33).

Although *The Couch* is a minor Blake Edwards film, it was made in 1962, the last year we have identified as the transitionary period between the early work and the beginning of the middle period. Like the much better-known

FIGURE 2.31   *The Couch*, © 1962 Warner Bros. Entertainment, Inc.

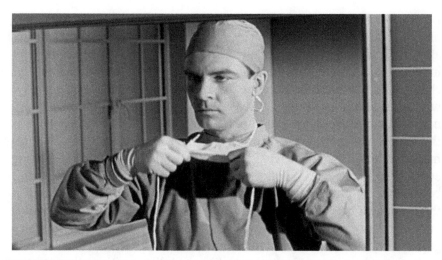

FIGURE 2.32   *The Couch*, © 1962 Warner Bros. Entertainment, Inc.

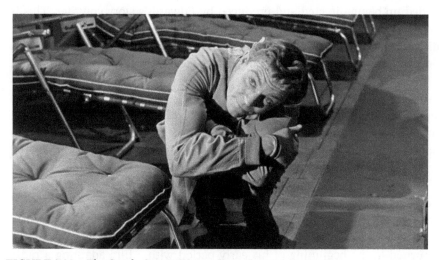

FIGURE 2.33   *The Couch*, © 1962 Warner Bros. Entertainment, Inc.

Days of Wine and Roses and *Experiment in Terror*, *The Couch* is a black-and-white film. Edwards made no black-and-white theatrical features after 1962. The circumstances surrounding the production, including his limited role as a cowriter of the story, make it an ideal way to summarize this chapter and introduce the next one. We have introduced Edwards's creative work style and his output as a writer-producer-director-actor working primarily in radio, television, and film. His early period from 1948 to 1962 was the richest mix in his entire career of working simultaneously in all three media while wearing all four creative hats. He seemed to be everywhere doing everything. Rather than privileging film directing, we're approaching this bewildering output by careful analysis of the works regardless of his role in their production. We have found his creative footprint on nearly everything on which he worked. The starting point of the story for *The Couch*, which goes back to an episode of a radio show he wrote and created at the very beginning of his career twelve years earlier, sheds light on his endless creative energy, his interest in exploring creative connections between various media, and his interest in how stories can be told and retold. That story was then significantly revised by his cowriter Owen Crump, and then the screenplay was written by a third party, Robert Bloch, well known at the time. But the film ended up being directed and produced by Edwards's story cowriter. This is about as far removed as possible from the traditional auteur privileging of the director in total control of the film. Although during his mid-career Edwards developed a reputation of a difficult director seeking total control of his films, *The Couch* shows Edwards capable of working creatively in a highly collaborative mode in a very busy, important time in his career. The film shows significant contributions by Edwards, Crump, and Bloch. Edwards could have simply canceled plans for the film, holding the story until there was an opening in his film directing schedule. Instead he embraced what others did with his original story. That itself is a form of creative flexibility.

Edwards would literally end his career with a theater production, *Big Rosemary*, in a manner that recalls *The Couch*. As we discuss in the final chapter, *Big Rosemary* is an adaptation of Edwards's second film, *He Laughed Last*, as a theatrical musical. Just as Edwards entered his middle period and returned to the beginning of his early period with a film adapting a radio show he had written, he ended his late period by returning to the beginning of his career by adapting a film he had written and directed for musical theater. Another sign of his creativity is that in both cases he cut the main characters out of the retelling! Neither Richard Diamond nor Walt Levinson are characters in *The Couch* and Gino Lupo (Frankie Laine), a nightclub performer, is not a character in *He Laughed Last*. Thus, he was not only

remaking and adapting from one form to another, he was also totally restruc-
turing how the story was told. And, to top the topper topper, he never formally acknowledges that he is remaking one of his own very early works in
radio and film. Not a mention of *"The Eight-O'Clock Killer"* appears in the
credits for *The Couch*, though the poster when the film was released playfully revealed that the working title of the allegedly secret production was
"Operation Icepick." The radio episode was in fact also known as *The Icepick
Killer*. And there is no mention of *He Laughed Last* in the Playbill program
notes for *Big Rosemary*. Although returning to his early work at key points in
his career was creatively important to Edwards, he did not want his audience
to approach the new works within that framework. Edwards's creativity
stands in direct opposition to the overused current figure of speech, "Been
there, done that." Going back there and doing it again held an immense
creative challenge for him.

NOTE

1. Mel Tormé, *It Wasn't All Velvet: An Autobiography* (New York: Viking Press,
   1988).

CHAPTER 3

Mister Cory (1957)

Written and Directed by Blake Edwards

Mister Cory, the first film that Blake Edwards directed under his new contract with Universal after leaving Columbia, highlighted that Edwards was not pigeonholed as a comedy filmmaker at this early point in his career. Edwards's previous films that he wrote and directed at Columbia had been under contract as Frankie Laine musical comedies. Although Edwards had written the screenplays for both, they had initially been scheduled to be directed by Richard Quine. However, when Quine moved into more prestigious projects, their direction fell to Edwards. After having demonstrated his talent with their direction, Edwards moved on to the prestigious Universal Studios. *Mr. Cory* is from this perspective the first film Edwards directed where he was free to work in a genre that he chose, and it is significant that it was "serious" drama and not comedy. Edwards did not envision himself as a comedy filmmaker but as a diverse filmmaker. His record of box-office and critical successes, however, quickly branded him that way and after the box-office successes of *Operation Petticoat*, *The Pink Panther*, and *A Shot in the Dark*, studios were reluctant to fund his other genre projects. However, he struggled throughout his career to make "serious" non-comic films, and he struggled against the widely accepted notion that comedy was not "serious."

Blake Edwards: Film Director as Multitalented Auteur, First Edition.
William Luhr and Peter Lehman.
© 2023 John Wiley & Sons Ltd. Published 2023 by John Wiley & Sons Ltd.

He knew and repeatedly demonstrated that comic filmmaking was as serious an art form as drama. His commercial and critical reputation as a gifted comic filmmaker has, however, obscured a stunning fact: he succeeded in making a number of dramas and a documentary which equal and perhaps even surpass his comedies. He thought his original cut of *Wild Rovers*, a serious Western, was his greatest film until the studio re-edited it and released a butchered shortened version. The restored version makes a reasonable claim for indeed being his masterpiece. We turn now to an examination of eight non-comic Edwards films, including *Wild Rovers*, in the hopes of shattering the old image and bringing attention to the diverse range of his creative achievements.

Mister Cory begins with a title, "Sangamon Street Chicago," superimposed over the first shot of a montage sequence of 11 shots showing the crowded streets of an inner-city ethnic neighborhood. We see peddlers, food carts, grocers, and crowds of people bustling about their business or simply standing together talking. The soundtrack is alive with the noise of the neighborhood, which, along with the visuals, combines to create a sense of intense vitality. We do not see the title character until he walks into the frame in shot 12 of the sequence and the dialogue begins. In contrast to this, the film will end with a shot of Mr. Cory, walking alone to board an airplane. That shot is also part of a carefully designed sequence which bookends Mr. Cory's journey from that working-class immigrant neighborhood to points unknown as he remakes his image, replacing the image of the T-shirt-clad working-class man he used to be with that of a well-dressed, highly successful businessman.

Within this structure, Edwards tells a picaresque tale of Cory's adventures and misadventures which is broken into five segments by geographical location: Sangamon Street Chicago, to the Wisconsin resort country, to a Reno gambling mecca, to a return to Chicago, to his departure for points unknown. In Wisconsin Cory (Tony Curtis) meets and falls in love with two sisters from a wealthy family, Abby and Jen Vollard (Martha Hyer and Kathryn Grant). He also meets Mr. Caldwell (Charles Bickford), a wealthy guest who hosts poker games in his room. In Reno, he unexpectedly meets Caldwell again, and they form a professional gambling relationship. When they return to Chicago, they form a new gambling partnership with Ruby Matrobe (Russ Morgan), and Cory pursues his romantic relationships with Abby and Jen. At the end, with his professional and personal life in chaotic transition, Cory goes off to points unknown to contemplate his future.

Within this framework, Edwards continues to examine key aspects of the world he created in his early multi-hyphenate period of radio, television, and film work. But storytelling within a narrative structure like this required feature-length filmmaking with him writing and directing. Foremost among the key aspects of the world Edwards had already created are his fascination with performance of many kinds and his equally and related obsession with masculinity and male bonding embedded in a sexual context including women and normative heterosexual marriage. Both Cory and the two women with whom he falls in love all seek marriage as their life goal yet, as in so many Edwards films, *Mister Cory* fails to end with an affirmation of any heterosexual monogamous couple. The film also explores performance as a mode of disguise and deception and continues Edwards's formal exploration of sound and the creation of space and off-screen space.

As we meet Cory in the film's opening, he stops to talk with a man on Sangamon Street who asks, "Hey, where you going?" Cory replies, "Any place, as far away as I can get." The exchange continues, "Are you coming back?" Cory replies, "Not if I can help it." He looks down on his neighborhood to which he considers himself superior. In order to escape the dreaded neighborhood, he in effect creates and performs a new version of himself. The first place he goes to is Green Pines, an exclusive lakeside resort in Wisconsin. He begins to create his new character when he interviews with Mr. Earnshaw (Henry Daniell), the maître d'hôtel of the fancy restaurant. To get the job he lies about a couple of guys he met who had worked there during the previous summer. We then see a remarkable long take of Cory working during a dinner. He has cleared a table and balances a large tray full of dirty dishes which he carries to the kitchen (Figure 3.1). He has trouble balancing everything, and he wobbles and winds his way around the dining room, directly passing in front of Mr. Earnshaw who stands watching with a severe

FIGURE 3.1   *Mister Cory*, © 1957 Universal-International Pictures.

critical eye. Cory succeeds in passing him and heading toward the kitchen entry door when two waiters come out through the swinging kitchen door, each narrowly avoiding colliding with Cory, much to Earnshaw's relief. Just when things look safe to Earnshaw, he and we hear an off-screen crash followed by a cut to the kitchen interior where Cory and another waiter lie sprawling on the floor amid piles of broken dishes.

The extreme long take with a near-comic tone ending in an off-screen catastrophe will become hallmarks of Edwards's comedies. As Sam Wasson points out, the characters who are victims of such mishaps are usually in some way arrogant or see themselves as superior. In this scene that is true of the maître d' who looks down on all his employees, demanding they call him "Sir," as well as Mr. Cory, who looks down on his entire neighborhood with contempt as he leaves, planning never to return. This scene is profoundly important to the development of what will become a major stylistic preoccupation of Edwards's dramas: the unexpected eruption of physical comedy into the world of dramatic action. Although perfectly executed with Curtis's acting, the elaborate long take, and the timing of the off-screen crash, it is a restrained comic moment. It is not laugh out loud funny, and it does not build with topping the topper topper. It is the sole moment of such comedy in the entire film, as if Edwards is introducing the very fine line between comedy and tragedy, between death and laughter. That fine line joins his comedies and his dramas at the hip.

As with so many things in this film, Edwards returns to a rhyming scene in the kitchen, this time with dark action. Cory's various guises that mislead people as to who he is lead to a dramatic climax when Abby Vollard, who he romances with various deceptions, enters the kitchen and stares in disbelief at Cory, whom she thought was a guest, washing the dishes. His being outed as a dishwasher leads to another worker making a sarcastic remark. An angry fight that turns into a brawl ensues with dishes and workers crashing to the ground. In the first scene, Earnshaw simply tells Cory the cost of the damaged dishes will be deducted from his pay. This time Cory is fired. In both cases he pays for his arrogant deceptions.

The formal use of the kitchen/dining room dichotomy pitting waiters and staff against the wealthy patrons pervades Edwards's work in all periods, including *Peter Gunn* and *Mr. Lucky* on television, and will include such classics as *The Party, Darling Lili, Victor/Victoria*, and *That's Life!*. Its thematic significance in this film is summed up by Earnshaw telling Cory, "The distance between your place in the kitchen and Miss Vollard's place in the dining room is considerable." The importance of space and the distances between spaces in this film extends from such literal spaces as that between

Sangamon Street in Chicago and Green Pines in Wisconsin to such metaphorical spaces as the class distinctions between the kitchen and the dining room.

The Wisconsin segment has multiple instances of Cory's performance masquerading as a wealthy guest while hiding the reality of being a kitchen staff member. He sees two patrons playing golf while betting and asks to join them. They presume he is a guest and lose their money to him. At one point we see Cory dashing out of the restaurant, discarding part of his uniform and transforming the remaining shirt into a seemingly classy, stylistic one as he then approaches Jen, who is fooled into continuing to believe he is a wealthy guest. Such moments are close to Edwards's use of farce in many of his comedies, but here it is not played for laughs. At one point Cory even fools Earnshaw into giving him time off due to being sick so that he can pursue his romantic quests. Both sisters and Earnshaw eventually see through Cory's masquerade performance, and he is forced to leave.

When we first see Cory in Reno, he is gambling at a card table in another complex rhyming scene. Caldwell walks into the backroom game where Cory is as surprised to see him as Caldwell is to see Cory. At Green Pines, Cory walked into Caldwell's private room with a card game in progress. But this moment intersects the performance masquerade when Cory is puzzled to hear that Mr. Caldwell is now Mr. Biloxi. Cory later asks whether he is really Caldwell or Biloxi. The startling reply is, "Neither!" He then explains that his real name is "Jeremiah Des Plains Caldwell." As he explains his background, he reveals that his name in Green Pines is itself a masquerade performance, hiding his true given name and his background. Hence, Biloxi in Reno is a masquerade of the Green Pines masquerade. Such performances pervade the film. When Cory returns to Chicago near the end of the film, he asks Earnshaw, "Have you ever been arrested, Mr. Earnshaw?" The startling reply is, "Only once, sir, for bigamy," at which point Cory realizes that both of the important older men he met at Green Pines masqueraded in a manner that hid their true past from him. The Reno sequence ends when Caldwell proposes a professional gambling partnership with Cory, and they go to Chicago to implement it.

The second Chicago sequence stands in stark contrast to the first one. They strike a new partnership with Ruby Matrobe. The deal gives Matrobe, who puts up most of the cash, 70 percent of the take and Cory 30 percent. Now Cory has advanced over Caldwell, who had been the experienced mentor to Cory. He now works for Cory. In another rhyming sequence, Cory now hires Mr. Earnshaw to work for him. Copying Earnshaw's snobbishness, since he had insisted Cory always refer to him as "Sir," Cory now asks Earnshaw to address him as "Sir." This masculine insistence on names and modes of address as signs of power and authority even carries over to titles of some of Edwards's works such as the TV series *Mr. Lucky*. The two main characters in *The Great Race* have comically ludicrous names and honorifics: The Great Leslie (Tony Curtis) and Professor Fate (Jack Lemmon). Again, the fine line between the comic and the dramatic. In *Darling Lili*, two male characters argue over the lead female character's name. One says to the other, "You say Smith and I say Schmidt. That precisely is the difference between us." And in Blake Edwards's comedies and dramas, such distinctions can be matters of life and death.

Whereas the first Chicago sequence is one set in a teeming inner-city neighborhood, the second is set in "the Gold Coast," an exclusive upscale neighborhood for the extremely wealthy. Cory insists that transforming a mansion there into a gambling casino is the perfect locale for their new venture. Matrobe is reluctant but finally gives in. The fancy mansion continues Cory's masquerade of being a wealthy upper-class man while emphasizing a new dimension to the persona he creates. The highly masculine, tough-speaking man who fights his way to the top reveals a traditionally feminine side to his gender performance. Edwards develops this via a complex interaction of camera position, set design, and wardrobe. Two rhyming sequences establish this using a large, winding stairway. In the first, Cory, impeccably and formally attired, appears at the top of the staircase, which is centered and framed by the camera at the foot of the staircase where we also see a group of men, including Matrobe, waiting for him. In one take, we see Cory descend the staircase while the men below and we in the audience watch the spectacle (Figure 3.2). Traditionally such staircase sequences are reserved

FIGURE 3.2 *Mister Cory*, © 1957 Universal-International Pictures.

for the appearance of a leading lady. The exact same setup repeats shortly after when Jen Vollard first visits the new mansion being transformed into the Dalton Club. Once again Cory appears fully attired and descends to speak with her at the bottom (Figure 3.3).

Cory's clothing also rhymes with an early scene in Green Pines. Shortly after Cory has won at cards with the wait staff and won at golf with guests, his fellow staff members rummage through his closet and angrily denounce Cory for the expensive clothes they find, which they note were paid for with their money lost in the card game. Sam Wasson insightfully quotes Blake Edwards in describing the *Peter Gunn* TV show as somewhere between soft boiled and hard boiled and incisively adds that Gunn's public masculine tough side is countered by the private side we see in his apartment where his somewhat feminine side emerges in how he dresses and behaves, including cooking and serving his girlfriend. Wasson cleverly dubs this aspect of Gunn's character as that of an "interior decorator." And sure enough, we also see just that side of Cory in this sequence. He carefully supervises the workmen as to where to place the classy furniture. In a remarkable moment, we see him standing with his back to a doorway as he holds a painting in one hand, carefully pondering one on the wall as he considers what to hang where. Cory's tough guy persona may appear as a further masquerade covering the interior decorating side, but Edwards undercuts and subverts all macho male personae as really having traits in common with women, as being on a continuum rather than being their polar opposites. Throughout his comedies, especially those made in the 1980s, he questions conventional notions of gender duality. This kind of duality also applies to *Mister Lucky*, where the

FIGURE 3.3   *Mister Cory*, © 1957 Universal-International Pictures.

film's title character who transforms his yacht into a floating casino also revels in beautiful clothing and the fine dining cuisine of the chef he hires for his club.

Cory has two rhyming business meetings with Matrobe which raise a further gender issue. The meetings are designed to secure Matrobe's backing of Cory's unusual business model of using a converted private mansion as a gambling casino. The first of these takes place in a steam bath where we see Cory's body displayed while he stands with a towel around his midsection (Figure 3.4). He stands next to Caldwell, who is fully covered with a bathrobe, while Matrobe sits against the wall with a towel around his midsection. The second such scene takes place as Matrobe lies naked on a table with a towel around his midsection as he gets a massage by a muscular, fit man. Many similar scenes occur in *Peter Gunn* and several of the early films such as Richard Quine's first film, *Leather Gloves* (1948), which features Blake Edwards as a boxer. The scenes continue throughout his career, including *Experiment in Terror* and, most notably, *Victor/Victoria*. On the one hand, these scenes reinforce the exclusive male space for such power transactions. On the other hand, such gendered spaces intensify a kind of male bonding with partially naked bodies that at times have connotations of potential homosexuality or paradoxically homophobia. This emerges most explicitly in *Victor/Victoria* when the implicitly homophobic central character, King Marchand, visits a virulently homophobic crime boss in a steam room. Many forms of male bonding, including men-only backroom card games with cigar smoking that we see in *Mister Cory*, are regularly part of Edwards's preoccupation with masculinity and the male body and the relation of women to such men in that world.

FIGURE 3.4 *Mister Cory*, © 1957 Universal-International Pictures.

As with the reversal of Earnshaw now working for Cory, the concluding segment in which the film returns to Chicago is full of complex formal rhymes which refer back to Wisconsin where Cory's journey to remake himself began. But the key rhymes center on his renewed relationships with Abby and Jen Vollard. Abby is still engaged to her old boyfriend, Alex Wyncott (William Reynolds), who remains a pitiable alcoholic, and Jen is still single and unattached. Jen's enthusiasm for Cory is therefore open; she clearly hopes she now has a chance with him since she has matured in the intervening time. But Cory clearly still has his desires set on Abby, even though she is engaged and even though she rudely rejected him when she discovered he was a kitchen worker and not a wealthy guest. When she and Alex come to Cory's club, he rigs the blackjack table so that Alex will win and stay engaged while he approaches Abby. Throughout the film, Cory is a manipulative, controlling man, never more so than in the finale. A dark tension remains between him and Abby and things come to a head on an evening when he tells her he is going to return to Sangomon Street.

The scene begins with Cory standing alone on the deserted street as he looks around, disturbed by sounds he hears recalling the now-nostalgic noises associated with the old neighborhood. This part of the scene is structured around sound more than visuals. The noises he "hears" arise and fall away into silence several times. In the opening scene the sounds were on-screen, and we now hear them as off-screen memories. After these confusing noises, Cory begins to hear off-screen fragments of dialogue from the past followed by the off-screen sound of a car approaching as the camera pans to show Abby driving in the family convertible. The present has just met the past. The use of sound to characterize an environment recalls Edwards's work on the *Richard Diamond, Private Detective* radio show. Working in radio had a lasting impact on Edwards's style of film storytelling.

Cory then talks to Abby about his past. "I just wanted you to see it. To know all about it. I'm not a dishwasher anymore. But I'm still from Sangomon Street." At this point we have a visual rhyme back to Green Pines. He assumes he now has become the man in Abby's life and walks over to the driver's seat of her car as she moves over to the passenger side and he takes the wheel as they drive away. In Green Pines he borrowed this same car to pick her up at the train station on a return trip to Chicago. She had expected Jen or someone else to pick her up, and she dismissively takes the wheel as Cory moves into the passenger seat and angrily drives away. The power reversal is now seemingly complete, but it will reappear in an ideologically disturbing manner.

Their final confrontation occurs at the film's climax. First, Alex angrily barges into Cory's suite as he eats breakfast, confronting him about his taking Abby away. Caldwell remains in the room, a background presence throughout the ensuing scene. In a brutal verbal exchange, Cory humiliates Alex with the ultimate insult, "I think you're a weak, no good excuse for a man." He throws the "coward" out of the room. Caldwell, who has witnessed it all, confronts Cory over brutally destroying the man's masculinity, leading to a parting of the ways between Cory and his partner.

The scene fades to black, and we see Abby in Cory's suite. Abby holds an engagement ring from Cory, but the scene quickly turns ugly when he is outraged that she will not agree to marry him but is willing to be his mistress and continue seeing him. He has even decided to leave the club for her. She remains unmoved and Cory denounces her for thinking that he's not good enough for her to marry him but only to see him on the side. He tells her that she is "nothing but a high-class tramp," and she calls him a "cheap, enterprising punk." Matrobe bursts into the room, interrupting their fight to announce that the cops are raiding the joint in half an hour. They have already seized a couple of Matrobe's other gambling sites. Matrobe blames Cory for the raids and declares that Cory has lost all his money invested in the club.

The film suddenly erupts into the second scene of violent action. Cory punches Matrobe in the gut and he collapses. He then ushers Abby out and they walk down the hallway where Alex shoots Cory in the back. Now he collapses to the floor. Matrobe rushes out and grabs Alex's gun, holding it on him. He sees an opening to reverse the power structure and stop the impending raid by using Alex as a pawn to get at his powerful father who can intervene with the authorities. But now another bizarre reversal takes place. Cory refuses to go along with this, telling Alex he didn't think that he was man enough to shoot him. Having shown that he is not a "weak man," Cory now sees that Alex can and should marry Abby. Without any consultation with Abby in determining her own future, Cory imposes their marriage on the couple and tells them to get away quickly before the raid which he now welcomes. In so doing, Edwards creates a variation on a common Hollywood narrative structure wherein a man saves a woman in a manner that seems noble but actually masks his abusive use of patriarchal power. Although he doesn't do this so that he can marry her, he in effect assumes the power position to not only make that decision but to pass her over to another man who now controls her. She is totally passive in the transaction, and, after she and Alex flee, we do not see them again in the film. This sets up the second disturbing moment of gender ideology.

In the film's denouement, Cory and Caldwell arrive together at the airport, their apparent earlier quarrel resolved. In a two-shot of the men, we see and hear Jen yelling at them and rushing toward Cory. We then see the three of them in the frame when Caldwell announces he will get the tickets, leaving Cory and Jen alone. Jen asks him to take her with him and Cory replies, "I can't. I've got some thinking to do. Jeremiah and I are going to sit in the sun, maybe do a little fishing, and settle the future." She playfully replies, "I bet you ten to one you marry me," and after a little banter we see Cory in a two-shot as he turns away to join Caldwell on the plane. The final image in that shot shows Cory alone in the frame with the plane in the rear (Figure 3.5). We see neither Jen nor Caldwell. What is going on here?

At the simplest level, the scene is open ended as Cory leaves Jen to await her fate, but it also avoids showing the male couple together. Wasson describes the relationship between Cory and Caldwell as a father–son relationship. If so, it is an odd one. Edwards has developed it in a manner that poses the father–son relationship in opposition to a normative heterosexual marriage relationship. This is not what most movie father–son relationships are about. Furthermore, as we've already mentioned, by the last section of the film Cory has surpassed and displaced the father figure; he is now the senior partner. Consider carefully Cory's explanation of why Jen can't come with him. It explains nothing but, rather, describes a world of male bonding and power, which, like the backroom card games and the steam rooms, excludes women. Within Cory's own logic there is no place for the woman he may marry because he's got some "thinking to do." A man apparently cannot think if a woman is present. But this seems to be no problem for both him

FIGURE 3.5   *Mister Cory*, © 1957 Universal-International Pictures.

and Jeremiah while they sit in the sun and go fishing (although not the heavy-duty "thinking" that also seems to require no women present). And most explicitly, Cory says he has to "settle the future." The woman he says he is most likely going to marry has no place in settling that future. She can wait to find out whether or not he chooses her. So, after telling Abby who she will marry and sending her off with a man we have seen she has serious doubts and reservations about, he leaves Jen waiting to see whether he chooses her or not. The women are excluded from the male spaces and from the power dynamics that determine their lives. Edwards does not offer a social critique of such deplorable conditions here but rather portrays Cory in a manner that invites the audience to identify with him as he solves HIS problems, which means treating both sisters in a controlling manner that suits his best interests.

Many of Edward's films and radio and TV shows involve odd male bonding couples. *Wild Rovers*, as we will see, is very complex in that there is a literal father–son relationship and what appears to be a central love relationship between an older man and a young man. But many such relationships do not turn on such age differences. The lead male couple in *Mr. Lucky* are men of similar ages. The same is the case with Peter Gunn and Detective Jacoby, Inspector Clouseau and Cato, Richard Diamond and Levinson, and so on. Edwards told us that he originally cast Robert Duvall in the Bruce Willis role in *Sunset* which would have made both the central male characters older men of the same generation. Casting Willis required him to change that dynamic.

Leslie Fiedler first drew attention to the role of such male bonding in American literature in *Love and Death in the American Novel* (1960) when he termed it homosocial as opposed to homosexual. The key issue with such male couples was not whether they had sex together but rather what Fiedler saw as their immature need to escape women for meaningful adventures with their male buddies. Consider this passage again within that light when Jen asks Cory to take her with him: "I can't. I've got some thinking to do. Jeremiah and I are going to sit in the sun, maybe do a little fishing, and settle the future."

Troubled endings like this that do not affirm the romantic heterosexual couple in Edwards's films combined with what will become an increasingly explicit representation of gays and lesbians clearly add that issue to the mix. Cory and Caldwell are not represented as men going off together to have sex, but there is something other than a mature father–son relationship. A poster advertising the film features big, bold letters asking the question: "WHO WAS THIS MAN THEY CALLED...*Mister Cory*?" It is an insightful poster about this film that asks that question about a character who performs many versions of himself in relation to not just class but also gender identifications. The mix of all these issues should not, however, obscure that the end of the film represses any questioning of the gender ideology by which Cory wields his position of privileged male power to control and shape the destinies of the two sisters central to the film's romance plot.

CHAPTER 4

Experiment in Terror (1962)

Produced and Directed by Blake Edwards

During 1961–1962, Blake Edwards made a trio of films that would mark a transition from his early period to his middle period: *Breakfast at Tiffany's* (1961), *Experiment in Terror* (1962), and *Days of Wine and Roses* (1962). These films, which brought new critical and popular attention to him as a film director, all share the following characteristics: none of them was written by Edwards; all of them were made in the 1.85:1 aspect ratio at a time when widescreen films were made in or close to a 2.35:1 aspect ratio; and all of them featured A level stars (Edwards was brought in to direct *Breakfast at Tiffany's* at Audrey Hepburn's request and Jack Lemmon requested Edwards for *Days of Wine and Roses*). Paradoxically, he rose to a new level of success which departed from a career as a developing writer-director (*Bring Your Smile Along, He Laughed Last, Mister Cory, This Happy Feeling,* and *High Time*) and as a skilled widescreen director (*Mister Cory, This Happy Feeling, The Perfect Furlough,* and *High Time*).[1] And, ironically, beginning with *The Pink Panther* in 1963, Edwards blossomed as a widescreen writer-director. But, as we shall see, these films were unusual and experimental in various ways linked to his highly personal middle and late periods which followed.

Blake Edwards: Film Director as Multitalented Auteur, First Edition.
William Luhr and Peter Lehman.
© 2023 John Wiley & Sons Ltd. Published 2023 by John Wiley & Sons Ltd.

Experiment in Terror opens with a disturbing sequence in which we see Kelly Sherwood (Lee Remick), a young bank teller, drive home from work and enter her garage, only to be seized from behind by an unknown and unseen assailant (Ross Martin). Most of the sequence is played out in extreme close-ups that show Kelly's terrified eyes, the hand of her assailant over her mouth, and partial views of his mouth as he speaks (Figure 4.1). He is a shadowy presence behind her. Although we never see him clearly due to the lighting which keeps him in darkness even when he leaves the garage, the scene is dominated by his perverse-sounding asthmatic voice. He tells her that he has been surveilling her, knows her routines as well as those of her younger sister with whom she lives, and demands that she steal $100,000 from the bank in which she works. His intimidation goes beyond physical entrapment and verbal threats; at one point when he talks about how much he knows about her, he recites her bodily measurements, and the film implies that, as he does so, he is deriving pleasure from fondling her body in off-screen space. This opening is intensely personal, intimate, and perverse, playing out between two characters isolated in a dark garage.

The film's closing works in the opposite way. We see much of it in long shot, at times via helicopter shots, as Kelly's assailant, Red Lynch, is cornered and killed in a large, empty stadium just after a baseball game has concluded and crowds of spectators are exiting the stadium. The game has not only been watched by thousands of spectators physically present in the

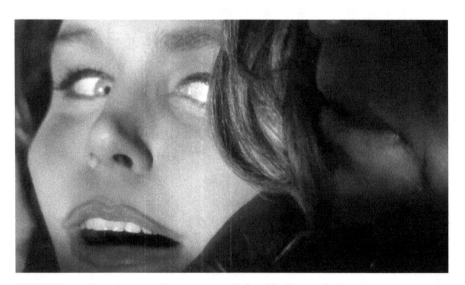

FIGURE 4.1   *Experiment in Terror*, © 1962 Columbia Pictures Industries, Inc.

stadium, it has also been televised. Where the film's opening was intimate and oppressively personal, the closing is extravagantly public and impersonal. After Lynch has been killed, we see his body stretched out on the pitcher's mound in a now eerily empty stadium and the film closes with increasingly distanced helicopter shots of the brightly lit, empty stadium surrounded by a sea of darkness (Figure 4.2).

Ken Wales considers it "one of the greatest endings of all time" and told us the entire final sequence posed many technical problems both on the ground and with the helicopter. At one point, Edwards ordered the bubble removed from the top of the helicopter to shoot the scene the way he planned it: "Then the grip said, 'We can't take the bubble off the chopper that we need to get off.' Blake says, 'I'll take care of it. Give me a hammer.' He took a hammer and went at the $25,000 – which was a ton of money then – plastic bubble, and it just shattered in pieces. He goes, 'Now it's off.'"

The film concerns Lynch's attempts to intimidate Kelly into stealing $100,000 from the bank in which she works by threatening both her life and that of her younger sister, Toby (Stefanie Powers). After their first encounter, Kelly contacts FBI agent John Ripley (Glenn Ford) and the remainder of the film becomes a cat-and-mouse game among her, Lynch, and the FBI. This involves elaborate surveillance, both direct and visual as well as indirect, particularly via the telephone. After terrifying Kelly in person, Lynch repeatedly threatens her on the phone and the FBI monitors her calls. On the day

FIGURE 4.2 *Experiment in Terror*, © 1962 Columbia Pictures Industries, Inc.

that Lynch wants her to steal the money, he kidnaps Toby and sends her clothes to Kelly to let her know that he has her sister. The film climaxes just after a baseball game ends at the cavernous Candlestick Park. In the large exiting crowd, Lynch seizes Kelly but is then himself seized by an FBI agent. As he attempts to flee and is about to fire at a descending helicopter, Ripley fatally shoots him.

One of the most experimental aspects of this film lies in its lack of any traditional character development among the main characters. None of them has a backstory. We don't know why and how Kelly has come to be living with and taking care of her younger sister Toby; we know nothing about Ripley's personal life including why he became an FBI agent; and remarkably we never learn anything that explains Red Lynch's perverse crimes. One character, Nancy Ashton (Patricia Huston), had apparently been involved in a relationship with Lynch that had recently become dangerous and, early in the film, had come to Ripley's office concerned for her safety. At that time, however, she would not reveal the details of the relationship because the film implies that it had included some criminal activity. Curiously, the only character with any backstory is Lisa Soong (Anita Loo), whose young son is hospitalized, recovering from a serious illness. She refuses to cooperate with the police as they search for Lynch because, over a period of several years during which she and Lynch had casually dated, he generously paid for her son's expensive hospital bills and came to the hospital regularly to visit the boy. Hence, her backstory, slight as it is, is profoundly ambiguous since it seems to give a caring, loving side to Lynch, a ruthless, perverted thief, kidnapper, and killer. The only thing we ever learn about Lynch comes via Soong's backstory: Lynch was attracted to Asian women.

Experiment in Terror centers on Kelly's victimization. A recurring image shows her terrified eyes as she reacts within perilous situations that are beyond her control. Both at the beginning when Lynch assaults her and at the end when Lynch is killed, she has little agency in the forces that determine her life. At the end she is abruptly seized by Lynch amid the crowd of spectators leaving the stadium but is then, as abruptly, seized and rescued by an FBI agent. All of these events involve her being watched and implicitly controlled by ever-widening circles of men, both malevolent like Lynch and protective like Ripley, as well as by random members of society like the man in the "Roaring Twenties" singles bar who picks her up, mistaking her for a woman who has come to the bar in hope of meeting a man to go home with. In fact, she is there to meet Lynch while she is being surveilled by Ripley!

While the omnipresence of surveillance adds to this film's dark and disturbing tone, Edwards has also regularly used surveillance in his comedies.

One scene in *A Shot in the Dark* (1964) encapsulates this. As Inspector Clouseau investigates a murder at a chateau, we see a shot of a maid (who is also the police's main suspect) in an adjacent room listening outside the door, then the camera pans back and we see a butler watching the maid from a doorway at the rear of the room. After a brief cutaway, we see a long shot of a third servant in the next room watching the butler, and, finally, transforming what had begun with a close shot into an extreme long shot, a fourth servant high on a staircase watching all three. Watchers are watching watchers who in turn are watching watchers.

The opening shots of Kelly's terrified eyes disrupt a common structure in Hollywood cinema – her eyes are wide open, but she is not seeing. In standard shot-reverse shot sequences, shots of characters who are looking are generally matched with shots of what it is that they are looking at, in effect completing a circuit that establishes the significant elements of the scene. But here that circuit remains open and incomplete since Kelly is not looking at anything because her assailant is behind her. She feels him and she hears him – he is holding her captive with his hand over her mouth and terrifying her with his threats. At the outset of the film, it would hardly matter if she could see him because, even though he has been extensively observing her, she has no idea who he is or what he looks like. We as the audience occupy a similar position since, until much later in the film, we do not clearly see him either. What we do see are grotesquely large close-ups of his mouth as he torments her on the telephone, and we hear his creepily asthmatic voice. The movie does not even name Ross Martin playing Red Lynch until its closing shot.

The strategy of keeping Lynch's face and identity a mystery via tight fragmented close-ups and dark lighting is profoundly related to Edwards's use of off-screen space throughout his career. In this variation, we see fragments of him mostly centered around his mouth and we see the full face a few times such as when we see him in the car mirror as he leaves the garage after terrifying Kelly, but we can't see any of his facial features since he stands in utter darkness. When Ripley asks Kelly to describe her assailant, she tells him that, since he attacked from behind, she has no idea of what he looks like but adds that she noticed his creepy, asthmatic voice. Edwards commonly uses off-screen space for comic effect where we have to imagine what happens since we can't see it. Sound frequently motivates our attention to off-screen space. For example, in *Mister Cory* (see Chapter 3) in one scene we see Cory in a restaurant precariously carry a loaded tray of dishes into the kitchen. Just when it seems like he has succeeded and the door has closed behind him, we hear a terrible crash. Another simple example of off-screen space in *Experiment in Terror* occurs when, as the camera follows a character walking through her apartment, we suddenly are shocked by a freakish-looking intrusion of what seems to be a disembodied arm from off-screen space from the top of the frame (Figure 4.3). But we quickly see that we have misinterpreted what we saw (see herein).

There is a profound connection between keeping Lynch's face off-screen and between making his asthmatic voice his most defining characteristic. Off-screen space heightens the viewers' active imagination in picturing what they can't see. This relates directly to Edwards's background in radio in which characters are regularly characterized by distinctive vocal characteristics, something he valued so highly since it left so much to the listener's imagination (see Chapter 5). In other words, keeping Lynch's face a mystery is not just a gimmick in this film; that aspect of visual style combines with the manner in which Lynch's voice recalls radio strategies to form a unified aesthetic based around a visual and sound design style that fully engages the spectator's *imagination*. In what deceptively appears to be a minor scene later in the film, Kelly is escorted into a back room at her bank where she meets Ripley for the first time. Ripley tells her, "Every time I speak to someone on the phone I get a sort of mental image of what they're supposed to look like. Usually I'm wrong and your case is no exception." Kelly replies, "I guess everyone does that," to which Ripley adds, "Yeah, I guess they do." Kelly can only *imagine* Lynch through his voice like Ripley can only *imagine* Kelly

FIGURE 4.3   *Experiment in Terror*, © 1962 Columbia Pictures Industries, Inc.

through her voice and we in the audience have to similarly imagine who characters are and what is happening.

A central strategy in this film involves the sudden, shocking reorientations of characters from situations of security into those of terror when they, and often the viewer, abruptly learn that what they had thought was going on has changed entirely, and that they must now deal with a radically new state of affairs. This is also a common practice in Edwards's comedies, but here the reorientations are not developed for laughs. The opening credits appear over shots of Kelly serenely driving home from work in the evening. We see her observant face as she drives and her car going over a bridge into her neighborhood and her garage; "normal" things she has done many times before. Then everything suddenly changes for her when Lynch seizes her in her garage. Such jolting reorientations occur repeatedly in the film, as well as throughout Edwards's career across multiple media. A man who thinks he has picked Kelly up in a singles bar is shocked when she leaps out of his moving car. He has thought he understood the situation when she accompanied him to his car but is disoriented at her reaction. It gets worse for him when armed FBI agents immediately surround him. Everything has changed in an instant.

A related, but more complex, reorientation occurs in a remarkable sequence involving Nancy Ashton in her apartment. As noted above, she had apparently been involved in a relationship with Lynch that had recently become dangerous and, earlier, had approached Ripley concerned for her safety. She would not, however, reveal the details of the relationship because the film implies that it had included some criminal activity. In the later scene she telephones Ripley, tells him that she is fearful of coming to his office and asks him to come to her apartment. She ends the call by alerting him not to be upset when he enters the apartment because she has "an unusual occupation." The ensuing scene repeatedly disorients the viewer. As Nancy arises and walks across her darkened apartment, we suddenly see what appears to be a disembodied arm and hand hanging from the ceiling. However, Nancy takes no notice of it. The camera follows her as she walks and we see that her apartment is filled with naked, life-sized female mannequins, some full body and others of body parts like arms and heads. Now we know her unusual occupation. Although Nancy is not disturbed by these sights, the viewer is as the camera slowly follows her through this eerie environment. As the scene proceeds, she casually disrobes, removing her head scarf and sweatshirt, and goes to a makeup mirror in her bra before putting on her bathrobe. She then thinks she hears something and returns into the large studio with the mannequins, sees nothing but checks the doors and quietly returns upstairs. As the camera follows her, the mood of the entire scene shifts from disturbing to terrifying when it reveals Lynch's inert silhouette concealed among the mannequins, and then he silently turns his head. When Ripley later enters the apartment, he takes little notice of the eerie-looking mannequins, but then is shocked to find Nancy's naked corpse hanging from off-screen space among them. Although we do not see it, we learn Lynch has just murdered her. Hence, in this scene, the viewer at first thinks Nancy is telephoning from a traditional apartment but is initially shocked to see a fragmented body part which then reveals her occupation. She has called Ripley because of her fear of Lynch and is troubled when she hears a sound, but then finds nothing. We are shocked to see Lynch concealed among the mannequins and Ripley and the agents as well as those in the audience are shocked to find Nancy's body. In each successive case, the meaning of what we see has changed abruptly and brutally. In addition, the scene involves various disguises. At first, we see Lynch passing for a mannequin and, later, we see that he has posed Nancy's body hanging among the mannequins to resemble one of them.

In this scene we have seen Lynch, in effect, disguised as a female manne-quin. In a later one we see him literally disguised as an old woman and dis-guised so well that he initially deceives not only Kelly but also the two FBI agents who are watching over her. She has gone to a local restaurant for lunch with a coworker who is apparently her boyfriend. The FBI agents sit unobtrusively at the lunch counter. When Kelly goes to a restroom, she is followed by what appears to be a stooped-over old woman wearing a bonnet (Figure 4.4). Inside the restroom, Kelly senses something is wrong and turns to look at the woman, who then stands erectly and removes her large glasses

FIGURE 4.4 *Experiment in Terror,* © 1962 Columbia Pictures Industries, Inc.

FIGURE 4.5   *Experiment in Terror,* © 1962 Columbia Pictures Industries, Inc.

to reveal that "she" is Lynch in disguise (Figure 4.5). He displays a pistol and tells her that Friday is the day he wants her to rob the bank. He then replaces the glasses and stoops over, once more looking like an enfeebled old woman, and leaves the washroom. The FBI agents at the counter outside have noticed nothing. When the shaken Kelly opens the door to exit the washroom, she encounters a woman of roughly Lynch's height waiting to enter and Kelly gasps in shock.[2]

While clearly the woman was not in disguise and had no intention of shocking Kelly, she provides one of numerous instances in the film in which someone or something is mistaken for something else. Nancy's profession is making mannequins that are carefully designed to resemble human bodies, and her dead body ends up disturbingly hanging among them, so here we have, in effect, a human body being masqueraded as a mannequin. There are also repeated close shots of the large stuffed tiger doll that Lynch has given Joey, Lisa Soong's hospitalized son, focusing on its menacing-looking face. Nothing is developed about it, but it remains a disturbing presence, and one that recalls numerous instances in Edwards's work in which inanimate objects resemble living beings in disturbing ways. *The Atomic Kid* (1954), based on a story by Edwards, includes scenes set in a nuclear blast site that has a model house populated with life-sized mannequins that disorient the main characters.

Mistaken identity is a staple in both comedy and drama, and often involves some kind of deception or performance. Kelly is not a performer and does not solicit male attention in her career as a bank teller, but we constantly see her being carefully observed by men – by Lynch, by the FBI, and by others such as the man in the singles bar. In this she differs from many of the female characters throughout Edwards's career who actively court such attention, and who inhabit narratives that naturalize that situation. Many are entertainers who perform onstage, and part of performing is to solicit and hold the audience's gaze, whether the nightclub or theater performers in *He Laughed Last* or Edie, the nightclub singer in *Peter Gunn*, or the movie star in *The Perfect Furlough* or Lili in *Darling Lili*, or Victoria in *Victor/Victoria*, among others. *Victor/Victoria* provides a complex instance since Victoria is not only a stage performer but also one whose private life necessitates a performance. She shares this need to make her private life a performance with such non-performers as Holly Golightly in *Breakfast at Tiffany's* and Amanda Brooks in *Switch*. And performance is central to *The Tamarind Seed*, dealing with the world of international espionage, in which the head of British Intelligence is revealed to be both a Russian spy and a homosexual masquerading as a heterosexual.

Lynch's disguises, whether he is hiding among mannequins or dressing as an old woman, are only one of his tools for intimidating people. He employs extensive surveillance of Kelly and Toby to control them. However, his actions trigger similar ones by the FBI, who set up elaborate surveillance networks around Kelly's home and job. They occupy a house across the street from Kelly, bring the bank manager into their confidence, and, when Kelly moves about in public spaces, we regularly see at least two agents nearby unobtrusively monitoring her movements, and all of this looks "normal" to a bystander. Although neither Kelly nor the audience has a clear sense of what Lynch looks like until late in the film, the FBI, fairly early on, assembles a detailed history of his past activities and distributes photographs of him. The audience first sees Lynch's face in the photographs. The film establishes multiple and omnipresent invisible layers of surveillance everywhere.

Some of this involves the telephone. Lynch repeatedly uses the phone to intimidate Kelly. We see him sadistically derive perverse pleasure by physically seizing and fondling her, but he can also torment her from a distance by phone and we see close shots of his leering mouth as he does so. At the same time, however, Kelly knows that the FBI is now monitoring her calls and derives a measure of comfort from that fact. We also see repeated shots of an FBI switchboard operator receiving and transferring calls, and some of the agents have phones in their cars. Edwards often uses the telephone as a disruptive device, one that can alter the meaning of a scene in an instant. The *Richard Diamond, Private Detective* radio series and the *Peter Gunn* television series, for example, provide many instances in which an intrusive phone call instantly disrupts an anticipated romantic scene, whether between Gunn and his girlfriend Edie or Diamond and his girlfriend Helen Asher. And, unusual for the late 1950s, Peter Gunn has a car phone.

Ripley inhabits a long list of detectives throughout Edwards's work. Although this film deals with crime, it works in different ways from Edwards's other work with detectives and police, such as in his radio series *Richard Diamond, Private Detective* or his television series, *Peter Gunn*. It has no suave and/or wisecracking private detective and no rumpled police detective, no comic relief, and no romantic subplot. It neither attempts to glamorize the detective nor, at the other end of the spectrum, to impugn the integrity of the FBI. It presents Ripley as a competent but faceless bureaucrat, very different from Edwards's witty private detectives like Richard Diamond, Peter Gunn, or A. Dunster Lowell (*The Boston Terrier*). He also differs from Edwards's situational detectives like Mr. Lucky, or Tom Mix and Wyatt Earp in *Sunset*, or Dr. Peter Carey in *The Carey Treatment*, all of whom are developed as likable characters with lives outside their detecting. And he is certainly a world apart from Edwards's most famous detective, the bumbling Inspector Jacques Clouseau of the Sûreté.

Where the villain Lynch is characterized by numerous quirks such as his asthmatic voice or his disguises and is even given a counterintuitive character trait in his generous support for Lisa Soong's hospitalized son, Ripley has no quirks; he is his job and nothing more. We have no sense of his private life, and he never disguises himself. Finally, and deviating from standard patterns in detective films in which a detective protects a vulnerable young woman, there is never a hint of potential romantic attraction between Kelly and Ripley.

At the conclusion of the sequence in which Nancy Ashton is murdered and as her body is being taken down, a fellow agent surprises Ripley by telling him that "Popcorn" (Ned Glass), an informant, had established a connection between Ashton's case and Kelly's. We then get an abrupt transition placing us in a silent slapstick movie with a wild Keystone Kops chase transporting us into an entirely different kind of movie. This is intercut with shots of Popcorn enjoying the movie in a theater while eating his trademark popcorn. The slapstick film also depicts the police at work but does so within radically different generic conventions. Although Edwards regularly mixes numerous genres in his films, this is the only instance in this one and the contrast involves more than a variation on the crime and police theme. It serves three functions: It underscores the non-comic nature of this film, its status as a "serious" film, which is significant in light of the popular association of Edwards with comedy. It also typifies one of Edwards's most basic and unusual strategies of using comedy in his dramas: Rather than integrate comedy with drama, he frequently uses comedy to erupt into or disrupt drama. The scene is formally structured to maximize this disruption by joltingly cutting to the Keystone Kops scene completely filing the frame. We have no context for it. Then he cuts to a character we do not know sitting in the audience of a film screening, eating popcorn. If Edwards wanted to integrate a point about the distinction between his usual comic style and love of silent film style, he could have done so easily by first introducing Popcorn watching a movie and then cutting to the screen in the theater. Furthermore, his love of silent film is the only thing we learn about Popcorn. Like the other characters, he has no backstory. All he seems to do besides his work as an informant selling information to the police is watch silent films and eat popcorn. The manner in which he dies while assisting the police capture one of his sources underscores the bizarre eruption and disruption of comedy into an intense drama: There is nothing funny or lighthearted in the unexpected shot of him lying with his signature popcorn carton and popcorn on his dead body.

Many of the terrifying situations in this film could be and in fact were used by Edwards in comedies, whether they are abrupt reorientations, the use of disguises, or extreme misinterpretations of what is going on. The sight of Lynch in a dress in this film is menacing but the sight of Bing Crosby in a dress in *High Time* is played for comedy. Many of the laughs inspired by Inspector Clouseau result from his often inept and preposterous disguises, and a central plot device in *What Did You Do in the War, Daddy?* involves an entire Italian town during World War II pretending to be involved in fierce fighting in its streets while actually having a festival, so, in effect, a jubilant, celebratory event masquerades as a brutal and bloody one.

Gender representation in *Experiment in Terror* is traditionally rigid. Everyone with power and agency in the film is male; all of the victims except Popcorn are women. Although Kelly is the central character and is presented as a responsible young woman, she has virtually no agency in her fate. She is utterly surprised at the beginning when Lynch seizes her and equally surprised at the end when an FBI agent rescues her. Comparably, her teenage sister Toby is kidnapped, imprisoned, and undressed by Lynch. She neither resists nor attempts to escape and is only freed when FBI agents burst into the place in which Lynch has imprisoned her. Like her kidnapping, her release comes as a surprise to her. Most of the troubled female images in the film are associated with Lynch, whether it is the undefined, but troubled, relationship with Nancy that ends in her murder, or his counterintuitive relationship with Lisa Soong in which he has paid the medical bills for her young son. Lynch disguises himself as an old woman as another of his ways to terrorize Kelly and he hides among Nancy's eerie female mannequins. The FBI is depicted as an all-male organization in which the only presence of women comes in the form of a switchboard operator. This is particularly curious in Edwards's career, which frequently involves women moving outside of contemporary gender expectations, whether having to act as a mob boss in *He Laughed Last* or dealing with gender confusion in *Victor/Victoria*.

Experiment in Terror appeared five years after *Mister Cory* at a time when Edwards had catapulted into the world of A-List filmmakers. After directing his first two B films at Columbia, *Mister Cory* was the first film Edwards directed for Universal. *Experiment in Terror* marked his return to Columbia but with new visibility. It marks a significant break from his earlier work. It is his first feature as both director and producer. With the exception of *Mister Cory*, all of the feature films he had directed had been comedies and the look and tone of this film marked an ambitious new direction for his career, signaled in the very title – an experiment.

At virtually the same time that Edwards left the *Peter Gunn* television series because, as he told us, the network would not allow him to expand the episodes to an hour and shoot them in color, he ironically made this film in black and white. Although he started his career by writing and producing two B Westerns in black and white, he then directed eight features in color.[3] *Experiment in Terror* is his first A feature film shot in black and white, particularly notable since the early 1960s was precisely the time when black-and-white cinematography was outmoded after Hollywood's move to color in the 1950s as one way of competing with television. When an interviewer brought up the subject of *Experiment in Terror* and *Days of Wine and Roses* being shot in black and white, Edwards replied, "Were I to do them again, I might very well choose to do them in color. I don't recall that I intentionally chose black and white because of some creative need."[4] But, significantly, *Experiment in Terror* refers back to Edwards's most successful 1950s black-and-white crime TV series, *Peter Gunn* and *Mister Lucky*. It is no coincidence that Philip Lathrop, who was a cinematographer on both those shows, and Henry Mancini, who scored them, both worked on *Experiment in Terror*. Lathrop's brilliant cinematography and lighting are integral to the film's success, as is Mancini's moody jazz-pop score. And both

Lathrop and Mancini would work on *Days of Wine and Roses*, a film which was also connected to late 1950s black-and-white TV; it was a remake of the 1958 black-and-white *Playhouse 90 television show, Days of Wine and Roses*.

Unlike the majority of Edwards's films, this one does not significantly mix genres. In this it resembles Edwards's 1954 television pilot, *Mickey Spillane's "Mike Hammer!"*, in being a straight-down-the-line crime story with no attempts at humor.[5] With the significant exception of brief scenes from a silent slapstick film, *Experiment in Terror* incorporates no elements of other genres.

Although Edwards's television and radio series during this time draw extensively on tropes of the genre, this police procedural is Edwards's first theatrical *Film Noir*. Intriguingly, he made it at precisely the time in which *Film Noir* was losing commercial viability due to the disappearance of black-and-white cinematography and the absorption and hence outmoding of *Film Noir* tropes by television (detective stories, police procedurals, domestic melodramas). It also has no normative couple at its center and no traditional romance developing in its narrative arc to climax at the end to parallel the defeat of the villain.

The endings of Edwards's films seldom involve definitive closure; they frequently incorporate elements of ambiguity, whether Mister Cory's walking alone to the airplane, the mysterious shooting from the nightclub balcony at the end of *He Laughed Last*, the disruptions that close some of the Clouseau films such as Cato attacking Clouseau in *A Shot in the Dark*, or the melancholic sense of loss in *Victor/Victoria* as Toddy and Victoria are split up and he performs in drag on stage as she sits with King Marchand in the audience. However, the ending of this film has a resolute sense of closure seldom evident in Edwards's films. Lynch is dead, both Kelly and Toby have been freed and can resume their lives, and Ripley will continue with the FBI. The major plot strands have been resolved; it is definitively over. However, the experimental nature of this film strongly qualifies that conclusion. It is precisely because the characters are not developed in the traditional Hollywood classical sense and have no backstories or close relationships that there are none of the usual elements of Edwards's films such as, for example, the tensions arising from romantic subplots and male bonding to resolve. Tellingly, Ripley has no close relationship with a partner, nor does he show any romantic or sexual interest in Kelly. Since we know so little about any of the characters to begin with, there is little to leave ambiguous at the end. The film lacks the traditional elements of character development so fully that there is not even any sense that Ripley, Kelly, or

Toby have been fundamentally changed in any way by the intense experiences they have undergone. They are left to go back to being who they were at the beginning.

NOTES

1. Edwards is an uncredited screenwriter on *High Time*, on which he worked with Tom and Frank Waldman who wrote many screenplays with and for him.

2. This use of cross-dressing differs somewhat from the way Edwards normally uses it. Like the other instances of cross-dressing in Edwards's films, it is a type of performance. It is normally used for comic effect even when it causes anxiety, such as when King Marchand fears he may be gay when he finds himself attracted to someone he initially thinks to be a female impersonator (see *Returning to the Scene: Blake Edwards, Volume 2*). Here, in *Experiment in Terror*, it causes genuine terror and relates to a cross-dressing scene in *Gunn* (see Chapter 6).

3. Edwards, however, had extensive experience in black-and-white filmmaking as a writer, producer, and actor, including *Drive a Crooked Road*, *The Atomic Kid*, *Leather Gloves*, and *The Notorious Landlady*, to name a few.

4. Darrah Meely, "Director-Writer-Producer-Father and Former Actor: Blake Edwards," in *Blake Edwards Interviews*, edited by Gabriella Oldham (Jackson: University Press of Mississippi, 2018), p. 60.

5. We cannot draw any conclusions about the mixed-genre tones the series might have taken had it been picked up. Edwards frequently began both his TV series and his movies with a different tone from what would follow. The pilot of the original *Peter Gunn* TV show provides a perfect example. It contains very little of what came to characterize the series.

CHAPTER 5

Days of Wine and Roses (1962)

Directed by Blake Edwards

Days of Wine and Roses (1962), arguably the most popular and critically acclaimed drama in Edwards's career, appeared at a pivotal moment. Edwards, who was becoming known as a rising star director of "A" films, significantly chose to remake a 1958 episode of *Playhouse 90*. During that same year of 1962, he also wrote the story for *The Couch*, itself a remake of the 1950 "The Eight O'Clock Killer," one of the most well-known episodes of his successful radio series, *Richard Diamond, Private Detective*. All of these works, combined with Edwards's previous feature, *Experiment in Terror*, point to the influence of a genre he had earlier avoided in feature films that he directed, *Film Noir*. The two films are his first directorial features photographed in black and white, and they deal with dark, often disturbing material. They mark a new direction from his earlier film directing, which had been in color and was often comedic.

It is commonplace to view Edwards's early work as a stepping stone to film directing, which is presumed to be his important work. Such an assumption views Edwards's career in radio, television, and film as hierarchical, with film perched at the top of the pyramid. Such an assumption is not only profoundly wrong but it also misconstrues Edwards's understanding of his

Blake Edwards: Film Director as Multitalented Auteur, First Edition.
William Luhr and Peter Lehman.

own career. In 1985 on the set of *A Fine Mess*, we asked him between shot setups which of the media forms in which he had worked was his favorite. Without a pause, he replied, "Radio because it leaves so much to the imagination of the listener." His primary role in radio had been as a writer, and he was referring to dialogue as the main element of radio drama which then left so much to the imagination of the audience.

On a parallel track, Jack Lemmon has perceptively remarked that Blake's use of off-screen space is the defining aspect of his great directing because it leaves so much to the viewer's imagination, "He's the best I've ever worked with at what is *not* shown on the screen."[1] Since we do not see what happens, we have to fill it in. Far from leaving radio and television behind, Edwards as a multimedia, multi-hyphenate creator constantly engaged and re-engaged with his work in those media.[2] How did he do this?

His radio show, "The Eight O'Clock Killer," was based on a simple but gripping idea: a killer would randomly strike at eight o'clock on a given day after notifying the police that it would happen. Since the caller was anonymous and the murders random, the police were stymied. They had no motive for what appeared to be the work of a madman. Edwards and his collaborators totally reworked this story for *The Couch* as a feature film in which the killer becomes a central character whose actions are integrated with the lives of the other characters (see Chapter 2). Edwards has long known that the ways in which he tells stories need to be fully integrated with the form of the medium in which he tells them.

We begin our analysis of *Days of Wine and Roses* by briefly looking at how Edwards's film works as a remake of the 1958 *Playhouse 90* television show of the same title. The most obvious difference is that the TV show begins with an Alcoholics Anonymous (AA) meeting, introducing the organization's charter and beliefs. This sets a serious, at times preachy, tone which pervades the show. We see everything in flashback narrated by Joe Clay (Cliff Robertson), who is sober from the beginning. The show includes five scenes in an AA meeting. In Edwards's film, AA doesn't even appear and is not mentioned until one hour and twenty minutes into the film; Frankenheimer's entire version is only one hour and seventeen minutes long! And it only appears once in the film. In contrast, the second sequence in the TV show takes place after Joe and Kirsten are married whereas in the film we learn of their marriage in an important scene when they tell Kirsten's father, 39 minutes into the film! The actors' styles are also quite different in ways which have a profound impact on each work. Although Cliff Robertson is a good actor, his facial expressions do not have the extraordinary range of Jack Lemmon's whose face at times seems made of rubber or putty, expressions which became his hallmark in many comedies. Piper Laurie's performance becomes increasingly theatrical as her voice takes on a shrill quality whereas Lee Remick is comparatively restrained even in her most emotional scenes. At first glance, several scenes seem similar in both works such as the destruction of the greenhouse and the ending with the flashing bar sign, but a primary assumption in our book is that form and content cannot be separated since how a story is told becomes part of the story. From that perspective, as we shall see, Blake Edwards has made an entirely new work. Edwards takes several of the show's themes and motifs but develops them in an entirely different manner, including adding many new ones.

The *Playhouse 90* episode was rebroadcast a number of years later and the Rhino VHS video (1993) of it includes interviews with the principals, one of whom is the director, John Frankenheimer. He recounts his immense and lasting disappointment that he was not chosen to direct the film. The reason he gives is that Jack Lemmon told him that he was not right for directing comedy, to which Frankenheimer sarcastically replied, "I didn't know it was a comedy." His response ironically shows that Lemmon was right. Near the end of his life, Blake told us in his home in Brentwood that, until the tragedy of Julie Andrews losing her singing voice as a result of a botched routine surgical procedure, he had always been able to find the humor in everything. And he meant everything. Whereas Frankenheimer's version is highly serious in tone, Edwards makes his film in many tones and it is in part a profound meditation on the fine line between comedy and drama and between pain and laughter, including what we may best term "painful laughter." Both Frankenheimer's and Edwards's versions, for example, deal with masculinity issues but Edwards develops Joe Clay's masculine crisis quite differently, including the use of humor in a manner relating to that in his comedies. The variation is formally specific and profoundly bound into the style in which the story is told.

The film begins with five important scenes and, significantly, it takes eighteen minutes before we even see one recalling the TV show. In the opening scene in a bar, we see Joe Clay talking with a colleague about "One of these big dames, but in proportion." The subject of the first dialogue we hear is about gender and sexuality, not alcoholism. Clay is looking for "party girls" for a rich client. Scene two takes place on a launch taking them to a yacht. They await one of the women who is late. When she arrives, Clay criticizes her, without knowing who she is: "You're late, you're dressed wrong." He thinks she is supposed to be in a "cocktail dress" which he describes as "something peekaboo." The editing pattern as they go to the yacht shows Joe surveying the other "party girls" with a depressed, dejected look on his face followed by shots of the women looking at him with disapproval. The castrating stare of the women is the beginning of a symbolic castration that Joe undergoes throughout the film, ending with him moving into the culturally defined feminine position at the time of being the caretaker of the child at home.

Scene three takes place on the yacht where Joe learns that the late arrival is Kirsten Arnesen (Lee Remick), the secretary of Trayner (Jack Albertson) and not a party girl. Again, his facial expression is one of humiliation as his masculinity is deflated. We then see Kirsten with a smug look on her face implying that he has been put in his place. Yet another castrating moment. Then after the party begins on board, Joe escapes to the deck where he sees Kirsten standing alone. He approaches her, asking, "Can I buy you a drink?" She responds, "Oh, no thank you. I don't drink," and walks away. Another put down.

Later, when they talk about his job, she inquires about Eddie, the previous PR man. Joe says, "Eddie didn't feel that getting dates for potentates was part of public relations." Kirsten asks, "Well, isn't it?" Joe replies, "There's a name for it, but it isn't public relations." Now he diminishes himself. "Well, whatever it is, you seem to do it very well." The entire scene is one of escalating castrating stares, actions, and dialogue which cut deeper and deeper into Clay's masculinity.

While scene four will continue this trajectory, significantly it is the first predominantly comic scene in the film. We see Clay entering an office building and getting into the elevator. This initiates a complex set of two comic scenes structured around elevators. Clay enters the elevator as it goes up. He then goes to Trayner's office, which is surrounded by a curving wall of glass from floor to ceiling, including glass doors. Edwards will build this and the next comic elevator scene around glass. When Joe sees Kirsten at her desk through the glass, she is about to eat some chocolate, which becomes a new motif foreshadowing her alcoholism. He carries a package as a peace offering to make up for his insults the previous night at the party. She is not interested and, when he persists by telling her it is peanut brittle, she blurts out, "I hate peanut brittle." She walks off and Clay is even further rejected when he offers it to a cleaning woman, who shakes her head. Twice rejected, he throws it down and storms off. This begins the elevator ballet first as he and Kirsten stand side by side waiting for separate elevators to take them down. She disappears into off-screen space as her elevator arrives and Clay is torn about what to do until the head of the elevator operator appears on screen asking, "Down?" Off-screen space will be in play throughout the sequence. Joe insults Kirsten's job much like she had earlier insulted his work on the yacht. He implies she has no qualifications and does nothing but please the boss who wants her around. He adds, "You spend half your day reading a book," introducing a new motif about books and reading (she will later refuse to read an AA brochure) and also setting up the continuing elevator gags since his comment reminds her that she forgot her book and has to go back up to get it. When the elevator stops, she slaps him and goes out into off-screen space, and we see Clay humiliated and exchanging glances with the elevator operator. The elevator operator fulfills the same function as countless such onlookers in Edwards's comedies (see, for example, in *Mr. Cory* the scene in which the maître d' watches Cory precariously balancing a tray of dirty dishes or a wealthy estate owner watching Inspector Clouseau destroy his pool table in *A Shot in the Dark*), who are sometimes just watching the crazy world around them, sometimes adding to the humiliation of a participant, sometimes identifying with a participant, and sometimes just giving up hoping to understand in disbelief or despair.

Clay once again pursues Kirsten to the office, then returns to the elevator where, this time, he stands behind her where he puts his fingers in his mouth and stretches it as he sticks his tongue out at her like a little boy (Figure 5.1). Seeming relieved, he walks out of the building ahead of her, only to hear her calling out to him and running up saying that she thought he was going to ask her to dinner. Scene five takes place in the restaurant where Kirsten acknowledges her ethics are no better than his. Having made up, Joe tricks her into tasting a Brandy Alexander made with chocolate.

FIGURE 5.1   *Days of Wine and Roses*, © 1962 Warner Bros. Entertainment, Inc.

Scene six takes place after dinner on a bridge with both of them having drunk too much but now telling each other the intimate details of their lives. The action, dialogue, and setting all recall the TV show but to a very different effect. Edwards has slowly developed both characters as complex and attractive human beings seeking love in their lives. Joe, in describing his job, calls himself "a eunuch in a harem," explicitly articulating the castration theme. We do not see Joe and Kirsten through the lens of AA but, rather, as troubled figures with whom we identify, even as we see them start on the road to becoming out-of-control alcoholics who will need AA. Equally importantly, recalling Edwards's strong belief that comedy and drama are always linked in life, he has begun intertwining both of them in telling this dark story about a man in crisis, about his failing masculinity, and about the road that both he and the woman he loves take toward a catastrophic alcoholism. We turn now to the development and function of comedy followed by that of castration.

The scene that rhymes with the one cited above that involves elevators and glass occurs after Joe and Kirsten are married and have a child. Joe returns from one of his professional parties totally drunk and Edwards shoots the first part of the scene in a remarkably complex single take typical of those he uses in his comedies. The camera is positioned in the apartment lobby behind a large window as we see a taxi pull up. Joe gets out and opens the door to the rear passenger seat to pay the driver before realizing his drunken error. He then stumbles over to the building's flower garden from which he yanks out some flowers and weaves his way back to the lobby, crashing straight into the window pane that he has not noticed. The moment is startling to both Joe and the audience, all the more so since the audience is acutely aware of Joe's pain but, bizarrely, he starts laughing. This inversion of the usual comic structure whereby the character is in pain but the audience is laughing becomes another major motif. As we shall see, the characters in this film frequently break out laughing while the audience cringes in pain and empathy for the terrible situation the characters are in. The long take continues as we see and hear Joe laughing to himself in the lobby as he stumbles to the elevator, holding the flowers behind his back (a rhyme to yet another comic scene) as the elevator door closes on them, slicing them apart (Figure 5.2). Castration. It is not until later in the apartment scene in the midst of another long take that Joe, taking off his coat and seeing the flower stalks without the blooms in his hand, even realizes what has happened.

To fully appreciate the structured use of comedy in this "serious" drama, we have to look at another scene between Joe and Kirsten that occurs after the elevator scene in the office but prior to this elevator scene in the apartment

FIGURE 5.2   *Days of Wine and Roses*, © 1962 Warner Bros. Entertainment, Inc.

building. Before they are married, Joe arrives at Kirsten's apartment for the first time. He brings chocolates for her and lots of liquor and, since she previously complained of roaches in her apartment, a can of roach spray. While she makes a drink for him, he begins to spray the apartment, stopping at the door and holding the spray can in a fixed position oblivious to the spray spewing out until a knock comes on the door. An angry neighbor begins attacking him for upsetting the entire roach balance in the apartment house and before long he and Kirsten are in the hallway being assaulted by complaining occupants on the ground floor and on the floor above them. Edwards has point of view shots down at the ground floor and up at the third floor, stressing the chaos caused by Joe's incompetent spraying in one small-enclosed space. As the uproar of the angry dwellers grows, Joe becomes scared and holds the hand with the roach spray behind his back as he backs into the apartment. Once inside, they slam the door and break out into hysterical laughter and can't even continue talking.

The scene is remarkable in how it intertwines several threads. It is entirely comic in tone, beginning with Joe's incompetent attack on the "roach kingdom" and culminating in his symbolic castration, as he fearfully backs into the apartment seeking safety. The castration theme is once again explicit in the image of the disappearing hand holding the can, looking as if it has been cut off. Joe first fails to even use the spray correctly, as he talks about the manner in which he was taken off the case at work. He hadn't asked to be removed. The combination of talking about being "taken off the case" as he incompetently causes chaos with a roach spray can is indeed a fine line not just between comedy and drama, but between Joe Clay and Inspector Clouseau, who is only a year or two away from upsetting everything and everyone while being repeatedly taken off cases and undergoing constant failures of masculinity linked to symbolic castration in *The Pink Panther* (1963) and *A Shot in the Dark* (1964). And once again, the scene inverts the usual comic structure since it is far removed from the hilarity of the Pink Panther films and, once again, the characters in the film laugh much harder than the audience of the film.[3]

Even the harrowing scene of wanton drunken destruction in the greenhouse invokes the fine line between comedy and drama. First, we see Joe and Kirsten in their bedroom as he playfully does a striptease for her (another step into moving into the feminine cultural position); they begin to drink and once again laugh together as they get drunk. But Edwards's sophisticated use of the formal strategies developed in the comedies begins when Joe decides to sneak out to the greenhouse where he has hidden several bottles of alcohol. We see Joe in long shot as he drops from the window. When he weaves toward the greenhouse he stumbles and falls down off-screen, only to jump up and reappear with a stick and attack a big cactus behind which he fell (Figure 5.3). This gag is structurally very similar to Clouseau spinning a globe, falling off-screen when he leans against it, and jumping back up into the frame in *The Pink Panther*, or

FIGURE 5.3   *Days of Wine and Roses*, © 1962 Warner Bros. Entertainment, Inc.

falling off a sofa and jumping back up in *A Shot in the Dark*. Joe continues into the greenhouse in search of the bottle. He has memorized a three-part combination of the row the bottle is in, the table it is on, and the plant pot in which the bottle is hidden. Predictably he confuses the numbers with his increasing agitation. After having destroyed many plants and made a mess of the greenhouse, he looks for a light switch, turns it on, falls through the door, and lands flat on his back in the rain (Figure 5.4). Again, this virtually fore-shadows the structure of a gag in *A Shot in the Dark* where Clouseau falls out of a window, landing flat on the ground.

At first glance, this might seem much like the greenhouse scene in the *Playhouse 90* version but, within the formal structures of comedy leading up to this scene and the manner in which Edwards shoots and edits it, it is entirely different. The horror of watching Joe virtually falling out of the tree, then falling to the ground to reappear clubbing a cactus at the beginning of the scene, much like Clouseau, and then watching him fall backwards through a door to land flat on the ground, again recalling Clouseau, is star-tling, not because it is funny (it is anything but), but because it delineates just how fine that line is between hilarity and horror. The only person laughing in this scene is Joe! By contrast, in the TV show we simply see Joe go out of the window and then cut to him entering the greenhouse. Similarly, he never goes to or falls through the doorway.

FIGURE 5.4   *Days of Wine and Roses*, © 1962 Warner Bros. Entertainment, Inc.

The scene in the film ends by once again intertwining comedy with castration. This time, instead of seeming to lose his masculinity or to become feminine, Joe becomes infantile. After falling through the doorway, he lies on his stomach and cries like a little child. He then finds the bottle and, rolling over onto his back, he gulps from it like a baby being fed from a bottle, another motif in the film. On several occasions, Joe berates Kirsten for not drinking with him because of her anxieties about its effect on her breast-feeding the baby. He crudely tells her that, in the modern world, they have milk in cans for babies and that if she bottle-fed their baby, she could party with him. Now he lies in the mud bottle-feeding himself like a baby.

Edwards adds another dimension to this odd discourse about humor with the equally bizarre use of cartoons on television. We see Kirsten watching cartoons on television twice and, in both cases, she is drunk and pathetic. In the first instance, Edwards cuts from Joe in Houston on a business trip to a close-up of a cartoon on television which, as the camera pulls back, reveals Kirsten in their apartment drinking and smoking. We see the back of her head as we hear off-screen sound. We only briefly see the Mel Blanc-voiced cartoon about a bear family with Mama Bear and Papa, but we hear the off-screen sound and dialogue throughout. In a remarkably complex moment, we hear a child, Debbie (Jennifer Edwards), call "Mommy" from a different off-screen space. In a startling contrast, Debbie's off-screen voice intrudes into the off-screen sound of the world in the cartoon. When Kirsten goes to the bedroom to check on Debbie, we still hear the off-screen sound and, when she returns to the living room, she passes out while drinking while we continue to hear the cartoon sound. We learn later that, after having passed out, she started a fire with her cigarette.

Near the end of the film, Joe, who is once again recovering with the help of AA, receives a phone call from a motel manager. Learning that Kirsten is drunk in one of the rooms, Joe rushes off to help her. As he enters the room, we hear a Bugs Bunny cartoon with Yosemite Sam coming from off-screen space. The camera pans right where we see the TV screen with rolling images; we can't even make out what the images are and Kirsten is in such a stupor that she doesn't notice. Joe turns off the TV before beginning a conversation with her and there is a startling contrast between the sounds of the comic cartoon we have been hearing and their conversation, which once again involves her castrating attacks on Joe. He wants to take her home, but she snaps, "What did they do to you at the AA place, anyway? Aren't you a man anymore? Can't you hear a woman calling you? I'm a woman. Can't you hear me? ... I don't want anyone who doesn't have the guts to take a drink." She starts to laugh at him and he takes a drink.

Edwards has often spoken about his love of cartoons, but in a way that relates to his comedies where he revels in images so painful and extreme that no one could survive them without serious injury or death. For a simple example, near the beginning of *A Shot in the Dark*, Clouseau gets knocked out of a high second-story window. We see him flattened against the ground like a pancake. He resembles Coyote in the Road Runner cartoons, who does such things as sail off a cliff and be flattened when he lands far below. Both Coyote and Clouseau simply reappear and the madness continues. *The Great Race* is a paean to such gags when Professor Fate (once again, Jack Lemmon) and his sidekick get hit by trains and crash planes only to stagger out and quickly resume their dastardly deeds.

In these films the logic of the cartoon-like humor is clear. But what are cartoons doing in a dark drama about alcoholism? We will return to the related question of the fine line between comedy and drama in Edwards's films later: What is alcoholism doing in so many of his comedies? Kirsten in *Days of Wine and Roses* does not behave like the characters in the cartoons, nor does she suffer a similar fate. She simply watches (or attempts to watch) cartoons much like Popcorn in *Experiment in Terror* watches silent movies. In both of these films cartoons and silent film offer abrupt moments of intrusion that erupt into the movie we are watching more than being integrated into it. They become part of the film's discourse about comedy and the fine line between laughter and tears. Much like the pattern of laughter is inverted in this film from that of traditional comedy, the glimpses of the cartoons and even more importantly their off-screen sound bring no joy or pleasure to the viewer of the film. Indeed, here both our laughter and the laughter of the characters in the room are denied. If Kirsten seeks escape from her world of addiction and pain through them, she fails. The cartoons in this film seem and sound like another world so far removed that Kirsten seems oblivious to them and we are baffled as to why they are in the film. It is almost as if Edwards, a life-long recovering alcoholic, has found the perfect film version of his maxim, that he could find the humor in everything except Julie Andrews losing her voice. In this film, he has found one context in which his love of cartoons and their zany vitality and energy are not funny. He can't find the humor in cartoons here anymore than Kirsten can.

Three final examples show bizarre instances of a character in the film breaking into laughter that is not meant to be funny. When Joe is in Houston meeting with two business colleagues in a bar, he is called to the phone. He returns to the table with an uncomprehending look on his face and after a long pause laughingly tells his puzzled colleagues that his wife set their apartment on fire. They sit speechless and dumbfounded by his behavior.

Then, after returning from Houston, he laughs when he tells Kirsten she doesn't have to worry anymore about his Texas business trips because he's been fired. For Joe, his apartment being burned down and his being fired are laughing matters, but his laughter has nothing to do with pleasure. Ironically, in the earlier scene during which he returned drunk from work late at night and picks the flowers that are destroyed in the elevator, he had berated Kirsten for not being willing to drink with him, declaring that they need "some laughs around here."

Later in the film when Joe goes to the motel where Kirsten is drunk and she talks him into joining her, he does and gets drunk again. He then goes out looking for more liquor. In a brutally ironic scene, after he breaks into a closed liquor store to steal a bottle, the owner catches him and, as Joe lies helplessly on the ground, we see the owner laughing sadistically as he pours the contents of a bottle over Joe's face. These are not the laughs Joe was looking for. In a sense, *Days of Wine and Roses* is a meditation about the many dark sides to humor, comedy, and laughter and this scene serves a perfect segue into a summary of the film's representation of Joe's symbolic castration tied to alcoholism. Edwards's films foreground two kinds of castration imagery: one involves destroying powerful public phallic images and the other is centered on characters whose masculinity is attacked and humiliated. In the former category we have such images as a submarine in wartime, painted pink and held together by women's undergarments (*Operation Petticoat*); bomber planes in wartime straining to rise in the sky only to fail and plummet to earth (*Darling Lili*); and the collapse of the Eiffel Tower (*The Great Race*). On the other hand, central male characters fail in their masculine and sexual behavior. Inspector Clouseau spends much of *The Pink Panther* trying to make love to his wife while trying to capture a notorious jewel thief. By the end of the film, he has failed with every effort at lovemaking with his wife who, in fact, has been having an affair with the thief, and he goes to jail for the crime he is trying to solve, but not until he falls over in his chair on the witness stand. As far away as he seems from Inspector Clouseau, Joe Clay is one of Edwards's castrated men separated only by a fine line from Inspector Clouseau.

The castration motif unites several threads: the office; interactions with other men such as his father-in-law and the liquor store owner; and his interactions with Kirsten. To briefly summarize, he begins by calling himself a "eunuch in a harem" when describing his job. It will go downhill from there. We see his boss come into his office twice and, after casting doubts on his performance, literally picking up the phone and removing him from the account on which he is working, much as Dreyfus regularly removes

Clouseau from cases, and then fires him. When Kirsten takes Joe home to meet her father, her father adopts a stern moral tone, denigrates the value of Joe's public relations work and implicitly questions Joe's worth as a son-in-law. When he learns that Joe and Kirsten are married, he silently slams the door on them. And Joe, as we have seen, had already symbolically castrated himself via his own incompetence while attempting to impress Kirsten with his skill in killing roaches and later to be romantic by bringing her flowers.

And Kirsten herself castrates Joe repeatedly, beginning with her moral attack on his PR job of supplying party girls, her refusal to date him, her dismissal of AA with the implication that a "real man" wouldn't need to humiliate himself in front of others to control his drinking, to her final brutal attack on his masculinity in the motel room with "Aren't you a man anymore?" This is ironic in its reinforcement of his long-held opinion of himself, since he had characterized himself at the film's beginning as a "eunuch in a harem." But the film has an unusual narrative arc for Edwards with regard to the castration motif. Joe and Kirsten trade places several times as one exerts power over the other in regard to their drinking. Joe initially tricks Kirsten into having an alcoholic drink but before long she entices him as in the scene where she introduces Joe to her father.[4] After her father has closed the door on them, she says she needs a drink. As we have seen, at times Joe has lured her into drinking as when he returns home drunk and she initially refuses because of nursing the baby. At times he insists that they both stop drinking, such as after he joins AA, but she refuses and he gives in to join her. This see-saw power dynamic culminates at the film's conclusion when Joe is once again sober and now taking care of their child. Kirsten, who still drinks and lives with her father, comes to see Joe. She says she hasn't had a drink for a few days but he once again refuses to take her back because she will not agree to totally giving up drinking. The scene is extremely complex in regard to Joe's narrative arc and also clearly delineates how Edwards's version of the story is far removed from Frankenheimer's, although the scenes may at first glance appear similar. Edwards and Lemmon bestow a calm dignity on Joe Clay. On the one hand, he now occupies the traditional female role of the late 1950s and early 1960s as the parent raising the child, but on the other hand he is *not* feminized. Far from seeming like a eunuch or castrated man, he exudes a confident and secure masculinity in how he interacts both with their daughter and with his estranged wife. He has never seemed more like a man in the entire film.[5]

The formal constructions of this final scene are profoundly different from that of the TV show. Edwards shows Kirsten approaching the apartment, walking along a street with a bar sign visible above one of the store fronts. After Joe turns her away, he once again returns to the same shot but now we see Kirsten walking away from the camera with the same bar sign visible. Joe is interrupted by Debbie calling and she asks if she heard "mommy." Joe explains it was a dream, puts her back to bed, and returns to the window. Edwards then cuts to a shot of Joe looking out of the window and we see the same exterior long shot but now the street is empty and Kirsten is gone. The film then cuts to an exterior shot of Joe looking out of the window with the reflection of the electric bar sign flashing off and on in the right side of the window and the camera moves slowly in to a close-up. Not a word is spoken in any of these shots of the street, nor in the film's final shot of the window, but they are emotionally powerful. Joe contemplates much more than alcoholism; these are complex characters with whom we have come to identify from the very beginning of the film. He deeply loves the woman walking away as he loves the child within. This is also heightened by Debbie calling for her mommy. The flashing bar sign of course stresses the role that alcohol has played in bringing their lives to this point and the visual motif is developed in four shots, all of which include powerful imagery of Kirsten or Joe both alone in the frame, the latter in the apartment and the former on the empty street.

In Frankenheimer's version, in an earlier scene in the apartment, Joe goes over to the window and looks out. The film cuts to an exterior shot and we see Joe looking out the window and a large bar sign looming in the right foreground. Shortly after that in the final scene, after Joe and Kirsten fail to come to an understanding, Kirsten walks over to the window and looks out and Frankenheimer cuts to the same exterior long shot that we earlier saw with Joe and the bar sign. She then leaves the apartment. We do not see the bar sign in the street as we do in the film when Kirsten comes and goes. In fact, there are no street shots of her. After Joe turns her away, he walks over to the window to look out and we see a large close-up of the bar sign outside. Then we cut to an exterior shot of the window where we see Joe and hear him reciting an AA prayer asking God for the power he needs, which recalls the beginning of the show and the many times we see the AA 12-step program on the wall behind Joe as he speaks at the meetings. The at times heavy-handed emphasis here is on alcoholism and AA. We know and respond to the characters as primarily alcoholics in what at times sounds like a promo film for AA. In Edwards's film, we know and care about the characters before they become alcoholics and continue to care about them throughout. Although Edwards respectfully includes the key role that AA plays in helping alcoholics, his film is not primarily about the organization. The scene in which

Joe introduces himself as an alcoholic is brief and respectful but it is the structural opposite of that in the TV show. The scene ends as soon as Joe comes to the podium and introduces himself with one line: "I'm Joe Clay and I'm an alcoholic." It is the only AA meeting we see in the film. The TV show starts and ends with AA and frames all the action through it. After Joe introduces himself as an alcoholic, he begins narrating all the events speaking to the audience in the AA meeting. The TV show is very much about AA.

The ending of Edwards's film also resonates strongly within his oeuvre in which many films do not end with the strong formation of a heterosexual couple. Kirsten says she can't give up drinking, leading to Joe turning her away. Before she leaves she tells Joe he'd better give up on her but he says not yet. This ambiguity is reminiscent of the end of *Mister Cory* where, as we saw in Chapter 3, Cory turns away the woman who wants to leave with him at the airport, but not before she says she will be waiting for him and he indicates he may be back. And another variation occurs in *Experiment in Terror*, as we saw in Chapter 4. That film is even more unusual in that its lead female character, also played by Lee Remick, has no romantic involvement with the main male character played by Glenn Ford, nor is she involved with any other man. And, since she lives alone with her younger sister, film convention in 1962 virtually cries out for the creation of a strong nuclear family. Instead, the two sisters go home together.

In a conversation we had with Edwards about alcoholism in *Skin Deep*, he told us about his own life experiences as an alcoholic. Although he had not taken a drink for decades, he stressed that alcoholism was not just part of his past, characterizing himself as a "recovering alcoholic." But he also stressed that he learned to control his alcoholism without AA. Edwards was not criticizing AA or the people who participated in it, nor was he trying to glorify himself as a man who beat it on his own. Like much in his life, he seemed to have a philosophically complex attitude toward it and he was not above making fun of it. His films are full of the hilarious antics of characters who drink too much. In *The Party* much comic mayhem results from a waiter who gets increasingly drunk since the central character does not drink and each time he declines a drink, the waiter drinks it for him. In *That's Life!* the Jack Lemmon character explains to a maître d' that the best way to cook a lobster is to poach it slowly in champagne so that the lobster will die happy. In *Skin Deep*, a psychiatrist simply tells the central character the best way to overcome his alcoholism is to stop drinking, as if strong willpower is all that is needed.

Alcohol and drunkenness pervade Edwards's films and television shows for many reasons. Most obviously he likes to explore human behavior when drinking has loosened the usual social constraints. But for our purposes here, the most important thing is to understand what that tells us about his view of the relationship between comedy and drama. We posed two questions above: What are cartoons doing in a dark drama about alcoholism? What is alcoholism doing in so many of his comedies? As we saw in Chapter 2, from the very beginning of his career nearly all his radio, television, and film work has defied fitting comfortably into any genre. For Edwards, genres are simply too restrictive. But he loves to play with them. A similar impulse lies beneath his love of comedy and drama. Since he views laughter and pain as going hand in hand in life, he believes they should go hand in hand in film. From that perspective, even something as grim as alcoholism can simultaneously be devastating and devastatingly funny. The concept of simultaneity is crucial for Edwards since the need to find humor is directly tied to the terrible pain it seeks to relieve (ironically, not unlike alcohol). He does not mix comedy and drama into a unified aesthetic whole to create what critics now call "dramedy" but rather comedy erupts into and disrupts the dramas in much the same way as pain and even death erupt into and disrupt the comedies (for example, the shocking death of the central male character in *S.O.B.*). As the title of one of his late-period dark comedies puts it, *That's Life!*. Perhaps not coincidentally, the full title of that films is: *Blake Edwards's That's Life!*.

NOTES

1. Cited in Kirk Honeycutt, "His Pain, His Gain," in *Blake Edwards Interviews*, edited by Gabriella Oldham (Jackson: University Press of Mississippi, 2018), p. 96.
2. Philip Lathrop, the cinematographer for *Days of Wine and Roses*, had worked extensively with Edwards on two black-and-white TV shows: *Peter Gunn* and *Mister Lucky* (see Chapter 3). He also worked on *Experiment in Terror*, another black-and-white Edwards film, in 1961 (see Chapter 4). In many ways, he was the perfect cinematographer for Edwards for these two black-and-white films.
3. Something similar occurs in *The Pink Panther Strikes Again* when Clouseau laughs uncontrollably, as the result of laughing gas rather than alcohol, and throughout *The Great Race* as Professor Fate laughs at his evil plans.
4. In the TV show Kirsten is already a drunk in the first scene before she even meets and interacts with Joe. Near the end of both the TV show and the film, Kirsten's father berates Joe for having started his daughter drinking. Joe denies it both in the TV show and in the film, but, in fact, in the film he is lying.
5. Blake Edwards similarly portrays himself as a father being the caretaker of his children in his documentary *Julie*. See Chapter 10.

CHAPTER 6

Gunn (1967) and Peter Gunn (1989)

Executive Produced (Uncredited), Created, Written, and Directed by Blake Edwards

Executive Produced, Created, Written, and Directed by Blake Edwards

Gunn opens with a dark screen that we soon realize is a long shot of the ocean at night as a distant vessel emerges from the darkness and steadily approaches the camera.[1] The film then cuts to an extreme close-up showing a distorted image of a huge eye looking through a nautical scope. We then get some narrative context as a man, with the name of his vessel, *Tempest*, on his jacket, lights a cigarette and quietly remarks to a crewmate, "Another boat, coming this way. What's he doing now?" That boat pulls up alongside and what appear to be Coast Guard men come aboard. In a lower cabin, a man leaves a woman in bed to go up and confront the boarders, asking, "Do you know who I am?" One of the boarders replies, "Yes, Mr. Scarlotti, we know who you are," and machine guns him to death. Then the woman and everyone else on the boat are slaughtered, with all but the last murder occurring off-screen. The killers quickly return to their boat, which seems to be commanded by a platinum blond man in a dark jacket, shown from the rear. The boat pulls away, a searchlight goes out, and all returns to darkness. Abruptly, the film's credits appear against a brightly colored, psychedelic-looking backdrop, with silhouettes of go-go dancers gyrating to Henry Mancini's hard-driving Peter Gunn theme music.

Blake Edwards: Film Director as Multitalented Auteur, First Edition.
William Luhr and Peter Lehman.
© 2023 John Wiley & Sons Ltd. Published 2023 by John Wiley & Sons Ltd.

This sequence establishes central strategies in *Gunn*. The contrast of the mysterious long shot of the approaching vessel with the extreme, distorted close-up of an eye points to the ways in which the film develops its central mysteries, many of which involve perceptual deception. The boat containing the murderers is not a Coast Guard vessel at all but has been disguised to look like one. The unidentified blond man directing the assault turns out to be Daisy Jane (M. T. Marshall), owner of The Ark, a floating bordello, who lives as a woman and orchestrates many of the film's murders disguised as one. Throughout the film, most characters presume that Daisy Jane is a woman, the madame of The Ark. Many of the women on The Ark who roam around its main salon appear to be twins, with some characterized by the different foreign languages they speak, presumably rendering them attractively "exotic" and reinforcing the doubling motif. And of course the doubling began at the outset with the disguised boat.

In the second scene following the credit sequence, the film establishes a common connection back to the TV series when we see Edie (Laura Devon) singing in Mother's jazz club. After the song is over, she joins Gunn (Craig Stevens), who is waiting for her, and they begin kissing. But Edie declares she senses "instability" in the kiss, implicitly questioning Gunn's masculinity. They continue kissing while she further undermines his masculinity, and he attempts to reaffirm his virility. The most interesting connection here, however, is not back to such scenes which occurred regularly in the TV series but, rather, to Edwards's 1962 film, *Experiment in Terror*. And the reference is neither in the dialogue nor in the narrative context but in the formal use of composition and space. Edwards shoots the kissing scene with extreme close-ups centered on Edie's face and only fragments of Gunn's off-screen face. This echoes the opening scene of *Experiment in Terror* where Lee Remick's character is terrorized by a male intruder in her garage. We see her face in extreme close-up, at times foregrounding her nostrils as the intruder grips it so tightly (see Figure 4.1). In *Gunn*, the most extreme close-up in the kissing series of shots also emphasizes Edie's nose with her head tilted back, foregrounding her right nostril (Figure 6.1). In *Experiment in Terror* the woman in the shot is terrorized by a dangerous pervert, whereas in *Gunn* the shot eroticizes the woman's face as part of a light comic, romantic scene with her questioning the man's masculinity. Questions about Gunn's masculinity will reappear comically throughout the film. The differing uses of these extreme close-ups foreground how Edwards explores formal preoccupations such as composition and screen space across his films and genres; his preoccupations do not separate narrative and theme from the formal manner in which they are represented.[2]

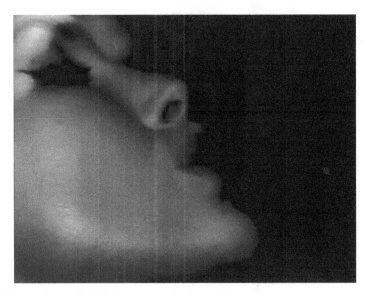

FIGURE 6.1   *Gunn,* © 1967 Paramount Pictures Corporation.

For Edie, Gunn's kiss may not be what it appears to be, but very little is what it appears to be in this movie, which is not surprising in a detective film. However, the ways in which this is formally developed throughout are surprising and powerful. What seems like a Coast Guard vessel is in effect a murder boat. For most of the film the main villain orchestrating the multiple murders appears to be the arrogant gangster, Nick Fusco (Albert Paulsen), but it is actually Daisy Jane who turns out to be a man living as a woman. "Sam" (Sherry Jackson), the seemingly ditsy, sex-addled young woman who furtively enters Gunn's apartment and awaits him while naked in his bed, is in fact a serious young woman seeking revenge for the murder of her father, Scarlotti, and she unexpectedly shoots Daisy Jane to death at the end. This pattern of deceptive appearances is echoed in the running gag of the bartender at Mother's, who repeatedly approaches patrons like Gunn with a drink and archly asks them to confirm that it is "ginger ale" when, in fact, it is hard liquor. At one point Gunn is shaving in his apartment with the radio tuned to "Captain Brady," a traffic reporter (Ken Wales). Suddenly, the sound of Brady's helicopter gets much louder, and Gunn hears a scream. Bewildered, he rushes to his window to see the helicopter leaving the area near his apartment and he also sees Sam standing below clad in a towel. She had sneaked into Gunn's apartment and was sunbathing outside. Clearly, Brady had lowered his helicopter to get a closer look at the naked woman while telling his radio audience that he was simply investigating a traffic incident.

The central deception lies with both Daisy Jane's gender and criminal agenda of consolidating underworld power while making it appear that Fusco is responsible for the criminal activities involved. When Gunn discovers all of this, the film climaxes in a shockingly graphic manner. Gunn yanks Daisy Jane's wig off (Figure 6.2), and Daisy Jane screeches and attacks him. Until this point Daisy Jane's voice had been carefully modulated and seductive, not harsh and animal-like. In the ensuing fight with Gunn, Daisy Jane's face repeatedly smashes through glass so that, at the end, we see it grotesquely mutilated and covered in blood. This scene follows another shocking one in which Gunn investigates Daisy Jane's apartment and discovers a bedroom lined with mirrors. An armed intruder enters, and the myriad of images that rapidly follow are confusing both about which are reflections, and which is the real intruder. Finally, Gunn kills the intruder in a gunfight that destroys the room. The mirrors are instantaneously shattered; an elegant-looking chandelier at the center quickly becomes a black, twisted tangle of metal and wires. The room that, seconds before, had appeared to be a brightly lit, theatrical showcase is now wreckage shrouded in darkness.

Characters are repeatedly disoriented by the differences between appearances and reality. In addition, the film is set amid a large-scale sociocultural

FIGURE 6.2   *Gunn,* © 1967 Paramount Pictures Corporation.

change between the 1950s world of jazz, including the cool jazz in Mother's, and the 1960s world of rock, in which cultural upheaval is everywhere.

Aside from the constant deceptions, the film is also built upon violent clashes of opposites. An explosion that destroys Mother's is one eruption, initially misunderstood as the work of Fusco. The larger clash is that of changing times. The "cool" detective Peter Gunn, who is rugged in his dealings with men, is repeatedly befuddled, generally in his interactions with women. In this he differs from contemporary examples of "hard-boiled" detectives like Mickey Spillane's Mike Hammer, who at times delights in brutalizing women. Sam Wasson has noted that Blake Edwards has described Gunn as "boiled somewhere between soft and hard."[3] This is amusing in his interactions with "Sam" and "Ernestine" (Carol Wayne), but explosive with Daisy Jane where it is no longer funky but horrifying.

The film also introduces a new heightened comic sensibility that first appeared in its mature form in the two earlier Clouseau films (*The Pink Panther* and *A Shot in the Dark*). It evidences Edwards's increasingly profound exploration of the relationship of comedy with drama which we have discussed, for example, in Chapter 5 with reference to *Days of Wine and Roses*. In that film, the Jack Lemmon character surprisingly resembles and foreshadows Inspector Clouseau a year before the release of *The Pink Panther*. Inversely, Peter Gunn in this film also recalls several aspects of his comic counterpart and, in addition, the film introduces bedroom farce in a manner recalling the plot of *The Pink Panther*. A recurring plot device finds Peter Gunn surprised in his bedroom by a woman that he had not known was there when his girlfriend Edie unexpectedly enters the apartment. In a near panic, he rushes out of the bedroom, slamming the door shut as he goes downstairs to greet and distract Edie. On one occasion he is so flustered that he continues walking past Edie, opening the door and walking into the apartment hallway until Edie calls attention to what he has done, and he comes back in with a befuddled look. These scenes involve off-screen space in a simple manner. There is the off-screen space in the bedroom from which Gunn emerges, the interior apartment space, and, quite unexpectedly, the apartment hallway. Edie's questions about who is in the bedroom bring our attention to that off-screen space. This is a much pared down but structurally similar use of a major scene of bedroom farce with off-screen space in *The Pink Panther*. In that scene Clouseau and his wife as well as her lover and her lover's young nephew, who also desires her, are all hidden and hiding from each other in the bedroom and the bathroom. Both Gunn and Clouseau lose their masculine composure in these scenes with highly sexual women.

Another example occurs when Gunn is making coffee in his kitchen after unexpectedly discovering that Sam, the woman he had previously discovered in his bedroom, has returned and is sunbathing on his patio with little or nothing on. He goes into the kitchen to make coffee when Sam suddenly enters from off-screen, wrapped only in a towel. Once again, Gunn gets so flustered that he turns around to avoid looking at her as he pours cream into his coffee, continuing to pour the cream until the entire mug overflows. Here there is an obvious sexual connotation of premature ejaculation from an overexcited man, a gag that recalls Clouseau holding a champagne bottle at groin level that explodes as the cork pops as he lies in bed awaiting sex with his wife. This kind of comedy will intensify in the 1989 *Peter Gunn* made-for-television movie, which fits a pattern in Edwards's 1980s films where his exploration of the fine line between comedy and drama is virtually erased and it is hard to tell if we are watching a drama with comedy or a comedy with drama. Edwards's belief that nearly everything in life has a humorous or comic aspect to it leads him to reject the notion of the most fundamental genre assumption in Western culture: the theatrical smiling mask of comedy juxtaposed with the sad mask of tragedy with a tear in its eye. By 1967, Peter Sellers as Inspector Clouseau, Jack Lemmon as Joe Clay, and Craig Stevens as Peter Gunn all resemble each other and much of that resemblance is based upon Edwards's use of similar formal structures in both his comedies and diverse dramas, including the structured use of screen space and off-screen space as well as sexual subtexts about masculinity and male sexuality.

The opening sequence in *Gunn* is shot in muted colors, evocative of the black-and-white cinematography of the *Peter Gunn* television series, which Edwards created and which ran from 1958 to 1961. That abruptly changes with the aggressively psychedelic coloring of the credits. What we see prior to those credits could have introduced an episode of the series, and in fact the film is partially based on "The Kill," the first episode of that series, created, written, produced, and directed by Edwards. Thus, the origin of the movie returns to the origin of the series.

A brief consideration of "The Kill" shows how Edwards approached related narrative material in a 30-minute TV series episode that he later adapted into a feature film.[4] The pre-credit sequence shows a police car pull over a large sedan but, when the officers approach, instead of issuing a citation, they pull out guns and kill all the occupants in the car. The first scene following the credits takes place at a funeral where Fallon, a new gang boss who has taken over from one of the men killed in the opening scene, threateningly tells Gunn that he is going to make changes "and you could be one of them," a line repeated in the film's funeral scene. The third scene takes place in Mother's as it also does in the film. The first three scenes in *Gunn* thus directly parallel those in the pilot. In the pre-credit shooting, we see a car which has been disguised as a police car and its occupants disguised as officers deceive their victims. The structure is the same as that of the disguised Coast Guard vessel in the film. Other similarities including lines of dialogue follow. When Gunn is escorted to Fallon's racquet ball court, Fallon threatens Gunn by warning that "Mother's," the bar where Gunn hangs out and where his girlfriend Edie sings, may be in danger. Shortly after that a bomb destroys the bar and Mother, who moments earlier had learned of a rat problem in her bar, lies in the wreckage and mutters, "When we get big rats, we get *big* rats." That exact line and others from this pilot reappear in the 1967 film. For example, when Jacoby warns Gunn against seeking revenge against Fallon for bombing Mother's, he says, "I'll go after you as fast as I go after Fallon," to which Gunn replies, "Then I've got nothing to worry about." When Lt. Jacoby fails to stop Gunn from vengefully pursuing the gang leader, Jacoby approaches Edie and asks, "Well, can't you do something?" to which she sarcastically replies, "Sure. What would you like me to sing?" In contrast to the film, however, the plot of the episode is straightforward, and all the main actions clearly interrelate. In the end, Fallon is found guilty of bombing Mother's and killing the tailor who made the disguises, and the gangsters disguised as officers and Fallon's other thugs are all killed. All in about 27 minutes minus commercials.

When Edwards expanded this origin story into a feature film it led to an entirely different structure. In the series, Mother's is blown up near the beginning of the pilot; in the film it is blown up near the climax. In the pilot, Gunn visits the responsible suspected gang leader playing racquet ball once while in the film he goes twice. Whereas, as we shall see, the film develops elaborate complex mysteries with many additional characters, the episode moves forward in a clear, linear, interconnected manner. But the premise of the starting point remains the same. Tension among rival gangs leads to one gang leader using a disguised police car to kill his rival, while in the film it will be a boat disguised as a Coast Guard vessel. And in the film, Fusco is innocent and has been framed. In this regard, Edwards's adaptation of a television episode from *Peter Gunn* into a feature film parallels his strategy that we analyzed in Chapter 2 of adapting an episode of his radio show, *Richard Diamond, Private Detective*, for a feature film, *The Couch*. We will return in Chapter 12 to Edwards's interest in remaking his earlier work from one medium within another medium, which continues into his late period where he remade his second film, *He Laughed Last*, as *Big Rosemary*, a musical theater piece, and remade his film *Victor/Victoria* as a Broadway musical.

As we have seen, the pre-credit sequence of the film *Gunn* is dark, both visually and thematically. It could also be the opening of a classic *Film Noir*, a genre that influenced much of Edwards's detective work in radio, television, and film. All of that changes instantly with the credit sequence. Where the television series, famous for its popular Henry Mancini score, evoked the 1950s world of jazz, the film credits abruptly plunge us into the rock-dominated 1960s and are also evocative of the stylish credits for James Bond movies of the era. The credit sequence also introduces the film's primary motif of doubling and disguising as we see one of the go-go dancers literally double in front of our eyes as she dances, three images of a man's head come together as one image, and a pair of already split images of a dancer split again and we see two pairs of two dancers.

The world has changed, and suddenly the cool Peter Gunn of the 1950s and early 1960s is beginning to be outmoded. This is not entirely new here. In the television series he was similarly out of place when visiting beatnik coffee houses or avant-garde artist's studios wearing his well-tailored suits with shirts and ties. But Edwards updates that theme in this film as when Gunn enters the "Monkey Farm," a counterculture bar, searching for an informant. He still wears the well-tailored suit and tie, but he is now surrounded by bikers and hippies. A hulking biker confronts him using the slang of the times, saying, "Hey, man, who are you?" and is so menacing that finally Gunn takes out his pistol and says, "I'm the man who's going to shoot you in the stomach if you don't let go, man." Although he extricates himself, Gunn is clearly out of place in the counterculture environment with its use of such popular 1960s terms as "man" and "groovy." Near the end we see Gunn and Lt. Jacoby (Edward Asner) in Mother's after it has been rebuilt following an explosion, but now the crowd is gyrating to rock music under a poster declaring "Freak In to Save Mother's." Jacoby, palpably annoyed by this change, comments, "When did Mother start attracting this segment of society?" and Gunn mocks him as reactionary by saying that he is upset because "Mairzy Doats," a popular 1943 novelty song, is no longer in the top 40, but it is obvious that Gunn's world is also disappearing.

The bright colors in parts of the film not only contrast sharply with earlier dominantly black-and-white imagery but also figure centrally in its strategies. The climactic sequence with Daisy Jane is shocking in its graphic violence, in its revelation of Daisy Jane's murderous villainy, and in the shocking revelation of her gender. We see Daisy Jane's previously elegantly controlled body violently crashing through glass partitions and ultimately lying lifeless on the floor, sliced up by shards of glass and covered in blood. Color is central to this shock of seeing Daisy Jane not as the well-appointed madame of The Ark but as a destroyed, boyish-looking, platinum blond man, now resembling a shattered circus doll whom we now recognize as the mysterious man with the platinum blond hair we have seen only from behind throughout the film at the various murder scenes (Figure 6.3).

Perhaps more than any other of his films, *Gunn* illustrates Edwards's career-long imperative of working across multiple media and adapting to the ever-changing industrial and formal imperatives of each. The movie was based on the successful television series he had created nearly a decade earlier, and that series would remain a presence in his career, emerging again in *Peter Gunn*, a 1989 made-for-television movie, and in unproduced projects near the end of his life. He told us that, even though the television series had been earning impressive ratings in 1961, he chose not to sign on for another season because he wanted the network to expand it to an hour and shoot it in color, but the network refused. It was a prescient plan on Edwards's part and indicates his sensitivity to the changing dynamics of the industry since, only a few years after this, many dramatic television series would be hour-long and in color. In a sense, *Gunn*, a 94-minute color film coming along only six years after the television series, fulfills that vision for the season that did not happen and illustrates other aspects of the changing industry. Not only was color unavailable to the television series but the film also touches upon content that television censorship of the 1950s and early

FIGURE 6.3 *Gunn*, © 1967 Paramount Pictures Corporation.

1960s would never have allowed. These include the graphic violence at the end as well as the revelation of Daisy Jane's disguised gender.

Nevertheless, the film draws substantially on components of the television series, including Craig Stevens returning as Peter Gunn, Henry Mancini's music, and Philip Lathrop's cinematography. Other central characters also return, although played by different actors, such as Lt. Jacoby, Edie (Gunn's girlfriend), and Mother. In addition, the movie bears numerous markers of other of Edwards's television work. One example is that the various shots of boats approaching The Ark directly echo similar shots of launches approaching Mr. Lucky's boat in Edwards's series, *Mr. Lucky* (1959–1960), about a floating casino.

Sam Wasson notes that "The idea was that Gunn would kick-off a James Bond-type franchise," but the poor box-office prevented a sequel.[5] Clearly Edwards was thinking of the series model, in which he had worked extensively, as well as with the popular James Bond films and his Pink Panther Inspector Clouseau films. Although Edwards directed and cowrote *Gunn*, Ken Wales, the film's associate producer, told us that initially Edwards did not intend to direct it and offered the job to William Friedkin, a young up and coming director. Due to conflicts in pre-production, Friedkin was fired. Edwards then asked Wales to direct it: "Blake said to me, 'You do it. It's time you directed one.' ... I said, 'I'm not ready.' He said, 'Yes, you are ... I'll be right there beside you.' I thought a moment. I said, 'That's the problem. If it doesn't work, it's my fault. If it works, you're the hero – that just isn't fair,' and he laughed about it. He said, 'Well, you got me on that.'" This history is instructive in several ways. Edwards's primary working relationship with the television series had been as the creator and producer. Within the television structure at that time a creator-producer was much more powerful than an episode director. Edwards's original creative plan showed him trying to extend that model from the black-and-white, 30-minute serial format to feature filmmaking. In fact, Edwards was the uncredited "executive producer" of the film.

Although the plan to extend the television creative production model did not lead to a series in this case, it appeared at a time in which Edwards was branching out into enterprises for which he assumed various creative and production roles as a multi-hyphenate, multimedia creator working in radio, television, and film simultaneously.[6] Many of these also involved regular collaborators of Edwards, including Henry Mancini and Philip Lathrop, among others. By the 1960s, the success of *Peter Gunn* and *Mr. Lucky*, combined with his growing prestige as a movie director, gave him much greater creative power with his projects.

The pilots he made in the 1950s and early 1960s were 30 minutes long, but in 1989 he would make the 90-minute made-for-television film *Peter Gunn* as a pilot for a possible series, acknowledging the different dynamics of the industry at that time. Feature-length made-for-television films did not exist in the 1950s but by the late 1980s they were gathering momentum.

In the 1960s, Peter Gunn developed into a franchise, and the franchise model is an important one in radio, television, and film. Commentators regularly describe Edwards as a movie director, and it is true that once he achieved that status in films, he prioritized it. He described it to *The New York Times* in 1988 regarding his made-for-television pilot film, *Justin Case*, as follows:

> Should "Justin Case" evolve into a series, the show's creator will oversee it from the sidelines, leaving the detail work to other writers and directors. "I'd much rather concentrate on feature films," said Mr. Edwards, who knocks off movies at a rate of one every 18 months. "Television is way down on my list of priorities. I have probably 10 films left in me," the 65-year-old director estimated, "and I want to be happy with them. If it looks like television will interfere with my film making, then I won't get involved."[7]

But he saw his work in complex ways. He valued television throughout his career, and he recognized how, with his multi-hyphenate, multimedia orientation, he could play a significant creative role in TV without it interfering with his film directing by pushing it to the back burner. It is remarkable how many hats he could wear simultaneously in radio, television, and film while rightly prioritizing his film directing. Within a year of making that comment, he was back with *Peter Gunn*, another made-for-TV film which ironically directly grew out of his original *Peter Gunn* TV series.

His primary credit on the *Peter Gunn* television series was "created and produced by Blake Edwards." Edwards's interest in franchise production was influenced by his work in series radio and television, starting with his work for Dick Powell. Edwards has remarked, "When I was looking for the actor to play Peter Gunn, for instance, I took my cue from Dick Powell in *Murder, My Sweet*: his whole career had gone downhill, he was an ex-musical comedy star singing by a waterfall – then suddenly he was playing a private eye and doing it effectively. I applied that same principle to Craig Stevens."[8] Craig Stevens has told us in detail how he came to play Peter Gunn, confirming that Blake took him to a tailor and to a barber to change his hairstyle and fashion style to remake his image as Powell had remade his.

It is not, therefore, surprising that Edwards returned once again to *Peter Gunn* in the 1989 made-for-television movie of the same name with yet another actor remaking Gunn's image. Peter Strauss told us how he came to be cast in the film. Edwards was considering casting the much-older Craig Stevens once again to play Gunn, but ABC wanted a younger actor who could attract a new audience. Strauss had done several successful shows with ABC and they suggested him to Edwards. ABC saw this pilot as bringing together a well-known franchise, a well-known director, and a popular TV star. Edwards had no interest in further hands-on involvement after the pilot, planning to turn over producing and directing to Tony Adams. For Strauss the elements of comedy in the movie were an exciting challenge and he recalls Edwards as being very calm throughout the production: *"No sturm und drang."*

It is also not surprising that that film returns to the origin story of the series and the previous theatrical feature as its points of departure with yet another tale of Gunn being caught up in a war between two gangs. As with *Gunn*, it opens with an elaborately conceived gangland murder, but here it is set in daylight and at a swimming pool, not at night on the ocean. We see a gangster emerge from his house and enter a swimming pool. A masked killer in black climbs over a wall and deftly rigs up a device by which he can hurl a long, grounded wire over nearby electric power lines that then lands in the pool and electrocutes the gangster. The killer quickly escapes but leaves the evidence behind, which shows that the gangster did not die of a heart attack, which might readily have been assumed without the evidence, but was in fact murdered, and is intended to ignite a war among rival gangs.

The scene echoes the opening killings in *Gunn* and much of the film bears substantial markers from the earlier one as well as from the television series. In fact, the image of the gang leader's dead body floating in his pool recalls a similar image of a dead body in a pool in *Gunn*. The film centers on Peter Gunn, the private detective, and revives characters and relationships from the earlier works (albeit played by different actors), including Peter Strauss as Gunn, Barbara Williams as Gunn's girlfriend Edie, Peter Jurasik as Lt. Jacoby (often called Herschel as a nod to Herschel Bernardi who had played the role on TV), and Pearl Bailey as "Mother," as well as settings such as Mother's nightclub and Gunn's apartment. There were however marked differences, such as Mother now being an African American character. It also revives the series practice of including colorful character actors who do brief turns as informants, including Speck, a pool shark (David Rappaport) (Figure 6.4), a little person whose presence recalls that of Billy Barty who repeatedly appeared in the similar role of "Babby" in the television series (Figure 6.5), and Willie, the drunkard who sleeps in a car trunk. Henry Mancini's music is central throughout.

FIGURE 6.4   *Peter Gunn,* © 1989 New World Television.

FIGURE 6.5   *Peter Gunn,* © 1958 Spartan Productions, Official Films, Inc.

But even though many characters and situations resemble those in earlier Peter Gunn works, much is different. At the center of this strategy is the fact that nearly everything operates by misdirection and that little is what it appears to be. The rival gangs are deceived into starting a war, but here the real instigators of it all are rogue police officers who hope to profit from the ensuing chaos whereas in the pilot "The Killing" the police are really just disguised gangsters having nothing to do with rogue cops. What is obvious from the outset in the 1989 film is the extent to which nearly everything operates by misdirection, how characters are *not* saying what they mean but often speaking in code or riddles, which sometimes echo their real meaning.

Early on, the gangster Tony Amatti (Charles Cioffi) sends two of his goons to bring Gunn to see him and he asks Gunn to find out who killed the gangster, Julius, at the opening. Later, Amatti's gangster brother Spiros (Richard Portnow), in a parallel manner, sends two of his goons to bring Gunn to him. When Gunn asks what he wants, Spiros says he wants the same thing as Tony, but with one exception – he is hiring Gunn *not* to find out who killed Julius. Hence, Spiros's demand directly echoes that of Tony, even though it acts in an opposed manner.

At times these parallel structures include private jokes with hidden meanings within a relationship and are developed in a manner that resembles improvisatory riffing among jazz musicians. The interactions between Gunn and Edie generally function in this way. At other times these parallel structures indicate genuine confusion, and at others dangerous deceptions. At times this heightens the mystery; at others, even in perilous situations, they become farce and slapstick comedy.

Early on, after exchanging some lame patter with Mother and the bartender, Gunn goes to a rooftop balcony where he and Edie quickly engage in similar patter. She asks where he has been, and he archly replies that he was buried alive after being kidnapped after having been mistaken for someone else. Both obviously understand that he is not speaking factually but they continue to riff on the silly premise and enjoy doing so. This goes on, establishing that they often speak in improvisatory code with one another.

On the simplest level, it points to the film's constant use of double entendre, not always sexual, but a pattern of talking around what one means, communicating with a dual level of meaning. As Gunn and Edie kiss after riffing in this manner, two of Tony Amatti's goons appear and force Gunn to leave with them to meet with Amatti. As they depart, a concerned Edie asks Gunn, "Shall I tell your sister you'll be late?" Since Gunn has no sister, Edie is obviously using a code term, asking Gunn if she should summon help, but Gunn tells her not to do it. Immediately after this, as Gunn and the goons move downstairs to leave, Mother asks him, "Shall I tell your brother you'll be late?" emphasizing these sibling stories are code. These echoes and parallel structures pervade the film.

In the film's final shootout, Gunn, who is lying in the street with his hands cuffed behind his back, grabs a pistol and awkwardly prepares to fire at a fleeing villain. Jacoby, who is also lying in the street wounded, comments on the near impossibility of the attempt, saying, "You're kidding." Then Gunn yells, "Halt, or I'll shoot," to which the fleeing villain, echoing Jacoby, replies, "You're kidding," before Gunn shoots him.

Nearly everyone misunderstands everyone else or speaks to other characters using a code or a complicated double meaning, or non-sequiturs resulting from the jumbled double meanings. Sometimes this is done in fun, but at other times it involves darker strategies, as with the killers. It is almost compulsive. Gunn repeatedly refers to his secretary Bernice's husband from Crete, neither of whom we ever see, as "Zorba," and other characters repeatedly ask, "Who is Zorba?"

A major difference between this film and earlier Peter Gunn works lies in its extensive use of farce and slapstick comedy. Confusion comes from multiple directions, and much of this is centered around Maggie Dugan (Jennifer Edwards), Gunn's new secretary, and a character without parallel in earlier *Peter Gunn* works. This marks another major distinction between the two films. If a viewer doesn't know that *Gunn* was intended to be part of a series, which was in fact the case for us in many past screenings of it, they would never know from the film itself. It is a complete, self-contained work. It has no loose ends, such as a villain escaping, that point to a sequel. Although the film's ending suggests that Mother's will thrive, this hardly screams for another film. It ties up one of the film's threads since we earlier saw Mother's badly damaged by a bomb. Tying up such loose ends conforms with the Hollywood model of good storytelling. The casting of Jennifer Edwards in *Peter Gunn*, however, adds to the likelihood of a planned sequel. At this point in the 1980s, Edwards was working with her on a hoped-for TV series. The year prior to *Peter Gunn*, he wrote and directed *Justin Case*, a "back-door pilot" made-for-television movie with Jennifer Edwards playing the female lead.[9] His script was even based upon a story idea which she pitched to him. Since the film failed to warrant a series, his casting of her in the role of a new character who is set up in the film to have a continuing relationship with the central male character continues his creative television efforts on her behalf. He may even have been partially motivated to create the new character with that in mind. When a new series did not happen, he returned to casting her in a feature film, *Son of the Pink Panther* (1992), which turned out to be his last film.

Early on, Gunn enters his office and is surprised to find Maggie sitting at his regular secretary Bernice's desk, greeting him. Neither has any idea who the other is. Each suspiciously asks what the other is doing there and they engage in a comically prolonged conversation with little enlightenment. Finally, Maggie reveals that Bernice, the previous secretary, who had a whirlwind romance and rushed off to Crete to get married, had asked Maggie to fill in for her. It is obvious to the viewer that something of the sort is going on, but the scene plays out with extensive non-comprehension until things are clarified. The scene then shifts from verbal comedy to physical comedy when she brings Gunn coffee as he sits behind his desk, and she spills the coffee on a document he is reading. The scene points to yet another major change in that, in the original television series and in *Gunn*, Peter Gunn does not even have an office, let alone a secretary.

Maggie is involved in a number of other, more elaborate comic scenes. She ends up in Gunn's apartment bedroom in a manner that recalls and then develops a variation on the structure of Sam in his bedroom in *Gunn*. Upon returning home, Gunn is surprised to open his bedroom door and finds her tied to the bed headboard. After he unties her, and they talk in the kitchen, she explains what happened and then faints. Gunn picks her up and carries her into the bedroom. He awkwardly tries to get her into the bed with her head near the top and her feet near the bottom but fails. Unable to figure it out, he solves the problem by walking over to the other side of the bed. No sooner does he get her to bed than the doorbell rings. He answers the door to find Edie, who then enters. She has come to return her key since she feels their relationship is on the rocks. He acts surprised but she interrupts to ask why he has left the door unopened, which we have seen in the rear right of the frame throughout. After he closes the door, she becomes suspicious and asks if he has another woman in the apartment. He denies it and is about to leave when Maggie opens the bedroom door, which has been off-screen left. Under the influence of what Gunn has spiked her milk with in the previous kitchen scene to help her relax, she acts drunk and looks horrible with makeup smeared on her face. Gunn tries to explain that she is in a state of shock, to which Edie retorts that she is also in shock and storms away.

Although this film was shot in the standard 1.33:1 television aspect ratio, the scene sets up a complex interplay of three screen spaces: the bedroom at the left, the hall in which they speak at the center, and the open apartment door bringing the exterior hallway off-screen space into play at the right.

This sets up the later rhyming scene which further develops the bedroom farce within these spaces. Edwards has remarked, "You can't get too involved in physical humor on television, because you just don't have the time. You have to focus more on verbal gags."[10] Nevertheless, he pushes the boundaries within those contexts, culminating in the scene when Gunn returns home late at night soaking wet from a rainstorm.

He opens his bedroom door to find Tony's moll, Sheila (Debra Sandlund), seductively posed on his bed in a negligee like a *Playboy* centerfold, suggestively opening a bottle of champagne which overflows, with sexual connotations, as she says, "Happy Birthday." He tells her she is three and a half months too late. He mentions that he smelled cordite when he entered the apartment and asks her if she shot the milkman and if she is wearing perfume put out by the National Rifle Association. As they engage in banter about sexual performance, she begins to undress him and the doorbell rings. He opens the door and Maggie enters dressed in pink pajamas. As she begins explaining her presence, there is a knock on the door and Edie enters, once again finding Gunn with Maggie. And once again, she interprets the circumstances as sexual impropriety on Gunn's part. As the three try to explain and understand what is going on, we hear an off-screen voice asking, "What's going on?" and then see Sheila standing in the bedroom doorway, holding her champagne glass. Edie has no idea who either Maggie or Sheila is but is jealously suspicious of both. Edie says it is a "full house" and asks, "Who's in the closet?" Maggie cluelessly responds, "I'll look" and opens the closet door in front of which they are standing. The bodies of two of Spiros's goons come tumbling out. Maggie faints and as Gunn is gently laying her down on the floor, another knock is heard on the door. Gunn opens it and two detectives enter. We now see in one shot the dead gangsters and Maggie lying on the floor as Gunn, the two detectives, and Edie stand around talking. Sheila once again enters from the off-screen bedroom space and, as the newcomers stare in disbelief, she walks past them toward the apartment door. Edie says she is going with her but, as they start to exit, Jacoby enters from off-screen in the hallway and they all return to the apartment with him. As Jacoby begins a new conversation, we see Maggie enter from off-screen space below the frame line, crawling her way up the body of one of the detectives. He grabs her as she loses consciousness again. In one remarkable shot we see seven living characters and two dead ones crammed into one small space. The two dead men are sprawled on the floor in the center, the detective is holding Maggie at the right, Sheila is standing in the left foreground, and Gunn and Jacoby are standing in the left rear with Edie sitting on a stair step next to them (Figure 6.6). The scene is pure farce with elaborate physical comedy structured around off-screen

FIGURE 6.6   *Peter Gunn,* © 1989 New World Television.

spaces in the bedroom, the hallway, and the closet from which we hear characters speak and see characters enter, leave, and from which we see dead characters fall. Most of the main characters are present and nearly everyone is confused and has no idea of who the others are or what they are doing there. The use of space, timing, and physical comedy shows how Edwards finds creative ways of continuing his explorations of screen space in his widescreen comedies adapted for the 1.33:1 television aspect ratio.

Throughout this scene, Gunn is helpless and frazzled. He even looks different than he does for most of the film during which he is stylishly dressed. Here, he is not only soaking wet but also partially dressed since Sheila has seductively opened his shirt. This contrasts with his behavior when confronted with masculine threats, such as when he was brought to Spiros's garage and menaced by his goons. In that situation, he behaves with aplomb and, when things turn threatening, readily subdues most of them before an unidentified masked intruder shoots another gangster.

Edwards has no interest in simply repeating himself, even when repeatedly engaging similar material. From the late 1940s on, Edwards worked in multiple media. He demonstrated not only that success in each of the different media necessitated different creative and industrial strategies, but also that those individual strategies do not remain fixed. What works well in one era can become outdated and even cliched in another. He adapted to changing times as the media, the entertainment industry, and the culture were constantly in flux.

The different Gunn iterations have different temporal components. The television series was set in the time in which it was made, the late 1950s and early 1960s. The 1967 film was also set in the time in which it was made but introduces the effects of changing times by underscoring the fact that the 1960s have arrived and that Gunn's era is fading. It shows both Gunn and Jacoby beginning to feel outdated as the era of cool jazz is supplanted by the era of rock and roll. *Peter Gunn* takes a different approach. Unlike the two prior Gunn iterations, this is a "period piece" set in the mid-1960s, roughly 25 years prior to its 1989 release, earlier than *Gunn*, and just after the TV series ended. It generates no sense of Gunn being at odds with his time, but here the disjunction is between the world of the film and that of its audience. This is a film about the past, rendered specific when we hear on the radio that LBJ is president and that the Vietnam War is heating up.

The television series was set contemporaneously with the era of its initial audience. Its clothing styles, automobiles, slang, and social norms would all have been recognized by its audience as part of their world. *Gunn* was also set contemporaneously with the making of the film whereas *Peter Gunn* is set in the past. In *Gunn*, the temporal disjunction appears within the narrative whereas in *Peter Gunn* the disjunction is between the temporal setting of the film and the time in which it was released. Its initial audience would have recognized it as a film not about their "today" but about the past.

Furthermore, each of these holds a different status within the rapidly changing entertainment media. The television series appeared during the heyday of similar half-hour, black-and-white, network series. The 1967 movie was part of an attempt to incorporate that model into serial feature filmmaking. The 1989 made-for-television film attempted to position that feature film as a pilot for a new series within the changed television landscape of the era. Near the end of his career, Edwards had planned to set a new Gunn television series in the near future, further engaging temporality in the mix of the works.

These temporal differences demonstrate more than Edwards's desire to approach the Gunn works in new ways, to reshuffle the deck; they influence nearly everything about the works. One example lies in the significance of Gunn's masculinity for different eras. In the television series, he is generally "cool" except in his interactions with Edie. In the 1967 movie, much more impedes upon him. When he enters the counterculture bar seeking information, he is clearly out of place, an older man among a younger generation. When Gunn stops the intimidation of the menacing biker by drawing his pistol, it is not a scene of simple triumph but rather one that indicates that Gunn is borderline desperate in this new environment. And he is utterly frazzled in his dealings with Daisy Jane. In *Peter Gunn* he is in his initial era but, particularly with the introduction of Maggie, unstable things seem to surround him. Scenes in the television series and the previous film certainly incorporated some slapstick comedy, but they seldom developed elaborate farce. Characters such as various eccentric artists and inhabitants of beatnik bars could be goofy and even bizarre, but they seemed to be oddball exceptions to the norm; with *Peter Gunn* and its compulsive pattern of indirection, doubling, and hidden meanings, we see a world that may have always been there, but viewed from a new, distanced perspective. For Edwards nothing remains the same. In his film *S.O.B.* one of the characters remarks, "Just when I think I know where it's at, it's somewhere else." Remarkably, Edwards created these various iterations of Gunn as a multi-hyphenate, multimedia filmmaker wearing multiple hats as a writer-producer, director, and creator working in classic 30-minute TV, feature theatrical film, and the made-for-TV film format, always trying to make Peter Gunn part of "where it's at."

NOTES

1. Although *Gunn* was shot in the 1.85:1 aspect ratio it has never been released on DVD in that ratio. All the prints we have seen and the one we use here were cropped for US TV and VHS tape. This kind of cropping cuts off the edges of the frames but does not involve panning and scanning as occurs in more extreme widescreen aspect ratios. The shots we describe will be generally accurate, though they may miss some details at the edges of the frame.

2. Philip Lathrop was the director of cinematography on both *Experiment in Terror* and *Gunn* and had served in that capacity in a number of episodes of the TV series *Peter Gunn.*

3. Sam Wasson, *A Splurch in the Kisser: The Movies of Blake Edwards* (Middletown, CT: Wesleyan University Press, 2018), p. 120.

4. For a detailed discussion of the series, the actors, and the character relationships, see Chapter 3.

5. Wasson, *A Splurch in the Kisser*, p. 127.

6. For a discussion of Edwards's work as a writer-producer-director in radio, television, and film in this formative period in his career see Chapters 1 and 2. When Edwards began his work in movies, series films had a secondary status within the industry, and were often relegated to low-budget, non-prestigious "B" genres like Westerns, horror, and science fiction. All of that would change in the 1960s, and Edwards played a part in that change with his Pink Panther films, which led to numerous feature films and extended to television cartoons, as well as merchandise such as Pink Panther dolls and T-shirts.

7. Susan Christian, "Blake Edwards: The Small Screen Can Be Funny," in *The New York Times*, May 15, 1988, Section 2, p. 41 (nytimes.com). Edwards only directed four of the ten feature films he estimated at the time of the interview.

8. Peter Stamelman, "Blake Edwards Interview – In the Lair of the Pink Panther," in *Blake Edwards Interviews*, edited by Gabriella Oldham (Jackson: University Press of Mississippi, 2018), p. 14.

9. Christian, "Blake Edwards."

10. Christian, "Blake Edwards."

CHAPTER 7

Wild Rovers (1971)

Written, Produced, and Directed by Blake Edwards

When *Wild Rovers* was released in 1971, many viewers probably considered this Western to be an unexpected genre for Edwards, who at that time was primarily characterized as a comedy director. But in fact, his first two films as a writer and producer were Westerns: *Panhandle* (1948, in which he also acted) and *Stampede* (1949). They were low-budget, black-and-white B films, but they already demonstrated Edwards's penchant for experimenting with genre conventions, particularly those involving pacing and tone (see Chapters 1 and 2). He would return to Westerns throughout his career. Ken Wales told us that a three-picture directing deal Edwards had with Paramount for *Gunn* included a Western, *Waterhole #3*, which he ended up only producing (uncredited) in 1967. He had also included a segment satirizing Westerns in *The Great Race* (1965). Late in his career he returned to the genre once again with *Sunset* (1988) in which he would play with the genre's conventions in a story about a popular Western movie actor, Tom Mix, and a legendary figure from Western history, Wyatt Earp, working together in 1920s Hollywood (see Chapter 11).

As is widely known, *Wild Rovers* was cut dramatically when it was released in the United States with a length of 106 minutes. Edwards was devastated

Blake Edwards: Film Director as Multitalented Auteur, First Edition.
William Luhr and Peter Lehman.
© 2023 John Wiley & Sons Ltd. Published 2023 by John Wiley & Sons Ltd.

since he considered his cut of the film to be his greatest achievement. That experience, combined with the production problems on his next film, *The Carey Treatment*, led to him leaving Hollywood for much of the following decade (see Chapter 9). Curiously, this is one of the few instances in Edwards's career where such production conflicts had a comparatively, if delayed, happy ending with the eventual release of a restored print that is 137 minutes long.

Ken Wales, the film's co-producer, has spoken to us about this process in great detail, recalling that, after Edwards had produced his final cut of the film, he and Edwards took a meeting with MGM executives:

> Doug Netter, head of foreign distribution, and Aubrey [James Aubrey, the studio head] had looked at it, and Aubrey had said, "Too long. Take 30 minutes out of it." We said, "What? Cut this down to 90 minutes? What for?" He said, "Well, you get rid of all the stuff that isn't about Holden." I said, "But that's how you tell the story – with Karl Malden, and the ranch hands, and all the other people – the characters – involved." He said, "No, no. They just came to see Holden. That's it." So anyway, I said to Blake, "There's got to be some way to do this." He said, "No, I've tried to persuade them. We just have to let it go and not worry about it. Maybe other people won't miss it as much." So, it did get out that way, but after we'd started the release, Doug Netter came to me in panic. He said, "We've got to have a longer film." I said, "Well, which way do you want it? You wanted it short. We did it. Now, you're wanting it long. Tell me, what do you want?" He said, "Well, we got a good chance to have it as a road show in Europe and opening in Paris. They want a Western. It has to be longer." I knew exactly what to do, just put everything back in they'd taken out. So, we did, and they didn't even realize what had happened. That's how uninformed they were. They said, "Great. It's wonderful. Where'd you get all the footage?" "Well, it's what you took out."

The restored version was released in France with the title *Men of the West*.

Prints of *Men of the West* were used in a series of restored videos in the United States. A word about them is necessary before turning to our analysis of the film. We are using the Warner Archive DVD edition, which is the closest to Edwards's cut with at least one notable major exception – the ending, which Edwards described for us in detail and which we discuss below. We have seen three different versions of the ending. Nevertheless, thanks to the Warner Archive, we now have a version that comes close to Edwards's version.

Wild Rovers appeared at a time in which the commercial viability of the Western, an industry staple from its early days, was in precipitous decline, and many Westerns produced at that time were often called "revisionist," meaning not traditional, full-throated engagements of the genre but rather commentaries upon it. Coincidentally, Sam Peckinpah's hugely successful *The Wild Bunch* had appeared two years earlier, which not only had "Wild" in its title but also starred William Holden, and some reviewers compared the two to the detriment of Edwards's film. This particularly irked Edwards, who told us that he had in fact written the script for and titled his film prior to the release of *The Wild Bunch*.

Wild Rovers tells the story of two cowboys, Ross Bodine (William Holden) and Frank Post (Ryan O'Neal), who decide to break the aimless monotony of their lives by robbing a bank. They are friends but, since Bodine is older, their relationship at times assumes a father–son dynamic. After robbing the bank, they are pursued by their former employer, Walt Buckman (Karl Malden), and his two sons, John (Tom Skerritt) and Paul (Joe Don Baker). The film explores broader family dynamics, including Walt's relationship with his wife and sons, as well as broader socio-historical tensions like those between the sheep farmers and the cattle ranchers. In a profound departure from the conventions of the Western genre, the film is structured around a series of conversations with only brief scenes of violent action, and even those sequences are structured around conversations, including the bank robbery sequence; we never see the actual robbery that sets the main plot in motion

Wild Rovers begins with a pre-credit sequence which continues over the credits. The opening shot shows a barren landscape with the tip of the rising sun. Cut to a coyote sitting atop a hill in the pre-dawn darkness. The coyote rises and walks down the hill and off-screen left. As the shot of the now empty hill continues, we see two riders appear at the top of the hill from the off-screen space behind it. As they ride on, we see them still in the early dawn light and then a shot of the rising sun over a hill fades in over the riders and then fills the frame with the cowboys off-screen. We then see the landscape with the rising sun as the two cowboys appear from off-screen space behind a hill as they ride directly toward the camera. Then, in a remarkable cut, we see the wide-open landscape with the tip of the rising sun recalling the film's opening shot as the two cowboys ride right to left in complete darkness, with the sun now off-screen. This astonishing long take with moving camera continues as the camera pans to follow them and we see daylight sweep over the riders and push the darkness away; daylight now fills the frame. As the riders approach a house, we see a title at the bottom of the frame, "Metro-Goldwyn-Mayer presents," followed by another title, "A film by Blake Edwards." The pre-credit sequence now seamlessly transforms into the credit sequence.

Edwards has already introduced several of the film's main visual motifs and formal strategies in this brief pre-credit sequence in which not a word is spoken. The opening shot introduces the rising sun and the vast Western landscape followed by the careful use of off-screen space. The coyote introduces an animal motif. The unidentified riders appear as small figures in the dark landscape with its hidden spaces. The elaborate single take as they approach the house ties everything together: without a spoken word and without any significant action, Edwards establishes his main theme of "men" attempting to control their destiny within powerful environmental and natural forces which surround and sweep over them. Edwards told us that, when they did that remarkable long take, they did not know that they would capture the light of the rising sun in such a breathless manner. Nevertheless, he binds it into the fabric of the entire film in which there will be much talk of free will as well as the elaborate development of the sun motif and the use of off-screen space. That one shot establishes the power of the sun to dispel the darkness in a manner that dwarfs the destiny of the riders who ride on as if they control their lives. They don't.

The credit sequence continues with a cut to an interior shot of the house in which a conversation is in progress between John Buckman and his father, the family patriarch. When Paul Buckman walks in, we hear John speak the first dialogue we hear in the film, "I don't know, but they say what he said," and his father cuts him off with, "I know what he said." The two continue talking as their mother, Nell Buckman (Leora Dana), appears from off-screen to serve them and then return to the kitchen, which we do not see. John and Walt continue to talk about the conflict developing between their ranch and sheep farmers who are letting their sheep graze on the Buckman ranch. The scene ends with Paul asking John to pass the eggs, to which he says, "What?" and when Paul replies, "eggs," the film cuts to a shot of eggs in a bowl with long rows of cowboys eating breakfast in their space. The first words we hear spoken in the film introduce the major themes of language and epistemology and Walt's reply that he "knows" emphasizes the role that knowledge will play in the film and how Edwards will formally develop that theme. The entire Buckman breakfast scene is shot in one long take with no shot-reverse shot editing that is so common in Hollywood conversation scenes.

The silent manner in which Nell serves the men introduces gender issues and the cut to the next scene on the word "eggs" introduces another key contrast: that between the nuclear family that owns the land and the cowboys who work the land. This theme in turn relates to images and themes of wealth, banks, capitalism, and prostitution. Furthermore, the scene contrasts with the family breakfast in that there are no conversations. Except for a few brief snippets we overhear about passing the food, there is no dialogue.

The credit sequence that follows is a montage of the cowboys riding out and doing their work for the day on the range: rounding up and branding cattle, mending fences, playing cards, and cooking lunch over a campfire. The sequence ends with the riders returning to the ranch and the final credit, "Written and Directed by Blake Edwards," appears against a wide-open vista in which a large image of the sun dominates the frame. We then see the cowboys riding into the corral and dismounting as part of the routine end of their workday when a horse suddenly goes berserk and kicks one of the cowboys into a wall, instantly killing him. One of the cowboys goes to the horse, now lying on the ground, and shoots him in the head. This sudden eruption of violence and death into what had been a peaceful scene introduces the last major component of the film's narrative and sets the story in motion. Bodine and Post are told to take the body into town.

Before analyzing the film's central structure of multiple conversations interrupted by brief, terrifying moments of deadly violence, a few preliminary observations are helpful. From early in his career, Edwards explored the use of the spoken word in relation to the formal positioning of the characters in the frame. What characters say to each other in these scenes and how they speak is inextricably linked with how they are positioned in the frame. Edwards approaches dialogue as fully formally integrated in his television shows and films. *Gunn*, discussed in Chapter 6, makes this clear. The film's first scene following the credits is set at a gangster's funeral. Peter Gunn stands removed from the mourners, looking on. The camera pans to follow Lt. Jacoby as he walks up to Gunn. After briefly glancing at Gunn, Jacoby begins to talk as he passes by Gunn and stands looking off-screen left. We see Gunn standing, looking straight ahead, not even acknowledging Jacoby (Figure 7.1). Jacoby then moves back, crossing in front of Gunn and turns away from him, continuing to talk. They both are now looking in the direction of the mourners. Jacoby once again positions himself looking off-screen left where he stays for the remainder of the conversation, during which time they only briefly look at each other. Then Gunn walks away, leaving Jacoby alone in the frame. The entire conversation takes place in one take with no shot-reverse shot editing.

In a later scene after a shooting has occurred in Gunn's apartment complex, Jacoby approaches Gunn again but this time Gunn stands at the left of the frame looking screen right smoking a cigarette while Jacoby stands in the center. Gunn never even glances at Jacoby. In another variation, as they prepare to question the brothel owner, Daisy Jane, Gunn stands in the center of the frame looking straight ahead while Jacoby is behind at the right playing with the keys on a piano (Figure 7.2). Even their conversation is confused as each misunderstands what the other is talking about. Then Gunn turns and

FIGURE 7.1   *Gunn*, © 1967 Paramount Pictures Corporation.

FIGURE 7.2   *Gunn*, © 1967 Paramount Pictures Corporation.

approaches Jacoby at the piano but, as soon as he gets there, Jacoby gets up, walks around Gunn, and stands where Gunn had stood. In a complete reversal, now Gunn is at the keyboard but as they continue talking Gunn walks up to Jacoby on the right, but instead of stopping and looking at him, he walks past him looking straight ahead!

In yet another scene, when Gunn and Jacoby question the gangster Fusco, Jacoby sits on a sofa and Gunn stands behind him by the wall. We see Jacoby and Gunn in a two shot and, once again, they both look in the same direction. In this variation, when Fusco asks questions of them, instead of getting straight answers, we see Jacoby ask Gunn the same question and he dodges answering the question inconclusively by simply rephrasing it to Jacoby who then repeats that to Fusco. This is a parody of a conversation, which Fusco points out. It is closer to a vaudeville routine than to a meaningful exchange of information. *Gunn* resembles *Wild Rovers* with a series of conversations by the two detective partners about the mystery they are trying to solve paralleling the conversations between the two bank-robbing cowboys as they try to understand the mysteries of life itself.

It is also instructive to examine Edwards's interest in language and how it is understood and misunderstood, as highlighted by the manner in which Inspector Clouseau mangles the English language in the Pink Panther comedies. Both the characters to whom he speaks and Clouseau himself are frequently baffled or flabbergasted.

In a pool-playing scene in *A Shot in the Dark*, the owner of an estate tells Clouseau to grab a cue stick. When Clouseau stupidly grabs a bridge and the onlooker points out he has a "bridge," he looks at it and calls it "the bridge cue" as if he knows what he is doing. The onlooker is speechless. Later in the film when Clouseau interrogates suspects, the estate owner mentions the problem of moths in the closet. Clouseau responds by asking, "What are these meuths (myths)?" Clouseau's mangled English became so widely known in popular culture that, when Peter Sellers died, a political cartoonist celebrated him standing before Saint Peter at Heaven's Gate as he asks, "Do you have a rheum?" referring to a scene in *Return of the Pink Panther* where Clouseau poses that question to a hotel clerk. Edwards's exploration of dialogue and language extends well beyond the comic slapstick world in the Pink Panther series; it started long before Clouseau first appeared and is also a strong component of his dramas and non-comic films.

In the first extended conversation scene in *Wild Rovers*, Bodine and Post sit on a buckboard talking to each other as they transport Barney, the dead cowboy, into town. They are of course sitting next to each other rather than looking directly at each other, but that is a favorite strategy of Edwards to disrupt shot-reverse shot editing. At the simplest level, placing people in such positions disrupts the usual pattern of people looking at and reacting to each other, motivating traditional shot-reverse shot editing. Edwards's resistance to such editing in many of his conversation pieces in film and television disrupts the comfortable rhythm of shot-reverse shot editing for the spectator, foregrounding the act of conversation and the use of language. We see and listen to these characters in a new way which complicates rather than simplifies language and sometimes even interrogates language. We do not feel part of it so much as spectators of it. Instead of drawing us in, it pushes us out, inviting critical engagement. Some of the major conversation scenes we will consider include an extended sequence related to the bank robbery and the final scenes between Bodine and Post.

Edwards establishes Bodine and Post taking Barney's body into town with an extreme side-view long shot of the buckboard. Then he cuts in to a two shot as the men begin their conversation ruminating about what has happened to Barney. Post tries to describe what happened: "You know what I'm trying to say is ... I can't even get to the way to say." Once again, the failure of language in relation to knowledge of what has happened is foregrounded. Bodine explains it as follows: "You know what scares a man the most is to find out and discover just how uncertain life really is." This prompts Post to reply, "There ain't nothing much you can do about it anyway," to which Bodine emphatically replies: "Ain't nothing much?! Ain't nothing!" The scene is shot mostly in two shots with both men in the frame together. In fact, the first cut just goes closer in while maintaining the view of both men seated next to each other as they talk. As the conversation progresses, a few cuts are close shots of, first, one man talking and then the other, but these are variations on the way the men talk while both are sitting facing the same direction. There is no strong sense of action-reaction cutting but rather a more intimate sense of each speaker's increasing emotional awareness as revealed on their faces. After they finish talking, Edwards cuts first to a longer front angle view of the riders and the buckboard and then, in a stunning unexpected cut to a shot from behind the buckboard, we see Barney's covered corpse as the wagon moves forward (Figure 7.3). Until that shot Edwards had carefully avoided even any glimpses of the dead man about whom they are talking.

After they pass the house of the town's banker and Post comments that the man is lucky to have a beautiful wife, the conversation continues with them ruminating about sex, romance, and heterosexual monogamy. Bodine tells Post he is fortunate not being tied to one woman of whom he will tire as she grows older. Post asks Bodine if he doesn't wish that he had settled down and had children, to which Bodine replies that he has children he knows of and

FIGURE 7.3   *Wild Rovers*, © 1971 Metro-Goldwyn-Mayer, Inc., Turner Entertainment Company.

probably more. Edwards then cuts to single take long shot which shows Walt Buckman, sitting at the head of the table, saying grace before a family meal. Remarkably, that single shot is all we see of their meal. The film then cuts back to Post and Bodine continuing to talk about Barney in a saloon. The single shot of the Buckman family develops the visual motif contrasting the normative nuclear family with the life and non-monogamous sexuality of the cowboys.

Having established all these conversations, we get an eruption of violence and the first and only sequence of comedy disrupting drama. Bodine precipitates a saloon brawl by loudly insulting the sheep farmers who come into the bar. The resulting barroom fight is light in tone and brief, ending with Bodine lying on the floor with Post lying across his body. Both have been somewhat comically clubbed on the head by the irate bartender. It is the only mix of violence and comedy in the film and the only time that violence will be treated in a lighthearted manner. The irony of Post leaning over Bodine to ask if he is okay and then being clubbed and falling over Bodine seems to be the end of both the violence and the comedy but, in fact, it marks the beginning of the only sequence of pure physical comedy in the film. Post and Bodine are unceremoniously dumped into the back of their buckboard and the horses begin to take them home. At this moment, Edwards underscores the very thin line in his work between physical comedy and serious drama with a startling image from behind the buckboard as it heads homeward with the unconscious cowboys mirroring the image of the dead cowboy in the buckboard in the shot that ended the long conversation sequence as they came into town (Figure 7.4). But just as quickly Edwards breaks the solemn tone with the unexpected eruption of slapstick comedy when a

FIGURE 7.4   *Wild Rovers*, © 1971 Metro-Goldwyn-Mayer, Inc., Turner
Entertainment Company.

prostitute on the second story of Maybelle's empties a chamber pot from her
balcony just as the buckboard passes beneath, soaking both men in urine.
Though it may appear as the topper to the previous scene, it is in fact the
beginning of a new gag built on Edwards's comic form of "topping the topper
topper." When a couple of cowboys discover the buckboard the next morn-
ing, one of them awakes Bodine and Post complaining about their foul stench
and telling them to get ready for breakfast with a description of what's being
served. Bodine quickly leans over the side of the buckboard and vomits. The
sound of him vomiting rouses Post, who looks over, sees what's happening,
and quickly leans over the other side of the buckboard and vomits. This
seems to be the topper ending the scene as Bodine moves to the front of the
buckboard, grabs the horses' reins and whips them into motion, but he does
not see that Post has gotten up behind him. As the buckboard lurches forward, Post falls off the back – the topper topper – and then we see him
running after the buckboard to get back on. There will not be another such
comic moment in this film, which grows darker and darker until an unimag-
inably dark ending.

Having laid the groundwork for this unusual narrative structure of a
series of complex conversations shaped and formed by how they are shot
and edited, interspersed with equally complex violent events and physical
comedy, we will now summarize the significance of this structure
throughout the rest of the film. The next major conversation scene takes
place between Buckman and his two sons. It is the most extreme version of
Edwards's experimentation of conversations between characters who are
looking in the same direction rather than facing one another. The scene

begins with a long take of Walt sitting in the foreground in the right of the frame with the very long, narrow front porch of the ranch stretching into the distance. Paul approaches from off-screen space to join him and stands midway down the porch, alternating looking out and over in the direction of his father. Walt asks if he'd like to come with him on business to St. Louis and Paul asks if he can take time to make up his mind. Walt responds, "About what?" and Paul says about coming to St. Louis. As they talk, the door opens and John emerges from off-screen space onto the porch. He stands even farther away in front of the door, stretching and looking out while overhearing them before joining the conversation (Figure 7.5) (with both of the brothers looking out). This is probably the most extreme example of deep focus cinematography in Edwards's oeuvre. The long narrow porch extends in sharp detail well past all three of the characters. John then walks past Paul, childishly slapping his butt as he passes, and asks, "What's that? What's, ah..." "What's what?" Walt interrupts him with another question. "What's up to him this time?" John asks, turning to look at his brother. As they talk, all three suddenly look off and the first cut in the scene takes place as we see Bodine and Post ride past. John comments with a questioning tone that he never knew Bodine to go off to town except on Saturday night. When Walt jokingly replies, "Well, he sure went to town last night," John says, "I meant under his own hoof..." Walt again cuts him off. "Yeah, I know what you meant." As they prepare to go in, John passes behind Paul and snaps his butt with his bandana. Then, as Walt passes John to enter the house, John asks, "What? What..." and Walt parrots back to him, "What? What?"

FIGURE 7.5 *Wild Rovers*, © 1971 Metro-Goldwyn-Mayer, Inc., Turner Entertainment Company.

All the questions organized around the word "what" foreground the way such conversations in Edwards's films and TV shows seem to raise more questions than they answer. This is precisely what happens in the above-described scene in *Gunn* when the gangster Fusco tries to elicit information from Lt. Jacoby and Gunn about a murder investigation. He asks questions about Gunn's actions and Jacoby says, "It's possible." Fusco then asks him whether Gunn may know more and Jacoby asks Gunn, who replies to Jacoby, "It's possible." Jacoby then repeats to Fusco, "It's possible." Both are obviously performing for Fusco rather than engaging in a traditional conversation. Throughout this exchange, Gunn stands by a wall to the left of and behind Jacoby. They both look in the same direction toward Fusco. No one in the scene makes direct eye contact with or speaks directly to anyone. This scene exaggerates how characters in such conversations speak indirectly, raising more questions than they answer.

A variation on this occurs in the next Buckman family dinner conversation scene.

When John tells Paul, "Maybelle Tucker is bringing in a new Chippie from Kansas City," he is abruptly cut off by Walt's authoritative voice: "Watch your mouth.... That's not something we talk about in front of your mother." Nell tells Walt, "I know about Maybelle Tucker." Walt replies, "Well, that's not the point," and after a pregnant pause asks, "Is it, Nell?" Edwards cuts from a medium close-up of Walt to Nell, who looks down submissively, saying, "No, I guess it isn't." This scene involves cutting between John, Walt, Paul, and Nell but, ironically, although they seem to be speaking directly to each other, Walt's intense response invokes language as a way to repress truth and knowledge, not facilitate or acknowledge it. He aligns the language proper to the nuclear family with deep repression involving both gender (women should not hear certain things or disagree with the patriarch) and sexuality (the fact that the cowboys including her sons visit a brothel regularly).

The Buckman dinner scene leads into the bank robbery sequence, which is structured around yet another dinner scene in the banker's home which the robbers interrupt. We then see a series of conversations intercutting between Post and the banker's family of his wife and baby as well as her mother as he keeps watch over them; between Bodine and the banker as they ride into town and as they rob the bank; between Bodine and the banker with John Buckman, who interrupts them as they leave town; between Bodine and the banker and his family when they arrive back after robbing the bank; and finally between the banker and his wife after Post and Bodine leave. In keeping with the pattern, the conversations are punctuated with unexpected violence. Post tries to explain and justify to the banker's wife why he is robbing the bank. Bodine talks with the banker about why he should follow the robbery plan to protect his wife and family as they ride to town. When the banker pulls a gun on Bodine in the bank and tries to talk Bodine out of going through with the robbery, Bodine convinces him that, if anything goes wrong, Post will kill his wife. As they are leaving town, John Buckman stops them in the street demanding to know where Post is. He is obsessed with the idea that Post is in Maybelle's having sex with the new prostitute, even though Maybelle has denied it. Bodine easily manipulates Buckman into believing Post is in Maybelle's through the clever use of language, which is another instance in the film of asking questions leading to more questions and confusion rather than revealing the truth. This leads to Buckman riding over to Maybelle's and shooting up the place. In the ensuing chaos of gunshots that follow as the sheriff tries to stop Buckman's behavior, Edwards cuts on a shot of a gun and the sound of the shot to a deadly serious eruption of violence as Post, back at the banker's home, shoots at a mountain lion who has killed a dog and lies in wait to spring on the returning riders.[1]

Once they have returned to the banker's home, Bodine says he wants to leave some of the stolen money to cover the wages of the R-Bar cowboys and some for the banker's family, but the banker refuses on self-righteous moral grounds. But when Post leaves the money anyway and walks out, we see the banker's wife talk him into keeping not only their share of the money but all of it, including that left for the cowboys. Later, in Maybelle's, Walt Buckman will give a self-righteous moral harangue about forming a posse to catch Post and Bodine. He speaks surrounded by Maybelle and prostitutes as well as his sons and the sheriff, all of whom are regular clients. The irony of the setting is entirely lost upon him, much like the irony of the morally upright banker whose bank is directly across the street from Maybelle's is lost on him; we see the brother in the rear of the dark frame as the banker enters the bank. Nevertheless, he denounces the immorality of Post and Bodine. The sheriff of the town is a regular at Maybelle's, where he stays all night. Prostitution, which Walt insists must never be acknowledged in front of Nell, pervades the entire community. When Post and Bodine rob the bank they hardly seem like moral miscreants in this community.

As Bodine and Post make their way to Mexico, they stop in a town where they visit a brothel to enjoy spending some of their loot before completing their isolated journey. Two scenes of violence erupt during this sequence. After we see them bathing, shaving, drinking, and relaxing, Edwards cuts to a scene at the R-Bar Ranch in which Walt discovers the sheep farmers on his property and rides to confront them. Chaotic shooting erupts in all directions both among the sheepherders and between them and Walt. The scene ends with Walt and the head of the sheep farm shooting each other with rifles as Walt charges in on his horse. Both men throw their arms into the air in slow motion when they are shot and the final shots are close-ups of Walt with a look of crazed vengeance mixed with the horror of his awareness of his mortal wound. These images will return in the film's climax.

From the eruption of brutal violence Edwards cuts to an interior scene of the quiet brothel, with only the soft sound of a muted guitar. We see Post telling Bodine that he's going to play poker. Bodine is in bed with a prostitute and for once silence dominates over conversation. Not a word is spoken between them as Bodine enjoys a cigar with a contemplative look on his face as the prostitute cuddles up with him under the blankets. The scene is serenely peaceful. Both of them know exactly what is going on and do not say a word to justify anything, explain anything, or dissemble in any way. And since neither Post nor Bodine ever speak in self-righteous terms, their actions stand in contrast to what we have seen and heard about Maybelle's.

Edwards cuts between Bodine in bed and Post playing poker with a table of men who also do not speak or say much, although their silence is part of a deception revealed when Post finally figures out that two of them are working together to rig the game and cheat him. Violence suddenly erupts when one of the cheating gamblers pulls his gun and shoots Post. Chaotic shooting then breaks out within the entire bar when Post, the other card players, and the bartender all respond to the first shot. We see one of the prostitutes brutally killed in the crossfire and, when Bodine rushes in amid the confusion, he mistakenly shoots and kills the bartender who is holding a shotgun which then discharges, blowing a hole in the roof. This is not a protracted action sequence; it ends almost as quickly as it begins and is highlighted by the extreme contrast with the wordless silence and peaceful stillness introducing the sequence and that Bodine enjoys with the prostitute in the room from which he rushes not even fully dressed.

A complex use of language and conversations occurs when John and Paul, who are pursuing the robbers, stop to talk with a sheriff. The sheriff informs them of the death of their father, which we neither see nor hear. Instead, the film cuts to Walt's funeral. We see the mourners gathered around the grave and hear the voice of the minister presiding over the ceremony, but then we hear Paul and John's voice-over conversation in the present tense. Paul says that they should go back since their mother needs them, but John says they should pursue Bodine and Post as their father had ordered them to do. The film then continues in the present tense as we see the sheriff and his posse as well as John and Paul as they pursue Bodine and Post. Paul again tells John that they should go back because the pursuit no longer makes any sense since their father is dead, but John remains obsessed with carrying out the irrational, vengeful search and killing both men. These conversations are central to understanding the film's ambiguously dark conclusion.

The rest of the film is devoted to the hunt for Bodine and Post with Edwards intercutting between John and Paul and the men they pursue. This pattern culminates in a scene with one of the most memorable conversations in Edwards's career. Three campfire scenes are devoted to Bodine's efforts to save Post, who has developed an infection from his gunshot wound. All involve fire and a knife and take place in the dark of night. In the first, Bodine tells Post that he has to remove the bullet and, to alleviate his pain, he gets him drunk. Post's part of the exchange is limited mostly to screams of pain and brief curses. It ends with Post unconscious and Bodine talking to himself as he says with grave doubt, "I hope this ends well." It doesn't.

In the next campfire scene, things have gotten worse. Post develops an infection and a bad fever. Bodine tells him that he needs a doctor and they should return to Benson, but Post insists they move on. As Bodine gets into his sleeping bag, it begins to snow and we see Post's body covered with a light dusting. The entire conversation in this scene is shot and edited with conventional eyeline matches beginning with a couple of long shots and progressing to close-ups of each speaker. They are always looking at each other with an intimacy and transparency lacking in many of their earlier conversations. In the third campfire scene, the visual motifs of the fire, the knife, the darkness, and the snow are fully developed, but this time there is no conversation and not one word is spoken. The scene has a surreal, slow-motion quality to it, starting with the first shot in which the camera is looking up along the rocky landscape at the left of the frame, which is filled with the black nighttime sky. As the camera moves into that sky the frame is filled with snow drifting slowly downward and the camera pans down to the campfire.[2] The rest of the scene shows a grim-faced Bodine preparing to sanitize and heat a large knife blade intercut with shots of a snow-covered Post with a dreamlike look on his face, a look which he has often had in the film including during the poker scene where he was shot. Bodine heats the knife until it is glowing. Throughout the scene he moves in slow motion, bringing the knife into horrific close-up as he approaches Post. The next shot shows the knife coming down toward Post's off-screen leg as we hear his anguished scream and the scene ends with a cut to a stream with running, cool water. That scream is the only sound uttered by a human in the entire scene.

The next scene returns to conversation as we see Bodine treating Post with a wet cloth as he lies on a travois. Post asks about Mexico and Bodine retells the romantic, utopian vision they have of this promised land as he mounts his horse and continues riding, spinning tales of the beautiful women awaiting them, but Edwards cuts to an ominous shot from behind the travois with Post's body, recalling the shots of the dead cowboy they took into town in a buckboard at the beginning of the film (Figure 7.6).

The last thing Bodine says is, "Hang on, partner, it won't be much longer now," and Edwards cuts to the ultimate campfire conversation scene as we see Bodine in close-up against the night sky continuing his conversation with Post, who is off-screen. Bodine philosophizes about the history of their unlikely friendship and the fact that everything seems predetermined. We mostly see him in a side-view long shot with a brief cut to long shot that shows Post unresponsive lying in the travois in the lower foreground as Bodine continues philosophizing: "When it comes to something special like loving a woman or judging a man, man don't know shit." On that line Edwards cuts to a brief close shot of Post with his face fully visible for the first time, appearing as if he may be dead. But the film then cuts back to the close-up of Bodine, who continues talking. On the next cut back to the long shot including Post, Bodine gets up and approaches the bottom of the travois and appears to be making Post comfortable with the blankets, but as he continues up the body while he looks at Post's face, we know he is covering the corpse. Post dies off-screen, much as, during the bank robbery that started the chain of events leading here, the actual theft of the money from the safe occurred off-screen. The scene ends with a close-up of Bodine's face in deep contemplation as he sits staring off into the darkness and a slow fade of the shot of the sun rising over the horizon which we saw in the film's opening replaces Bodine's face. The environment dwarfs human efforts.

FIGURE 7.6 *Wild Rovers*, © 1971 Metro-Goldwyn-Mayer, Inc., Turner Entertainment Company.

As Bodine continues the journey alone, Edwards once again stresses the environment with a series of long and extreme long shots and suddenly the camera zooms back, revealing that Paul and John are watching from what had been off-screen space. John has a turbulent, troubled look on his face as Paul, whose horse is next to his, sees in a sideways glance. This shot foregrounds Monument Valley, known for its use by John Ford in a series of Westerns, including *The Searchers* (1956). As we shall see, the use of the location goes well beyond an homage to John Ford since it references a profound connection to *The Searchers*. As Bodine, unaware of their presence, rides on, Edwards once again uses off-screen space in a chilling manner. In the far upper rear of the frame, we see two riders emerge from off-screen and slowly move along the ridge. Then the film cuts to the brothers riding in pursuit down in the valley, and John draws his rifle and shoots. Bodine falls to the ground and gets up as John bears down on him, waving his rifle at his side as if to club Bodine rather than shooting from a safe distance. Bodine, however, pulls John to the ground, and then picks up the rifle, raising it above his head to use as a club against John. But just as he prepares to swing it, a shot rings out and we see Paul, who has caught up, shooting at Bodine. We then cut to a slow motion shot of Bodine throwing his arms up in the air and his body writhing as he falls to the ground (Figure 7.7). Edwards then cuts to a close-up of John's face, which is intensely perverse with sexual connotations as he looks at Bodine's body and his face sinks slowly to the ground with his eye open, looking like he has climaxed (Figure 7.8). He begins to crawl toward the dying man, but Paul comes up behind him and pulls him backward.

FIGURE 7.7   *Wild Rovers*, © 1971 Metro-Goldwyn-Mayer, Inc., Turner Entertainment Company.

FIGURE 7.8   *Wild Rovers*, © 1971 Metro-Goldwyn-Mayer, Inc., Turner Entertainment Company.

Paul approaches Bodine and treats him humanely by shielding him from the sun with his hat as he says, "Bodine, I'm sorry," and Bodine's last words are "Me too." We see John in the background with a crazed stare as he watches. Paul remains kneeling with a look of respectful regret as to what the search has come to as John then crawls toward them saying, "He was mine, you son of a bitch. He was mine, Paul." As John continues speaking, he begins to manhandle the dead body. Paul looks on in horror and disgust and gets on his horse and rides away, ignoring John's pleas for help. John drags the body while talking to it, even calling the corpse a "son of a bitch" while also incoherently talking to his dead father about how he's bringing Bodine back as he was asked to do. At one point he momentarily falls onto the body. After he has dragged Bodine to his horse, he stands up and looks into the distance with a crazed expression on his face, then says, "Pa?" and, after pausing, shouts "Paul" in the direction his brother has ridden. Since both "Pa" and "Paul" begin with the same two letters and sounds, the film makes another strange connection between characters. John then sinks to the ground and collapses on Bodine's body, recalling Post's body falling on Bodine in the barroom brawl. The last words spoken in the film are John's desperate pleas, "Paul, please help me ... Paul." The camera slowly pulls back and up, with the final image an extreme long shot with John on the ground slumped over Bodine's body while Paul is far in the distance, riding away against a beautiful vista of Monument Valley's majestic buttes.

The image of Bodine being shot and the cut to Paul's head falling to the ground recall two other violent deaths. When Walt attacks the sheep farmer, he shoots him and we see the man's writhing body with hands up in slow motion as he falls to the ground (Figure 7.9). But the sheep farmer also

FIGURE 7.9 *Wild Rovers*, © 1971 Metro-Goldwyn-Mayer, Inc., Turner Entertainment Company.

manages to shoot Walt out of his horse, and we see his writhing body with his hands raised in slow motion before he falls from his horse (Figure 7.10). We then see Walt's face in close-up with a crazed look in his eyes as he falls, reflecting a dark mix of emotions including the vengeful satisfaction of seeing the man die while also realizing with surprised horror that he also is dying as he hits the ground dead (Figure 7.11).

Although the above may seem to be the film's climax (all three of the central characters played by the film's stars are now dead), it isn't. Instead of a denouement, the film moves into a totally unexpected deeper darkness which has no denouement. In the Hollywood sense of the word, the film

FIGURE 7.10 *Wild Rovers*, © 1971 Metro-Goldwyn-Mayer, Inc., Turner Entertainment Company.

FIGURE 7.11   *Wild Rovers*, © 1971 Metro-Goldwyn-Mayer, Inc., Turner
Entertainment Company.

does not "end" with all the main actions explained and questions answered
but, rather, it stops. In this print we hear Post's voice-over from the earlier
bronco busting scene, followed by the desolate sounds of the wind blowing,
and the closing credits appear over a still of the final shot accompanied with
music. With the exception of the final shot, this cut of the restored film is
very close to Edwards's cut. In the US release version of it and later videos,
the film cuts away from the action and we see and hear a reprise of part of the
bronco busting scene with Post doing slow-motion somersaults in the snow.
Blake told us that he was upset by this ending, which sentimentally softens
his brutal ending. While this version is much stronger than the US theatrical
release version, the use of Post's voice-over still introduces a sentimental
element. Blake's cut ends with a remarkable shot of the camera at near
ground level rapidly pulling back over the barren landscape until the film
suddenly stops as if the camera has run out of film. That ending is even more
grim than the last shot in this version, which nevertheless emphasizes the
nearly incomprehensible bestial behavior of John's disrespectful handling of
Bodine's body. And the vast expanse of the landscape with Paul a mere dot
on the horizon emphasizes the dominance of the Western landscape dwarf-
ing humans. But the camera racing along the ground in Edwards's cut doesn't
just minimize humans, it excludes them.

A number of reviewers have called Post and Bodine "dumb cowboys,"
which mischaracterizes them. Blake told us that even characterizing Clouseau
as stupid missed a very important admirable element of his character – that he
never gave up. Richard Brody more interestingly notes of Post and Bodine that
"Their hyperbolically comic dialogue en route, about life and death, fate and
hopelessness, evokes Vladimir and Estragon on the prairie."[3] Post and Bodine's

conversations, like those of Samuel Beckett's famous characters in *Waiting for Godot*, are indeed their effort to understand the absurd world in which they live. But their language is best understood in relation to their class; they are uneducated, working-class cowboys, but this should not obscure the manner in which their insights into life are very similar to those that Blake Edwards holds and develops through much of his oeuvre. When his characters say something like, "at least things can't get any worse," they invariably do. In *Tamarind Seed*, one of the educated characters says in a deadly serious context, "No one is to be trusted, nothing is to be believed, and anyone is capable of anything." In other words, "Man don't know shit." Once again, one could characterize these comments as "hyperbolic," but Edwards's view of life requires that kind of hyperbole and its relation to comedy is complex. Edwards's penchant for dialogue scenes is also part of his comedies such as in *The Pink Panther* where, instead of disrupting action or drama, they stop slapstick comedy cold in its tracks. For example, Sir Charles Litton (David Niven) attempts to seduce the Princess via conversation in a long static scene where she lies on a tiger skin rug directly facing him.

Edwards's unusually staged conversation scenes frequently disrupt genre conventions in his dramas and serious films as well as in his comedies. In *The Tamarind Seed*, for example, the two central characters played by Julie Andrews and Omar Sharif engage in conversations about the difference between communism and capitalism (see Chapter 10). Although they are upper-middle-class educated characters, they parallel the working-class conversations between Post and Bodine in *Wild Rovers*.

Wild Rovers in its representation of the nuclear family also points to an important aspect of Edwards's work across radio, television, and film and across the comedies and dramas. Edwards's films typically do not involve nuclear families. In fact, *Wild Rovers* is the first major project he created, produced, and directed to deal centrally with the nuclear family. Most of his early work in radio, television, and film belonged to genres such as crime featuring single detectives; service comedies dealing with mostly single service men in pursuit of a woman in the service; or musical comedies with related shenanigans. His first drama, *Mister Cory*, dealt with the exploits of a single man. Significantly, the first two films he made that dealt centrally with families were films he did not write, *Days of Wine and Roses* and *Experiment in Terror*, which he did produce. In those films, however, the nuclear family is either torn apart, in the former by alcoholism, or inexplicably fragmented as the two sisters living together in *Experiment in Terror*. We will return to this issue in Edwards's documentary about his family in *Julie* (see Chapter 9) and his late-period generically complex semi-autobiographical film, *That's Life!*.

Wild Rovers is the first major work of Edwards's in any medium to deal centrally with parenting within the context of the complete nuclear family and its vision is dark and disturbing, as the end of the film highlights. When complaining about John and Paul going to Maybelle's, Walt abuses Nell authoritatively and coldly blames her, referring to John and Paul as "her children" since she raised them. He mistreats John for being slow in his ability to understand the world or to even articulate his questions about it (in two scenes he mocks him saying, "What? What?") and openly flaunts how he favors Paul. He is a sadistic, moralistic hypocrite. John has an inappropriate, immature, childish need to snap Paul on his butt at every opportunity, like an adolescent in a locker room. All these issues return in the final scenes, beginning with Paul saying there is no reason to continue the search. He is logically correct when he says that since their father is dead it makes no sense to carry out his order to bring Bodine and Post back dead or alive. It would be in the best interests of the family to be home with their mother working the ranch, but John's deep psychoanalytic need to kill Bodine and Post drives him on and Paul, despite his misgivings, goes along in the hopes of stopping John.

John's mental breakdown in the final scene shows that he is driven by dark repressed motives which he rationalizes as carrying out his father's wishes. The exhausted manner in which he drops his head on the ground after seeing Bodine lying mortally wounded has sexual connotations; he is "spent" in a way that has nothing to do with fulfilling the law. And when he collapses on Bodine, that image also has sexual overtones recalling John's intense overinvestment in Post's and Bodine's sex lives in regard to the new prostitute at Maybelle's. Paul, on the other hand, acts in a sane, controlled manner showing full awareness of the human dimension to Bodine's death. John looks on like an animal crawling toward finishing off his prey. His total breakdown involves his inability to even articulate what drives him as well as his profane, barbarous mistreatment of the corpse. His final inarticulate invocations of the family by calling out to his brother and, apparently hallucinating, to his dead father, fall on deaf ears. Neither he nor we know exactly why he maniacally continued the search and then atavistically regressed to an animal-like state in completing the hunt.

This ending occurring in John Ford's iconic Monument Valley with its majestic buttes references the ending of *The Searchers* where Ethan Edwards, the John Wayne character, driven by a deep racism to find and kill his niece, instead suddenly reverses himself and humanely cradles her in his arms to take her home. Nothing in the film, including any dialogue, clearly explains Ethan's motives or behavior. Like *Wild Rovers*, *The Searchers* also complexly deals with issues of language and epistemology. Although the two films are otherwise unlike each other, they share a dark vision of the family, language, and the characters' ability to know and understand the world in which they live.[4] In *The Searchers*, Ethan's nephew Marty tries to stop him from carrying out his murderous intentions, much like Paul tries to stop John. Although Marty fails, Ethan overcomes his dark obsession. *Wild Rovers* is in this regard even darker than *The Searchers*. Paul fails in stopping John from shooting Bodine dead, but then, apparently to save John, he shoots Bodine a second time. But even this is ambiguous since he then prevents John from the bizarre satisfaction of further brutalizing the dying man. The look on Paul's face in the previous two shot of John's grotesque contemplation of the pleasure of killing Bodine as they look on from the ridge shows his utter contempt for his brother's motivation. Paul did not go along to save his brother, but to save Bodine and Post from his brother. And there is no reunification of the family in Edwards's dark film as there is in *The Searchers*. Even the brothers are now torn apart as one rides away in the distance and we see the other insanely and perversely left in the desert with his grim trophy.

NOTES

1. The unpredictability of animals is a major visual motif and theme throughout the film: the horse that goes wild and kills the cowboy at the beginning; a cat that suckles a puppy along with her kittens; a mountain lion that kills the suckling cat and threatens Bodine and Post; and a wild horse that Bodine catches and breaks in only to then be thrown off by the horse he thought he'd tamed.

2. Throughout his career, Edwards has inserted surrealistic slow-motion scenes of the air suddenly being filled with floating white things such as pillow feathers in *Breakfast at Tiffany's* and soap bubbles in *The Party*. For a discussion of such scenes see William Luhr and Peter Lehman, *Returning to the Scene: Blake Edwards, Volume 2* (Athens: Ohio University Press, 1981).

3. Richard Brody, "*Wild Rovers*," *The New Yorker*, October 14, 2019 (new yorker.com).

4. For a detailed analysis of ambiguity, language, and epistemology in *The Searchers* see Peter Lehman, "'You Couldn't Hit It on the Nose': The Limits of Knowledge in and of *The Searchers*," in *The Searchers: Essays and Reflections on John Ford's Classic Western*, edited by Arthur Eckstein and Peter Lehman (Detroit: Wayne State University Press, 2003), pp. 239–264.

CHAPTER 8

The Carey Treatment (1972)

Directed by Blake Edwards —A Blake Edwards and William Belasco Production

From a traditional auteur perspective, *The Carey Treatment* may appear to be a complicated film to discuss with its troubled production history. Due to differences during production with James Aubrey, the head of Metro-Goldwyn-Mayer, and William Belasco, the film's producer, Edwards quit after the completion of principal photography and sued, unsuccessfully, to have his name removed from it, and left Hollywood. Ironically, the film's first opening credit boldly labels it as "A Blake Edwards and William Belasco Production." What the credits present as a promising partnership was an experience so bitter for Blake that it was the only film he directed that he would never discuss with us.

Ken Wales, however, did talk with us about the film's origin and production history:

Well, Bill Belasco was a friend of Aubrey's and kind of a semi-agent. Aubrey brings him in to produce stuff at the studio. Somehow, Belasco wants to do a film with Blake. When Aubrey or somebody says, "Well, Ken Wales is his producer, so...," Belasco says, "Well, so what?" So, Blake came to me and said, "I'm in a terrible spot. I'm

Blake Edwards: Film Director as Multitalented Auteur, First Edition.
William Luhr and Peter Lehman.
© 2023 John Wiley & Sons Ltd. Published 2023 by John Wiley & Sons Ltd.

trying to get things back on track so we can maybe do something with Julie there [Paramount]. They're just insistent that Belasco be the producer and I don't know what to do," and I said, "Blake, it's very simple. Let me step aside." He said, "Well, I don't want to do that to you." I said, "But, let me solve the problem for you." He said, "Would you?" and I said, "Sure. What I'll do is be around a bit and just make sure the video system works." He says, "Yeah, please do that." I saw the world's biggest mess. I thought, "God's taken me. You're out of it, Ken, so just be grateful."

Julie Andrews tells a related anecdote about Edwards and Aubrey: "One evening at dusk, he was driving home from Beverly Hills, thinking about Aubrey and deeply preoccupied, when a jogger appeared. Blake swerved, missing him by inches. Glancing in his rearview mirror, he realized that the jogger was in fact James Aubrey. Afterward, Blake said that if he hit Aubrey, no one would have believed it was an accident."[1]

The stormy relationship between Edwards and Aubrey on this film was well known at the time of its release, leading Andrew Sarris, who liked the film, to quip in his *Village Voice Review*: "In these matters Jungle Jim Aubrey is always judged guilty until proven even guiltier." His point was that in this instance even with Edwards quitting after principal photography, not overseeing editing the film and then disowning it, it was still a very good Blake Edwards film. Good enough, in fact, for him to list it in his 1972 10 Best Movies list in *The Village Voice*.[2] Since Sarris was the founding father of American auteurism which enthroned directors and usually sided with them in disputes with studios while valorizing director's cuts, this is all the more astonishing. Edwards had claimed that the studio had broken promises with him about script changes they had agreed to, including developing the love interest, and had cut off two weeks of the production schedule including the entire conclusion. And, in fact, those are the weak areas of the film. Ironically, and perhaps fittingly, the film's three credited screenwriters – Irving Ravetch, Harriet Frank, Jr., and John D. F. Black – were unsatisfied with changes made in their script and took screen credit under the pseudonym of "James P. Bonner."[3]

We have largely avoided film reviews in our analyses in this book as well as discussions of our likes and dislikes or of how good or bad we think the films might be since our goal is to examine how Edwards worked as a multi-hyphenate, multimedia director and creator. In other words, we are not defining him through traditional auteurism which is centered on film directors, their personal visions, and control over their projects. When, for example, analyzing films that he wrote and had no further connection with (see Chapter 2), we do not anguish over not knowing what his vision would have been, script changes the director may have made, or how he might have directed it. If our analyses reveal important features of style, theme, dialogue, and characterization related to the films that he did direct and over which he had control, the evidence lies in the examples we use to support our argument. Either his footprint is there, or it isn't. This approach is well suited to *The Carey Treatment*.

It is also well suited to another aspect of Edwards's multi-hyphenate career: he worked repeatedly, for example, with the same editors, in this case Ralph E. Winters. We spoke with editor Robert Pergament while visiting the sets of *A Fine Mess*, *Sunset*, *Switch*, and *Son of the Pink Panther*, all of which he edited. He was Edwards's regular editor during that period in Edwards's career, having also edited *Blind Date*, *Skin Deep*, and *Peter Gunn*. He told us that working with Edwards was ideal for him as an editor since Edwards told him throughout the production how he envisioned the editing and that he printed very few takes. He also used very few cameras, frequently with little or no coverage. In other words, his editors knew what he wanted and had a limited amount of film to choose from in most scenes. We witnessed this throughout our visits to his sets and it holds true for much of *The Carey Treatment*. Ralph E. Winters was Edwards's regular editor when *The Carey Treatment* was made. Ken Wales told us that the same held true of the restoration of *Wild Rovers*. John F. Burnett, that film's editor, had served as assistant editor to Winters for years. When the opportunity came to restore the film, he knew exactly where he could find what had been cut and knew exactly where it had been in Edwards's original version.

A close continuing relationship with editors, cinematographers, and composers was tied to Edwards's multi-hyphenate status within the industry. Therefore, when he left after completing principal photography on *The Carey Treatment*, he did not totally abandon the project. Indeed, that may be why he finished shooting principal photography. We do not know whether he stayed in touch with Winters or if Winters had access to him. Nor does it matter. Winters was perfectly positioned to do the best job possible of retaining Edwards's vision with the footage that they shot and of which he would have had detailed knowledge. Winters could not alter the decisions that had been made about script changes, nor could he restore anything with the ending since Edwards had not shot any of his planned footage. Regardless of Edwards disowning the film, Sarris understood that it was in fact consistent with his multi-hyphenate output, which in this case included a strong, hands-on studio head injecting his vision into the final edit. One might think of Aubrey as just one more collaborator, albeit an unwanted one, in the production process.

Consider for a moment another prominent review of the film at the time. Roger Ebert, who did not like the film and only gave it two stars, noted that "most dialog on television is devoid of useful information," which he said was "especially true in doctor and nurse programs, people speak only in order NOT to say what is on everybody's mind." Applying this to *The Carey Treatment*, he remarks, "There are long, sterile patches of dialog during which nothing at all is communicated."[4] As usual Ebert is a perceptive, smart critic and he is right about the television genre and its use of many extreme close-ups to give great meaning to a slight facial expression that conveys meaning in place of dialogue.[5] We will, however, offer a different reading of such dialogue in the film and relate it to our analysis of Edwards's unusual manner of structuring and shooting conversation scenes discussed in Chapter 7 with reference to *Gunn*, which was, of course, based on the television show he created and produced, and in his widescreen Western masterpiece, *Wild Rovers*, which had nothing to do with television and its small screens. As a multimedia creator Edwards did, in fact, often bring things from both radio and television into film, frequently in a creative, rather than a detrimental, manner.

The Carey Treatment opens as Dr. Peter Carey (James Coburn), a brash, middle-aged pathologist from California, arrives in Boston to assume a new position at a prestigious hospital.[6] This brings him into the world of entrenched Bostonian class structures, especially old money privilege, and he quickly encounters abrasions. When he first enters the hospital's physician's parking lot, a security guard challenges his right to be there and Carey defiantly flashes his credentials. Soon afterward, after a gross of morphine ampules have gone missing in the hospital in what is presumed to have been an inside job, Carey witnesses the Boston police chase a hospital employee fleeing from a drug checkpoint. Carey intervenes, preventing the police from shooting the young man but leading the police to retaliate by searching him. From the outset, then, the film establishes Carey as an outsider unafraid of challenging the authorities.

The powerful head of the hospital is Dr. J. D. Randall (Dan O'Herlihy). When Carey first enters the hospital, he pauses to look up over a main interior entrance at an oil painting of "Adam Randall, 1790–1861," which is encircled, halo-like, on the wall with a quotation from Hippocrates: "I will preserve the purity of my life and my art." We presume Adam Randall to have been the hospital's founding patriarch and an ancestor of its current head, indicating an embedded line of Boston Brahmin power and privilege.

A colleague brings Carey into the cafeteria and introduces him. They join a table of white-coated MDs, with the only exceptions being Carey in a brown leather jacket and the hospital dietician, Georgia Hightower (Jennifer

O'Neill), also in brown. The camera quickly unites them in a two shot linking them and foreshadowing their romantic involvement. When Dr. David Tao (James Hong), a friend with whom Carey had interned years earlier, invites him to dinner that evening, Carey invites Georgia to accompany him. She agrees, but says that she first has to feed her son, Jesse. When Carey asks why her husband can't feed Jesse, she replies that her husband has gone to Aspen skiing, with no expected return date.

The film reflects post-1960s counterculture and social turmoil. Georgia's never-seen husband irresponsibly abandons his family to go skiing in Aspen on the grounds that he finds everything "synthetic." Carey clearly holds his behavior in contempt. However, Carey's later impassioned speech to Randall about the need for "fresh air" in ossified social institutions is also reflective of the era's mores. Carey reflects some anti-establishment elements of the times, but at the same time he is also clearly and safely part of the establishment.

At dinner, Tao fills Carey in on the staff. He describes J. D. Randall as "celestial," adding that, "If you're under 60 and white you call him 'Sir.' If you're black, yellow, or somewhere in between, you evaporate." Carey says that that's awkward and Tao replies, "Prudent." Responding to Carey's questioning look, Tao says, "You wouldn't know," and Carey replies, indicating his awareness of the racial divide between Tao's Chinese background and his own, "Oh, you mean being white, Protestant, etc., etc." Tao quickly changes the subject.

The sympathetic center of the film resides with the three outsiders to this white, male, Bostonian environment – Carey, who is newly arrived from Palo Alto, Georgia, the female dietician, and Dr. Tao. The plot triggers when Randall's 15-year-old daughter Karen (Melissa Torme-March) dies of a botched abortion and Dr. Tao is blamed for it. Carey initially tells Dr. Tao that by doing abortions he is "playing God," but he defends him, certain that the talented surgeon could have never done such a botched job, and he takes it upon himself to find the real culprit. However, within the Catholic context of Boston in 1972, the revelation that Tao has performed other abortions has reverberations. One character comments about Tao's plight: "In Boston, with a jury half-Catholic, they'll convict him on general principles."

A central formal structure of the film involves mirrors, glass, and doubling, and a pivotal scene occurs when Carey questions Karen Randall's roommate, Lydia Barrett (Jennifer Edwards), in her dorm room. The room is lined with mirrors (Figure 8.1). As they enter, the first thing we see is a black-and-white poster of Karen's father, J. D. Randall, that is riddled with darts. Lydia says that Karen threw darts at it every night before going to bed. We then see various 1970s-era counterculture posters on the walls, such as

FIGURE 8.1 *The Carey Treatment*, © 1972 Metro-Goldwyn-Mayer, Inc., Turner Entertainment Company.

one featuring Ringo Starr and another with a red-tinted "Viva La Revolucion" above an image of the Mexican revolutionary Emiliano Zapata. The scene quickly focuses on mirrors, starting with a three shot of Lydia before a mirror, which presents her, her reflection, and Carey. She talks about Karen's crudeness and promiscuity. While they talk, in a second mirror shot that shows Carey standing before a different mirror, he looks behind him and finds a small bottle of pills. Then Lydia walks across the room and stops in a complex shot that shows the dart-filled poster of J. D. Randall on the left, Lydia in the center, and a mirror on the right showing Carey, a rear angle reflection of Lydia, and the Ringo Starr poster (Figure 8.2).

FIGURE 8.2 *The Carey Treatment*, © 1972 Metro-Goldwyn-Mayer, Inc., Turner Entertainment Company.

Carey quickly realizes that Lydia's accusations about Karen's promiscuity actually apply to Lydia and not Karen, and that the pills he found on her dresser are birth control pills, reinforcing his sense of Lydia's promiscuity. In effect, Lydia has created a mirror image of herself and ascribed it to Karen. Later, Karen's brother confirms the fact that Lydia and not Karen was the promiscuous one. Lydia's false narrative about Karen parallels the false one about Tao's guilt for Karen's abortion. Lydia later admits that she had been angry at Karen for stealing her boyfriend, Roger Hudson (Michael Blodgett). Hudson is also involved with the nurse, Angela Holder (Skye Aubrey), and will later try to kill Carey when he learns that Carey has discovered that it was Angela, not Dr. Tao, who performed the botched abortion on Karen with Roger's help. After interviewing Lydia, Carey drives her to an appointment but, while doing so, locks her in his car and drives recklessly, smashing through a barrier on a bridge and purposefully terrorizing her, finally getting her to confess to the truth about herself and Karen. He is ruthless and, when Lydia leaves his car, she bitterly calls him a "son of a bitch."

This echoes what Police Captain Pearson (Pat Hingle) will later tell Carey, saying, "Jesus, doctor, you're a worse son of a bitch than I am." He has just watched Carey terrorize the morphine-addicted nurse, Angela Holder, in a comparably brutal way. She had just been murderously attacked by Roger and is lying bloody in a hospital bed. Knowing that she is a morphine addict suffering withdrawal, Carey threatens her with a hypodermic needle that he tells her is filled with a drug which could throw her into cold turkey and possibly kill her. She watches him empty it into her IV tube. Pearson, who is watching, is visibly upset at this. Carey also shows her another hypodermic filled with morphine, saying that if he chooses he can use it to relieve her pain. When she tries to stop him by telling him that, if he kills her, he will also be in trouble, Carey brutally retorts by describing the privileges he holds in the hospital: "In this room, I'm God [earlier, he had accused Tao of playing God]. I can label it anything I want – heart failure, respiratory arrest, shock. I make out the death certificate." Although he has actually used a harmless saline solution, she believes it to be dangerous and begins to go into convulsions. Brandishing the morphine, he tells her to confess to her involvement in Karen Randall's death quickly because, in a few minutes, she will be unable to do so. It is a painful scene, and also one in which he is presenting a mirror narrative to the truth, since he is only using saline. The normally hardened Captain Pearson of the Boston police watches in the shadows, becoming increasingly upset. Finally, Angela confesses.

Those at the hospital mostly reflect well-to-do Bostonians, and the film gives us different perspectives on both the city and the hospital. It begins almost like a travelogue, starting with a stately helicopter shot of the city followed by shots of Carey driving into it and then up to the hospital in which he will work. The hospital initially appears majestic and formal, a center for healing, but we quickly see ruptures within it and the film climaxes with murderous activities in its bowels. Like the city, the prestigious and curative hospital is simultaneously a horror zone. Carey's description of himself as "God" in the hospital room mirrors Tao's initial categorization of the powerful J. D. Randall as "celestial." At times Carey resembles those he battles and, at the end when Captain Pearson bursts into Carey's hospital room and prevents Roger from murdering him, Roger is standing directly in front of Carey as Pearson shoots him. Visually, both are united as Pearson's targets.

Carey's first significant interaction with Randall occurs in Randall's office. It begins politely but quickly becomes confrontational. Randall opens the conversation by saying that Carey is seldom at his job. When Carey says he is conducting his own investigation into Karen's death, Randall berates him as a dissident, one resistant to the norms of his profession, and Carey retorts that ossified institutions need fresh air and should be fumigated. During the first part of the interview, Randall has left his desk to greet Carey but, when he returns to sit behind it, we see him frontally at his desk for the first time. Behind him is a large picture window covered with sheer yellow curtains, and the intensity of the light surrounding him makes him appear intimidating to anyone sitting before him; now he is playing God on his heavenly throne (Figure 8.3). Edwards returns to the same composition and lighting in a later scene once again in Randall's office.

In the scene immediately following the one in Randall's office, Carey visits Evelyn Randall (Elizabeth Allen), J. D. Randall's new, younger wife. She

FIGURE 8.3   *The Carey Treatment,* © 1972 Metro-Goldwyn-Mayer, Inc., Turner Entertainment Company.

is alternately flirtatious and snarky with Carey. Drinking straight Scotch in the middle of the day, she smugly describes herself as "a member of the club with all dues paid," indicating that, although she comes from what she terms a "shanty Irish" background, she has now married into the Boston upper class and enjoys the prestige. Carey also meets Dr. Joshua Randall (Alex Dreier), J. D.'s brother, who greets him with, "And who are your people, and what do they do?" emphasizing the importance of family ties in his world. But Carey also investigates another section of Boston, a rundown, working-class area. When he connects Roger Hudson with much of the corruption, he enters a steam room at which Hudson works and requests a massage from the vain, heavily muscled Hudson, who had been romantically involved with Karen, with Lydia, and with Angela Holder. As Hudson massages Carey, Carey questions him about the case in ways that quickly become confrontational, with close shots of Roger's hands pressing firmly on Carey's body and with Carey vocalizing gay and sado-masochistic inferences, which infuriates Roger.[7] He lets Roger know that he suspects him of having been involved in Karen's death and, at the end, punches him. Roger embodies a dark eroticism in the film, one that attracted Lydia, Karen, and Angela. When Angela is undergoing morphine withdrawal in the hospital, she deliriously speaks of Roger, particularly about the erotic attraction of his hair, saying, "all summer long his hair kept getting blonder and blonder like a halo," yet another reference to celestial, Godlike imagery.

Immediately after leaving Roger, Carey tries to call Captain Pearson from a street telephone booth to tell him that he knows who killed Karen, but Roger tries to kill him by driving into and smashing the booth. We see Carey in the street, covered with shattered glass and bleeding profusely (Figure 8.4).

FIGURE 8.4　*The Carey Treatment,* © 1972 Metro-Goldwyn-Mayer, Inc., Turner Entertainment Company.

The scene reinforces the film's formal concern with glass, whether in its use of mirrors or other structures indicating entrapment, such as the phone booth, the mirrors in Lydia's dorm room, and a remarkable single long take extreme depth of field focus interview scene that opens with a shot of a physician's hand lowering a squirming rodent into a large glass beaker. Hudson, presuming that he has killed Carey and wanting to avoid all suspicion, sneaks into the darkened hospital to kill Angela. When he approaches her in her lab brandishing a knife, she smashes a beaker to defend herself. As the film reaches its climax, we see Carey, who has been brought into the hospital covered in blood, as well as both Angela and Roger, who are comparably covered in blood from their encounter. At this point, the film resembles a slasher movie, with the now-bloody Roger, after having killed a hospital employee to steal his clothes, prowling its halls hoping to finish off both Carey and Angela. The sequence also creates an unexpected visual link between the two men, both of whom have put on spotless white surgical jackets which disguise their bloody wounded bodies (Figure 8.5). He finally locates Carey and is on the verge of killing him when Pearson bursts into the room like an avenging angel and shoots him dead.

The Carey Treatment creates a maze of connections among seemingly dissimilar and even opposite characters such as the striking similarity between Roger and Carey, who mirror each other while roaming the hospital in their surgical disguises hiding their wounded bodies. Dr. Carey, Dr. Tao, and Dr. Randall are dramatically diverse characters who appear to be quite different from one another, but all are linked together by the way they wield Godlike medical power. Randall is described as "celestial" and looks like a god sitting

FIGURE 8.5 *The Carey Treatment,* © 1972 Metro-Goldwyn-Mayer, Inc., Turner Entertainment Company.

on his throne in front of the blinding light behind his desk; Carey accuses Tao of "playing God" by performing abortions, and Carey declares to Angela Holder, "In this room, I'm God." Yet all three of the doctors are dramatically different characters. Even Roger Hudson with his "halo" relates to this pattern. Yet, in addition to being linked to Randall, Tao, and Hudson, Dr. Carey is even linked to Pearson who, after watching Carey torture Angela, declares, "you're a worse son of a bitch than I am." These connections across such disparate characters complicate simple good–bad dichotomies.

The shock of the image of shattered glass in the destroyed phone booth recalls the horrifying images of shattered and mutilating glass in the climactic fight scene between Gunn and Daisy Jane in *Gunn*, which itself follows the destruction of Daisy Jane's mirror-lined bedroom discussed in Chapter 6. Edwards often uses glass and mirrors for diverse purposes, including Jack Lemmon's drunken and disorienting walking into the window of his apartment house in *Days of Wine and Roses* as well as, in a less shocking mode, the constantly performing Holly Golightly's signature opening image showing her looking into, and being reflected by, a picture window of Tiffany's in *Breakfast at Tiffany's*. In *The Carey Treatment*, Carey has a huge skylight directly above his bed. A photographer, presumably hired by J. D. Randall, resembles a Peeping Tom in furtively climbing upto the roof to photograph Carey and Georgia in bed making love. Carey chases the man, seizes the film, and, soon after, brings a huge blowup of the photo into J. D. Randall's office and aggressively presents it to him, indicating that he knows that Randall commissioned it. He takes what was presumed to be something that would embarrass him and flips its meaning around, now turning it into something that embarrasses Randall.

Such a use of glass, mirrors, and reflective surfaces also points to Edwards's career-long interest in mixing genre conventions. Characters and situations that may initially appear to be one thing often shockingly turn out to be something else entirely. *The Carey Treatment* initially appears to be a hospital procedural of the type popular on network television from the 1950s in diverse formats such as the soap opera, *General Hospital*, in series such as *Dr. Kildare, Ben Casey*, or *St. Elsewhere*, or in feature films like *The Hospital* (1971), but it quickly echoes other genres, including the detective and horror films. Interestingly, given Edwards's strategy of having slapstick erupt into many of his dramas, including *Wild Rovers*, he does not employ slapstick here.[8] Dr. Carey is yet another instance of Edwards's long interest in detectives, whether situational, amateur, private, or police detectives. This film not only includes Dr. Carey (a situational detective) but also the police detective, Captain Pearson. This extends all the way back to his early work in radio (the *Richard Diamond, Private Detective* series) and television (see Chapters 1 and 2) and includes the two Peter Gunn films we discuss in Chapter 6, which feature his most famous private detective, as well as the Inspector Clouseau Pink Panther films. Wyatt Earp and Tom Mix in *Sunset*, which we discuss in Chapter 11, are late-period examples of his amateur detectives.

Edwards's private detectives are generally paired with actual police detectives, like Lt. Jacoby in *Peter Gunn*, Lt. Rovaks (Tom Brown) in *Mr. Lucky*, or a detective is paired with a higher-ranking officer such as Inspector Clouseau and Chief Inspector Dreyfus in the Pink Panther films. Here, Carey's profession of pathologist involves a kind of detecting and, like the others, he is paired with a police detective, Captain Pearson. Edwards uses these pairings to create hostilities between the two, leading to laughter in the comedies or tension in the dramas. And in both the comedies and the dramas they often take on complex attributes of male bonding. For example, while Gunn and Jacoby frequently oppose each other as they work to solve the case, they also bicker in a manner that reveals their affection for each other. The relationship between Carey and Pearson is not as well developed as many of these others but it contains similar dynamics. Throughout much of the film Pearson threatens Carey and Carey strikes back. Indeed, one such exchange with Carey in his parked car with Pearson standing beside it and talking to him leads to the only truly comic moment in the film. As Carey begins to drive away, Pearson exaggeratedly puts out his hand to stop oncoming traffic while waving Carey ahead with the other hand. It is funny but is, of course, Pearson's stinging response to Carey's Godlike presumption of power. Yet, by the end of the film, they work together to solve the case, with Pearson even saving Carey's life.

Another major structuring device in the film involves Edwards's complex staging of conversations. In fact, the detective genre is particularly well suited for Edwards's interest in foregrounding conversations and exploring how his characters use language to obfuscate the truth or to lie (see Chapter 7). Detectives are literally in the business of finding the truth through interrogation. Once again, Edwards stages many of the conversations with characters who do not look directly at each other, frequently moving around and changing positions while talking, and even engaging in an activity totally unrelated to the conversation. These strategies also largely dictate how the scenes must be edited. One such strategy involves long takes and, significantly, they begin with the above-cited scene as Carey enters the hospital for the first time. In a 1-minute shot, we see Carey in close-up and the camera tilts upward as he looks at the imposing portrait of the founding Dr. Randall (Figure 8.6). The camera pulls back and follows him walking away from the reception desk

FIGURE 8.6   *The Carey Treatment*, © 1972 Metro-Goldwyn-Mayer, Inc., Turner Entertainment Company.

FIGURE 8.7   *The Carey Treatment*, © 1972 Metro-Goldwyn-Mayer, Inc., Turner Entertainment Company.

(Figure 8.7). Just as we see the head resident walking down a corridor in the center of the frame toward the camera, Carey exits screen right (Figure 8.8). The camera then follows the resident to the reception desk where he is directed to Carey (Figure 8.9). The camera then pans right as he approaches Carey, who had been off-screen (Figure 8.10). After introductions, they begin to walk away down the long corridor in the rear of the frame, and the camera now follows them from behind in conversation (Figure 8.11).

Edwards uses a similarly complex long take in the above-mentioned scene where Carey enters a lab to interrogate a doctor who is experimenting with a rat in a large bell jar. The entire scene is a single take and, as the characters talk, they move around. Carey enters the room from the extreme rear of the frame in a deep focus shot which includes a looming close-up of the rat

FIGURE 8.8   *The Carey Treatment*, © 1972 Metro-Goldwyn-Mayer, Inc., Turner
Entertainment Company.

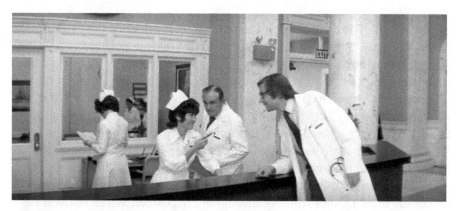

FIGURE 8.9   *The Carey Treatment*, © 1972 Metro-Goldwyn-Mayer, Inc., Turner
Entertainment Company.

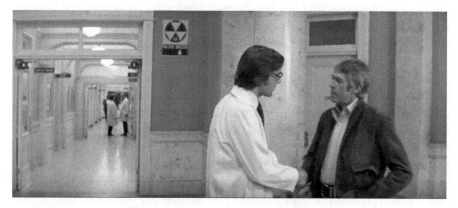

FIGURE 8.10   *The Carey Treatment*, © 1972 Metro-Goldwyn-Mayer, Inc., Turner
Entertainment Company.

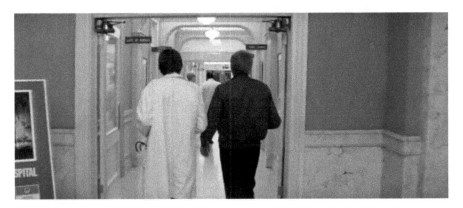

FIGURE 8.11   *The Carey Treatment*, © 1972 Metro-Goldwyn-Mayer, Inc., Turner Entertainment Company.

in the bell jar. The doctor continues to work at his desk in the front of the frame as Carey questions him. They virtually reverse positions as Carey, while talking, moves to the right foreground to look carefully at the rat while the other doctor is now behind him at screen left. Neither of the two long take scenes can be edited in any way short of cutting them from the film.

Edwards's strategy of positioning characters in conversation so that they avoid looking at each other or do so only occasionally dominates the film. When Pearson first meets Carey as he leaves Tao's jail cell, another long take follows them as they walk down a long corridor toward the camera. The scene concludes with cutting between the characters as Edwards foregrounds one of the main themes running throughout his career. When Pearson suggests that Carey himself might be involved in the abortion, Carey replies, "There's always that possibility." Pearson retorts, "That means you are?" and Carey says, "It means that is a possibility." The exchange echoes the one we analyzed in *Gunn* where Fusco asks Jacoby two questions about Peter Gunn's actions and Jacoby then asks Gunn the same question, and Gunn replies both times, "It's possible." Edwards always foregrounds language as a potential deception, a variation on "Anyone is capable of anything." During a party in his new apartment, Carey approaches a nurse who he thinks might have valuable information about the abortion case. As she is flirtatiously evasive, Carey says, "We can begin a real conversation, or we can begin a phony one." That applies not only to much of *The Carey Treatment* but also to much of his oeuvre. The endless conversations in his dramas and comedies revolve around characters trying to use language to conceal the truth or penetrate the deceptions. It is comically summarized in *Darling Lili* when two characters on opposing sides talk about the central character, Lili Smith, who may be a spy. One calls her Smith and the other Schmidt, which defines the difference between them. Everything in the film depends upon that one-word difference.

A final example of Edwards's formal structuring of conversation scenes in *The Carey Treatment* occurs when Carey interrogates Dr. Joshua Randall, J. D. Randall's brother who is also a doctor in the hospital. He is busy stirring a delicate gourmet sauce on his stove when Carey enters. He continues his careful attention to the sauce for the first part of the conversation while Carey remains standing in the background. Then he asks Carey to take over stirring and, as Carey moves to the foreground, Joshua Randall moves to a counter top in the right rear of the frame where he chops vegetables. Unlike Dr. Tao who performs his abortions for free, only charging women in need with no place to go a modest fee to cover the lab costs, Joshua Randall performs abortions only for the very wealthy Boston upper-class women who can afford his services. He brushes this off by saying that some doctors believe in a woman's right to choose and control their own bodies, as if who his patients are says nothing about his motives. It is not until the end of the conversation that they directly face each other, at which point Carey explicitly and emotionally confronts the avoidance strategy. He tells Randall to stop his "Julia Child routine" in light of the seriousness of their conversation. As he pleads for any information about the abortion that killed Randall's niece, he directly approaches Randall, forcing him into eye contact as he underscores that they are talking about the death of a 15-year-old girl. Finally, at that moment, Randall drops his charade and is visibly moved by the tragic circumstances. The conversation is now "a real one" instead of a "phony one."

Although some elements of *The Carey Treatment* relate to significant patterns in Edwards's career, some others deviate noticeably. The centrality of abortion as a serious and timely social issue in the United States the year before *Roe v. Wade* would legalize it nationwide is unusual for Edwards. In that regard it resembles *Days of Wine and Roses*, another drama that Edwards did not originate and for which he did not write the screenplay. When Edwards's films take on a serious contemporary social issue such as homophobia and cultural prejudice against homosexuals during the highly visible Gay Rights movement in the United States, as they do in *Victor/Victoria*, he approaches the subject entirely within the framework of entertainment and comedy, in the latter case even further removed by situating it decades earlier in Paris.

The way *The Carey Treatment* ends with a clear resolution of its plot elements and the non-problematic formation of a romantic couple is also unusual in Edwards's work. Dr. Tao is exonerated and even J. D. Randall apologizes to him, the guilty parties are punished, and Carey and Georgia are in a romantic relationship, so much so that Carey plans to drive her and her son, Jesse, to California to meet his parents. Hence, not only is the relationship secure, but it is enfolded into Carey's pride in his family history of happy relationships. The film's closing line reflects this upbeat pattern. When Georgia warns him that Jesse gets carsick, Carey glibly responds, "Oh well, we can work that out." From the beginning, their relationship has been largely monochromatic. They date the first time they meet and he quickly offers her a key to his new apartment. There is no hint of either of them having or desiring another relationship. In fact, Carey, in stark contrast to Edwards's many womanizers, repeatedly brushes off flirtatious overtures, such as those by the middle-aged Dr. Barker (Olive Dunbar) at the hospital who invites him to come to see her apple orchard in Dover, or by J. D. Randall's drunken wife. Georgia almost instantly becomes subservient to Carey and remains so.

Even Dr. Tao appears to be happily married, and at the end tells Carey that his mother is saying Buddhist prayers for him. In addition, he tells Carey that J. D. Randall has apologized to him for presuming him to be guilty. Such a pat wrap-up is unusual for Edwards, as illustrated by examples such as the unresolved or partially resolved endings of *This Happy Feeling, Mr. Cory, Days of Wine and Roses, The Pink Panther, A Shot in the Dark, Darling Lili,* and *Victor/Victoria,* among others. A central trope of the *Peter Gunn* television shows and films is the instability of the relationship between Gunn and his long-term girlfriend, Edie. No sooner do they seem to be uniting as a couple than Gunn will get a telephone call that calls him away, again and again.

Throughout his career, Edwards seldom devoted much time to developing the family histories of his central characters. In most cases, we learn little if anything about their backgrounds. When we raised this issue with Craig Stevens about his long-term role of Peter Gunn, Stevens agreed, simply commenting about the character, "what you see is what you get."

In *The Carey Treatment*, however, there are two counterpoints to Carey's unproblematic pride in his family. The first is with the broken family of Georgia, whose husband had abandoned her and their son in search of a "free" lifestyle skiing in Colorado. A second counterpoint is Randall's dysfunctional family, indicated in the dart-punctured poster featuring his face in Karen's room, in the palpable unhappiness of his drunken wife, and in the lack of affection vocalized by his son when he comes to Carey's apartment to attack him in the mistaken belief that Carey is defending Tao's killing of his sister. In the next chapter we analyze *Julie,* Edwards's documentary about his family life with Julie Andrews, within the context of families, and their frequent absence, in his films. The untroubled, upbeat family ending in *The Carey Treatment* may be one of the strongest markers of Edwards's limited control over this project and its conclusion.

NOTES

1. Julie Andrews, *Home Work: A Memoir of My Hollywood Years*, with Emma Walton Hamilton (New York: Hachette Books, 2019), p. 174.

2. Andrew Sarris, "Best Films of 1972," *The Village Voice*, January 11, 1973, Vol. XVIII, No. 2 (www.villagevoice.com).

3. For a detailed account of *The Carey Treatment* including problems with the script and with the production schedule, see Peter Lehman and William Luhr, *Blake Edwards* (Athens: Ohio University Press, 1981), pp. 203–212.

4. Roger Ebert, Review of *The Carey Treatment*, April 5, 1972 (rogerebert.com).

5. Edwards himself may have humorously winked at this near the film's conclusion when the doctor who has treated Carey for his wounds releases him from the hospital with orders "to sit home and watch a lot of daytime television."

6. Carey shares something in common with Cory in *Mister Cory* and with Feodor Sverdlov (Omar Sharif) in *The Tamarind Seed*. In all three dramas the central male characters undergo a major geographical and cultural shift. Cory escapes his inner-city ethnic neighborhood to travel the country as he rises in his economic and social class before returning to Chicago in a new wealthy neighborhood. Carey leaves California, the center of the new counterculture, to come to Boston. When someone asks him why, he simply says for "the bread." A major dramatic turning point occurs in *The Tamarind Seed* when Sverdlov, a Russian, defects to the West, escaping communism for capitalism and Russia for Canada. Cory, Carey, and Sverdlov all struggle as they seek something new and better in a new location.

7. Edwards's oeuvre includes many steam baths and massage scenes tied to issues of masculinity and the male body, including episodes in the *Peter Gunn* series and most famously *Victor/Victoria*. Interestingly, he even played a boxer in *Leather Gloves* (1948), a film which includes such a scene. The steam bath scene in *Victor/Victoria* where a homophobic gangster discusses homosexuality makes the masculinity issue explicit.

8. Although Edwards never made another hospital film, aspects of the genre will return. A central scene in the film involves Carey observing Karen Randall's

autopsy. Looking at the face of her young body, when water starts flowing on the table, we see him imagine the teenage girl, frolicking in the ocean in slow motion. His fantasy stands in stark contrast to the bitter reality. In *Justin Case*, a bizarre autopsy scene shows the dead main character's ghost watching his own autopsy! *That's Life!* starts with coldly impersonal imagery of the hospital medical procedure and technology involved in a biopsy. Later, in a hospital emergency room scene, we see comically exaggerated images of bloody patients who appear like cartoon characters having survived violent slap-stick mayhem.

CHAPTER 9

Julie (1972)

Executive Producer and Director, Blake Edwards

When we interviewed Ken Wales in 2011, during a discussion of the difficult time Edwards had after the problems he encountered on *The Carey Treatment*, Wales remarked, "We were working on some little documentary thing, behind the scenes thing," but he quickly passed on to the events that led to Edwards's next theatrical feature, *The Tamarind Seed*. We had no response to or questions about the "little documentary" since we did not know about it and had not seen it. We, like Wales, assumed the next important film was *The Tamarind Seed*. That changed dramatically in 2020.

On March 26, 2020, Richard Brody published a commentary in *The New Yorker* entitled "What to Stream: Blake Edwards's Masterwork Documentary of His Wife, Julie Andrews."[1] The masterwork to which he refers is, of course, the "little documentary" mentioned by Wales and which credits Wales as the producer. Brody's essay is itself a virtual writer's version of Edwards's beloved gag routine of "topping the topper topper." After acknowledging that "Edwards (who died in 2010) was a comedic genius, the most skilled and inspired director of physical comedy working in Hollywood in his time" (the topper), he goes on to make the claim, "Yet Edwards has also made some of the best movies of modern times, including 'Experiment in

Blake Edwards: Film Director as Multitalented Auteur, First Edition.
William Luhr and Peter Lehman.
© 2023 John Wiley & Sons Ltd. Published 2023 by John Wiley & Sons Ltd.

Terror,' 'Days of Wine and Roses,' 'Wild Rovers' and even 'Sunset,' which has been much, and wrongly, maligned, including by Edwards himself" (the topper topper). Then he makes the startling claim that "The documentary 'Julie,' starring Blake Edwards and Julie Andrews, is the director's secret masterwork" (topping the topper topper).

We have not critically analyzed film reviews in this book but want to comment on this one due to the importance it has for Blake Edwards studies in general and this book in particular (see Chapter 1). Were it not for Brody we probably would not have been aware of the existence of the film *Julie*. Brody describes it as "a secret masterwork ... hiding in plain sight" and classifies it as "a sort of genre mashup – combining the portrait film and the personal documentary with the exotic category of documentaries by filmmakers who mainly made dramas." Curiously, the film has slipped between many cracks and is barely known. One symptom of this lies in the fact that until 2023, IMDb did not list it anywhere under Blake Edwards's filmography and only listed it under "Self" (1972) in Julie Andrews's filmography along with 220 other entries.

Brody's brief analysis relates to ours in yet another way: "The documentary starts with a closeup of Andrews that is both intimate and glamorous, personal and radiantly cinematic. A seemingly infinite variety of such close-ups of her recur throughout the film *and sustain that abidingly dramatic tone, at once authentic and virtually fictional*" (emphasis added). Our analysis shows that the entire film is structured around this seeming paradox of the portrait of Julie being about both her authentic and fictional character. One might ask, "Who is the real Julie?", a question the film wisely does not answer since profound ambiguity lies at its center, and the film resists choosing between such conventional polarities.

The film begins with a close-up of Andrews singing intercut with shots of her using a hairdryer and performing.[2] This brief introduction is followed by the film's first of many conversation scenes, this one with Andrews in an executive's office as he tells her that the five-year contract for her television show will enable her to "make pictures in between shows." She replies, "Oh God, that doesn't leave me very much time to be at home." This is followed by the film's second conversation scene showing Edwards and Andrews walking along the beach as she expresses the anxiety that the contract will be "ten times more work" than she thought. We then cut back to the opening of her singing, followed by another shot of them walking along the beach and Andrews continuing to express anxiety, with Edwards responding that obviously, "it appeals to you, or you wouldn't be talking about it." Andrews is frustrated both about being away from the family and about the fact that she hasn't worked for several years. Edwards also adds that she won't have as much time to write her books, referring to the children's books she has been writing and publishing. Andrews replies that she could "just get *Whangdoodles* [*The Last of the Really Great Whangdoodles*] finished," but it would then require the time needed to edit and revise. Edwards then encourages her by noting that "it should work out fine as it did for Carol [Burnett]," her close friend. Andrews notes that "it will be worse at the beginning until we get a routine." We then cut to a rehearsal which includes shots of the television cameras and back to the beach, then back to Edwards and Andrews as he says, "I think what you're asking for is someone to make a decision," to which Andrews replies, "Yes, I am, I guess." Edwards then definitively says, "Okay, do it."

These brief scenes set up a pattern that Edwards will develop in a complex manner throughout the film. We see Julie from two different perspectives, as a performer creating her persona with attention to her hairstyle, and as a wife, which will soon be augmented by seeing her as a mother. This establishes one of the film's major thematic concerns, the sometimes tense relationship between the creative singer/performer/actor and her private life as a wife and mother, and raises the profound question: Which is the "real" or "authentic" Julie of the title? As we shall see, Edwards uses mirrors throughout the film to emphasize the construction of her multiple personae. Edwards's role in the film as husband and father becomes part of a similar doubling motif, with him also serving as the film's executive producer and director and with his on-screen persona which includes that of a film actor. A related thematic concern raised in these brief scenes involves Edwards showing in detail the hard, time-consuming work that goes into creating Andrews's seemingly effortless singing and performing.

Many of Edwards's films explore the relationship between creativity and private life, including *Darling Lili*, *"10,"* *S.O.B.*, *Victor/Victoria*, *Skin Deep*, *The Man Who Loved Women*, and *That's Life!*, to name a few. The creative figures run the gamut from singer-performers, composers, writers, sculptors, architects, and film producers and their private lives involve romance, family, womanizing, alcoholism, and midlife crises. *Darling Lili* is particularly interesting here since it stars Julie Andrews as a singer-performer who is also a spy and is romantically involved with the Rock Hudson character. Since spying is itself a performance, she really has three "roles" in this film: singer-performer, spy, and lover. Similarly in *Victor/Victoria* she is a singer-performer, a cross-dresser who is a woman pretending to be a man pretending to be a woman, and a lover with the James Garner character.

The beginning also establishes the documentary style of the entire film in that it consists of cutting among different types of professional and domestic scenes edited in a surprising manner without any narrator or voice-over supplying a clear continuity. We quite literally have no idea of what we are going to see next and how it may relate to what we have seen prior to it. Furthermore, Edwards disrupts any unified, coherent temporal progression by returning to interviews we have already seen but that we now re-see in entirely different contexts. For example, the early interviews focus on Julie's anxieties about whether or not to sign the contract and make the commitment to a television series while worrying about how she will have time for her family. But well after the film has shown her make the commitment and balance the hard work with her family time, Edwards will cut back to using other segments from those same interviews in which we recognize the setting, the interviewer, how everyone is dressed and so on. If an interview was done before she even committed to doing the series, how can it be relevant to what we are seeing after she has signed the contract and we have seen her hard at work? Edwards is boldly exploring a new kind of temporal space in this film, dispensing with traditional chronology. Thus, we find ourselves going back to the same walks along the beach, or the same conversation taking place around a patio table, or the same family barbecue around a bonfire on the beach. Not only is there no narrator; there is also not even a coherent narrative time frame. We're here, we are there; we're back there and back here.

Consider for the moment the Google Dictionary definition of *cinéma verité* as "a style of filmmaking characterized by realistic, typically documentary motion pictures that avoid artificiality and artistic effect and are generally made with simple equipment." An internet film glossary entry also notes: "Other elements typically identified with cinema verité are portable sound equipment, the handheld camera, and impromptu interview techniques."[3] Much of this seems to apply to *Julie*, but Edwards's film is most accurately described as an "observational documentary" combining verité elements with various forms of "direct cinema" wherein the filmmaker is a participant. First and foremost, *cinéma verité* filmmakers do not make films about themselves or their family but adopt the position of distanced "observers" of the events and people they "record." But, as we have seen, Edwards presents himself and his family life as integral to his film. The film is ostensibly about Andrews but Edwards's home life and even professional involvement with her career are inextricably interwoven into the film's fabric.

It is important here to also note that Jim Songer is co-credited with "Sound" in making the film in addition to Ken Wales. They, along with Edwards, had strong interest in developing and applying new technologies to filmmaking. They named their company Video West, with the last word being an anagram derived from the first letter of the names Wales, Edwards, and

Songer with the "t" added to identify the geographic location of the Hollywood company. Their most significant contribution to filmmaking was with _The Party_ (1968) when they invented and introduced a parallax video assist recording system that enabled instant review of footage shot through the exact same lens as that captured by the 35 mm film camera. This history accounts for Wales's calling it "a little documentary," not little in a dismissive sense but rather in a production sense. This film was not made for theatrical distribution and exhibition; it was made for television. At first glance _Julie_ looks and sounds nothing like Edwards's polished, big-budget Hollywood films, stemming from the fact that much of the footage does not appear to have been shot on 35 mm film but, rather, using a wide range of cameras and sound equipment ranging from video, to super8 mm, to large professional soundstage television cameras. But even here Edwards innovates with some very careful compositions, including playing with off-screen space and in the stunning concluding sequence using two mirrors positioned directly across from each other. So much of it is like the portable equipment favored by _cinéma verité_ filmmakers such as when they shoot on a beach at night around a campfire or around a dining room table during a meal, but much of it is also carefully constructed to emphasize sophisticated use of space and visual motifs that match carefully planned Hollywood filmmaking. As with so many of the films we have been analyzing, the documentary genre Edwards invokes in _Julie_ is complicated, using techniques and elements from other genres.

After Edwards resolves the issue of whether or not Andrews should sign the contract by telling her, "Okay, do it," we see Andrews in rehearsal, talking with one of the creative team members, then the film cuts back to Andrews on the beach but now we see her romping and playing with the children, followed by a brief cut back to rehearsal, and then we see Edwards and Andrews again back on the beach and Andrews tells him that, ten years from now, she might not have the energy or desire to take on these projects. Then we see her in discussion with an executive who tells her, "You've never been allergic to hard work," and we then see her at work with her choreographer followed by seeing her at another session, this time in costume, followed by a cut to a full costume rehearsal with television cameras. Julie is dressed formally in tails while holding an umbrella. Then we see Edwards and Andrews having a conversation in their back yard at home. While they are seated, the film cuts back to a longer shot with the children playing tennis with Edwards and Andrews in the rear of the frame. Then in a cut back, we hear Edwards telling Andrews that "the strain will be enormous" and that she needs someone with great experience: "Someone is going to run the show who understands your problem ... to make it worthwhile."

This sequence introduces the children for the first time. We have heard Andrews worrying about them but now we see her playing with them and then discussing the professional problems with Edwards as they play nearby. The children become prominent in the film's structure as it progresses. We also see Edwards becoming actively involved in shaping her role in the project. After telling her to do it, he then gives advice on how she should deal with the strain. In addition to being the executive producer and director of this film, Edwards will also become more prominent in it as both a husband and father and an experienced film and television producer and director. This sequence also introduces Andrews in tails with an umbrella and top hat, an image that will become the focus of the arc showing the hard creative work involved in this type of performance: she must master the difficult choreography of knocking her top hat off with the umbrella and catching it on her foot with her leg extended, all while singing and dancing! The costume in the number also bears an uncanny relationship to how Edwards will later cast her in *Victor/Victoria* as a woman pretending to be a man in her private life and then extending that on stage as a man pretending to be a woman.

Having laid out the basic style of the documentary as intercutting short scenes in varying personal and professional settings, we will now trace through a few of its main themes and motifs. In this style of documentary filmmaking, Edwards uses film form to shape and tell his story in a quite different manner than that of the feature narratives. Much of the time he foregrounds editing over such aspects of film style as the complex structuring of screen and off-screen space or careful lighting. Tracing the images of Andrews practicing the choreography of catching the top hat with her foot is a good jumping off point while simultaneously showing how Edwards intricately develops and intertwines other strands of the film with it.

Later we see Andrews with top hat and umbrella in a dance studio working with her choreographer on the foot trick, which she fails to accomplish. Edwards then cuts to a television soundstage showing another dress rehearsal of the big production number with Andrews in top hat and formal wear in which Andrews once again fails to catch the hat with her foot. During a break, we see a shot of Edwards at the left with Andrews sitting cross-legged near the edge of the stage with her hat and umbrella and Geoffrey standing in front of her. She gives the hat and umbrella to Geoff, and they clown around with Geoff wearing the hat. He then knocks the hat off his head and catches it with his foot on the first try! Andrews and Edwards are both broken up in joyous disbelief and Edwards turns to his left doubled over with laughter. Edwards then cuts to another clip from an interview, a portion of which we have already seen, with the interviewer now asking Julie, "Now you're going to take a vacation from motherhood. How do your children feel about it?" She replies that each child is different and, while we hear her voice-over, we see home movies of each child which ends with Jennifer. Edwards then cuts to Jennifer in the audience watching Julie once again perform the number with the hat and umbrella. After it appears to be over, Andrews bows to strong applause, which continues as she stands erect and knocks her hat off and, with her leg extended, successfully catches it with her foot. The applause continues, and at 22 minutes into the 51-minute film, Edwards freeze-frames Andrews's triumphant moment of mastering the choreography, thus emphasizing both her success and Jennifer's watching it.

Edwards then cuts to Andrews answering questions at a publicity event about her book, _The Last of the Really Great Whangdoodles_. This sequence shows how richly intertwined the elements of the film become. Edwards connects the theme of Andrews and her children in a way that leads to another aspect of Andrews as a mother: she writes children's books. Near the beginning of the film, we heard Edwards telling her that he thinks this project will give her the time she needs to pursue her writing. The film increasingly portrays her as a multi-hyphenate, multimedia creator. She not only writes books but, as the next sequence shows, she becomes a songwriter: She is a Broadway star, a film star, a television star, a singer, a performer, a songwriter, and a dancer. Edwards pursues this thread as Andrews tells the audience attending a book event about _The Last of the Really Great Whangdoodles_ that she has just written her first song. Cut to her walking with and talking to Leslie Bricusse, her songwriter for the television show. They go inside and Andrews sits at the piano and plays the song for Bricusse for the first time, asking for feedback. Cut to Andrews, Edwards, and Bricusse around a table. Edwards participates in a discussion and makes suggestions about creative issues. Then cut back to Andrews playing the piano and singing her song for Bricusse. When she finishes, he jokes, "That is the worst thing I ever heard." They laugh and he says, "I love it." Cut to a recording session for the song with Jennifer carefully watching and listening. Cut to Edwards and Andrews in a car talking about scheduling issues. Edwards says, "I'll be a housewife for a while" and playfully sticks his tongue out. Again, many threads are intertwined in these sequences. We see Edwards repeatedly throughout the film in many roles including being a father, husband, and a professional advisor and participant in Andrews's new television project. Both become intertwined here when we see Edwards offering to be a "housewife" while Andrews works, but we see him with her at the television rehearsal and in conversation with Bricusse.

While further pursuing scenes in this vein, Edwards totally breaks the tone and expectations by cutting to a home movie of Andrews and Jennifer in goofy costumes acting out a story in the manner of old, silent films. The entire segment, which lasts just over a minute, is played at fast speed, an exaggeration of the speeded-up silent films that were commonly shown on television and in cheap 8 mm films and later video copies. The speed of those resulted from showing old films shot at a slower speed of 18 frames a second and then projected on modern sound projectors with the speed of 24 frames per second. And this points to the other feature of such screenings: the addition of soundtrack music. Once again, the commonly used cheap prints for such television and video releases simply placed "canned music" over the images. Edwards also uses this technique by placing a kind of hectic, "canned" music over the actions instead of any sophisticated music fitting in with and contributing to the mood of the action we see. Once again, this contributes to the goofy, exaggerated feel of old silent films projected at the wrong speed with slapdash music on the soundtrack. The home movie itself shows Andrews and Jennifer in various tableau poses recalling early cinema and dashing around in action scenes. They employ a once again exaggerated version of acting styles used when actors had to convey meaning and emotion without the benefit of their voices being heard. In this home movie they appear to be wildly gesticulating rather than acting. This also contributes to the tone of goofing around and appropriately the sequence ends with them jumping into the swimming pool and toweling off.

This sequence recalls aspects of Edwards's theatrical features, including the scenes we have previously analyzed in *Experiment in Terror* of "Popcorn" in a movie theater watching an old silent comic short resembling the Keystone Kops dashing madly about as well as the scenes of Lee Remick as Kirsten watching classic cartoons on TV as she lies drunk in her apartment in *Days of Wine and Roses*. In all of these films, the use of silent film and cartoons seems to interrupt or disrupt the dominant tones of the films: a grim police procedural about a serial killer in *Experiment in Terror*, a grim drama about alcoholism in *Days of Wine and Roses*, and a documentary about the real-life hard work and creativity that goes into creating a television show and balancing it with family life. Whereas much of *Julie* shows the grueling schedule, hard work, and immense talent Andrews puts into her work, here she simply clowns around, having fun.

All of the family scenes in the film are harmonious with everyone interacting as a group. In one sequence, for example, Edwards cuts from a clip of Andrews talking with a TV executive who asks how she is going to do all this, meaning balancing the grueling work schedule with her family obligations. Andrews once again replies that she has weekends and certain evenings free. Edwards then cuts to a family dinner in the house in which we see him and Andrews, with their children, Emma, Jennifer, and Geoffrey, pleasantly interacting over dinner. He then cuts to a major scene shot at night with a family barbecue around a bonfire on the beach. They are eating and toasting marshmallows. Edwards jokes about the tide coming in, and, when one of the children asks how to toast the other side of a marshmallow, Edwards jokingly tells him to go over to the other side of the fire. The lighthearted mood changes when Edwards requests that Jenny and Andrews sing a song they had done in Ireland. As the two of them sing beautifully, Edwards watches and listens intently, as do Geoff and Emma. Cut to another rehearsal.

The sequence interweaves several of the film's major preoccupations with Andrews's work schedule in relation to her private life as well as Edwards's role in both. The dinner scene, followed by the bonfire on the beach, is the answer to the question the executive asks Andrews: we see her happily interacting with her entire family. We also see Edwards seamlessly weave the two worlds together by asking Jennifer and Andrews to sing together and then cutting directly to Andrews singing in rehearsal. In fact, throughout the film many of the family scenes stress Andrews being creative at home in a manner related to her professional life. In one scene, for example, we see her reading a story to the children with everyone, including Edwards, looking on. The creative way she voices the story reminds us of her being both an author of children's books and a performer. This aspect of her multi-hyphenate career would continue after Edwards's death not only with her collaborating with her adult daughter Emma in writing children's books, but also in her voice-over role of reading portions of a mysterious book of social gossip and commentary written by Lady Whistledown, an unknown and unseen writer in the television series *Bridgerton* (2021). Hearing her read is one of the highlights of the series.

Other scenes of creative role playing in her home life show Andrews acting in the silent film parody discussed above and then in a later scene learning to ride a unicycle by the family pool with Emma and Jennifer by her side. The scene ends with Emma falling into the pool, and they all have a laugh. Again, while it shows Andrews having quality time with her family, we see her learning a new skill in a manner recalling her hard work rehearsing skits for her television show, such as the hat and foot routine. Throughout the film Edwards stresses that hard work, including a poignant moment only minutes from the end of the film when, during a break in a full costume television soundstage rehearsal, Andrews remarks, "Oh, God. I have to sit down.

Either I'm getting too old, or they ask too much. I'm not quite sure which," and she mockingly flops back on the floor.

Throughout the film, Edwards represents himself as a father who repeatedly strives to bring the entire family into a creative atmosphere. These are children being raised in a rich creative environment. But even his serious conversations with Andrews are tied in with her creativity. In one of the cuts back to them talking by the tennis court near the beginning of the film, they discuss Andrews's dilemma of undertaking this ambitious work and family schedule. Edwards tells her that he wants her to be happy, "because if you're not happy, they, your audience, isn't going to be." Later, we see and hear Andrews singing a song with the title "I Want to Be Happy" with lyrics that recall Edwards's advice to her: she wants to be happy "but won't be until you are too."

The final sequence of the film is extraordinary: the compositions, editing, structured use of off-screen space and visual motif are as rich and complex as those in his theatrical features. It begins with a cut to Andrews in her dressing room. She moves back, revealing a mirror image with another mirror image within that one (Figure 9.1). Then a man enters from off-screen right and as he moves back and left, his head momentarily blocks the images (Figure 9.2) as he walks past the mirror images to greet Andrews. We then see him in the mirror as another man enters and blocks our view as he passes the mirror (Figure 9.3). We see the two men greet Julie Andrews as one of

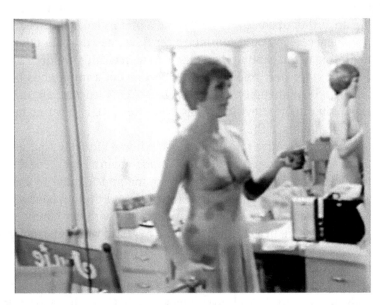

FIGURE 9.1   *Julie,* © 1972 Anjul Productions, Inc.

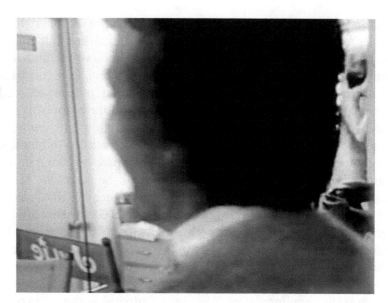

FIGURE 9.2   *Julie*, © 1972 Anjul Productions, Inc.

FIGURE 9.3   *Julie*, © 1972 Anjul Productions, Inc.

them kisses her (lower left) while the other man looks on (screen right) and the kiss is reflected in the mirror (Figure 9.4). We had been watching two mirror images of her and her actual presence becomes the third image. Edwards then cuts to a television studio soundstage and then cuts back to reveal an audience seated awaiting the beginning of the actual live performance. Cut back to the dressing room with Andrews applying make-up. Cut to an announcer addressing the audience telling them when and where they can view the television broadcast. Cut back to Andrews, who checks her makeup in a handheld mirror as she prepares to go out on stage. The camera follows her and the men as they exit the room. We see dual images of them, one of which is clearly a mirror (Figure 9.5). But instead of cutting to Andrews on stage, Edwards briefly lingers on the shot after they have left, and we are startled to see not an empty room but, rather, two identical mirror images of the door they have just walked through (Figure 9.6). The shot shows two mirrors directly across from each other and we have seen them walk "through" the mirrors. Edwards then cuts to a shot of the stage wing as the announcer says, "Miss Julie Andrews" as she walks out and up to the mic, at which point the film ends on a freeze frame. The credits then begin to roll in large, single line lettering, one following the other: "Executive Producer Blake Edwards, Producer Ken Wales, Directed by Blake

FIGURE 9.4 *Julie*, © 1972 Anjul Productions, Inc.

FIGURE 9.5 *Julie,* © 1972 Anjul Productions, Inc.

FIGURE 9.6 *Julie,* © 1972 Anjul Productions, Inc.

Edwards." The credits roll over a close-up of Andrews wearing headphones in a recording studio as she sings "Time Is My Friend." There is no simple answer to the question, which is the "real" Julie of the title.

While this is the only documentary that Edwards directed (he appeared as himself in *I Remember Me*, a documentary about chronic fatigue syndrome), it bears a significant relationship to two of his later films, *The Man Who Loved Women* (1983) and *That's Life!* (1986). Both blur the line between comedy and drama, star Julie Andrews, include Blake's and Julie's family members, and are semi-autobiographical for Edwards. And *That's Life!* is his only theatrical feature that deals centrally with family life. Paradoxically, while most of his films seldom focus on family life, surrounding himself with his family while making the films was important to him, frequently giving them various roles in the films from acting to writing. Julie Andrews told us that she was not always certain that this was in the children's best interests. Both films belong to Edwards's late period where his increasing experimentation of blurring the lines between comedy and drama often led to bad reviews and poor box office. One could almost just as easily describe them as dramas interrupted and disrupted by comedy or as comedies interrupted and disrupted with dark drama. And since we are not devoting individual chapters in this book to Edwards's comedies, we conclude this chapter with brief observations placing *The Man Who Loved Women* and *That's Life!* within the context of such other dark late-period comedies as *Skin Deep*.

Edwards wrote the screenplay of *The Man Who Loved Women* with his analyst Milton Wexler and with his son Geoffrey. Julie Andrews has a major supporting role and Jennifer Edwards has a supporting role. IMDb classifies the film as comedy and drama. It starts and ends with the funeral of the lead character, David Fowler (Burt Reynolds), a compulsively womanizing Los Angeles sculptor whose creativity is blocked and whose womanizing is wildly out of control. Jennifer Edwards plays Nancy, one of Fowler's assistants. Many of the scenes in the film involve psychiatric therapy about his womanizing with his analyst, Marianna (Julie Andrews). Although light comedy is scattered throughout much of the film, a sequence which takes place in Houston is wildly funny, but in this film it is disruptive.

Fowler goes to Houston on business where he has a wild, impassioned affair with Louise Carr (Kim Basinger), the wife of the collector, Roy (Barry Corbin), who hosts Fowler's visit. In one scene, just as Louise and Fowler are beginning to make love in the penthouse master bedroom, her husband unexpectedly returns and a classic Edwards-style bedroom farce ensues, following his topping the topper topper gag structure. Louise shoves David into a closet where he immediately falls over, creating a mess. Roy surprises

Louise with a gift of a small dog, who creates chaos by trying to get into the closet with David. After running back and forth between the bathroom where her husband showers and the closet where David hides, she discovers David has gotten his finger stuck in his mouth along with a tube of super-glue. He ends up with the dog glued to his right hand, while his left hand is glued to his mouth. To get him out of the closet, Louise has to cut the carpet into large squares since David's feet are glued to it. Just when it seems like everything has been topped, the topping continues for two more scenes! First, David goes down to a garage barely able to walk, talk, or use his hands. The comedy builds as he tries to explain his situation to the clueless parking lot attendant. Finally, David gets in the car and drives away using the hand with the dog glued to it on the steering wheel and a finger in the other hand still glued to his mouth.

Again, it is instructive to look at an important review. Roger Ebert, who only gave the film a two-star review, gets right to the heart of the matter: "Here is a sad movie with a funny movie inside trying to get out."[4] Although we assess it differently, Ebert's perception that this is in some sense two films in one that are not unified in a traditional way is astute. The sad movie, which begins and ends with a funeral, is the story of David's compulsive womanizing and his failed efforts with his analyst. Ebert again concisely gets at the heart of David's womanizing: "He thinks he loves them, but he's not a lover, he's a collector." He then notes:

> The funny movie inside is another matter.... The Texas movie is funny. It reminds us of some of the best farcical work by Blake Edwards, the director, whose movies include "10" and "Victor/Victoria." Unfortunately, the Texas sequence lasts only 30 minutes or so, and the rest of the movie is an uncomfortable mixture of psycho-babble, fake sincerity, and scenes we are supposed to take seriously even though they contain obviously impossible elements.

Some of his criticisms here are valid, and we will return to them, but we want to point to the way the "sad story" also intertwines with Edwards's oeuvre in a significant manner. Edwards has made a number of semi-autobiographical films about mentally disturbed artists who are womanizers; they include the Dudley Moore character, a composer, in _"10,"_ the John Ritter character, a writer, in _Skin Deep_, and the Jack Lemmon character, an architect, in _That's Life!_. All of them as well as Felix Farmer, the crazed, suicidal film producer in _S.O.B._, represent aspects of Edwards's own creative personality. Indeed, in _"10,"_ _That's Life!_, and _The Man Who Loved Women_ he cast his wife,

Julie Andrews, as the supporting woman in the troubled man's life either as his wife or as an analyst. This reverses his focus on Julie Andrews in *Julie*; there Edwards is the minor character and the supportive one, easing Julie's doubts and anxieties. In all these theatrical features, Edwards centers upon the male autobiographical character and in that sense centers upon himself. Many of the men in these films suffer from severe anxiety disorder, including panic attacks. For example, in *The Man Who Loved Women*, David wakes up in a deep panic and calls his analyst in the middle of the night, screaming that he can't breathe and is dying of a heart attack. She assures him it is just a panic attack and gives him breathing instructions. In *That's Life!*, Harvey Fairchild has a middle-of-the-night panic attack while riding his exercise bike and his wife, Gillian, finds him in near-collapse trying to ride himself to death.

In her memoir, *Home Work*, Julie Andrews has written about Edwards's struggle with anxiety disorders, something we do not see in the documentary *Julie*. She details an account of how she once found him lying on the floor in a fetal position in a hospital room where he was supposed to be comforting her seriously ill mother.[5] Edwards described to us in detail how he comically bungled a suicide attempt at his home in Malibu much like what happens to the character of Felix Farmer in *S.O.B.* These are truly serious and indeed often sad situations, but they usually connect with a sad autobiographical reality in Edwards's life in a manner different than that of the wildly farcical scenes of physical comedy. In *S.O.B.*, interestingly, the two come together since Felix's suicide attempts fit Edwards's topping the topper topper comic style. And the last time we see David in *The Man Who Loved Women*, the sad and the physically comic come together. David, lying in bed on life support, looks at his nurse as she leaves. We then see his POV shot of her standing in the doorway with bright backlighting emphasizing her legs in a manner recalling the way several of the other women caught David's eye. Edwards cuts back to David who, bandaged and hooked to IV machines and breathing tubes, pathetically reaches out toward the nurse, in the process falling out of bed, knocking everything over with a crashing sound. The next time we see him, he is in his coffin.

The Man Who Loved Women contains another extraordinary anxiety attack scene which also bridges physical comedy with the "sad story." It occurs during a session between David and his analyst which is about much more than "psycho-babble." After he relates his latest woes to Marianna at the beginning of the session, she asks him to lie down on the couch as usual. As he does so, he remarks that things are so bad they can't get worse. He no sooner says it than an earthquake shakes the office on the 12th floor of the high-rise building. David, of course, goes into an immediate panic, running madly around the office, while Marianna calmly collects some material from her desk. One second David wants to help, the next he runs away as fast as he can. Ultimately, he calms down and returns to the couch. A mirrored cabinet door has been flung open, and he finds himself looking at Marianna's shapely legs and up her skirt to her genital area. Immediately his entire persona is transformed. He is "in love" with her. At a later session, he shows her what happened when the mirror allowed him to see up her skirt.

This scene recalls the Freudian-Lacanian account of the mirror phase and fetish formation in which the male infant understands his separation from other's bodies including the mother's, which later enables the boy's desire to see the mother's body. The anxiety created by the "lack" he sees sends his eyes elsewhere, seeking comfort from a part of her body that he then overvalues. In David's case, legs. In several key shots in the film, David's attention and erotic desire are riveted not on an entire woman, but on her legs. Indeed, that touches off the final mad dash that sends him rushing across the street, where he stands paralyzed when his legs momentarily fail him, and he is hit and mortally wounded by a car.

This recreation of a key scene in psychoanalytic theory via set design connects with several other such scenes in Edwards's films.[6] In *"10,"* George Webber (Dudley Moore) has a telescope mounted at the edge of his property, overlooking a ravine with a house on the other side. He becomes a voyeur, constantly watching his neighbor's sex party–oriented lifestyle. This leads to hilarious physical comedy when George gets hit in the head by his swinging telescope and gets knocked down the steep hill and desperately claws his way back up, only to fall again.

In *Victor/Victoria*, an astonishingly complex scene takes place in a hotel where King Marchand (James Garner) has booked a room to spy on Victor (Julie Andrews). Like David and George, Marchand is compulsively anxious, motivated in this case by intense homophobic fear. He became aroused when he first saw Victor performing as a woman. At the moment she pulls off her wig and reveals herself as a man, he panics. How could he make such a mistake? As in *"10"* the key aspect of the set design here involves the hotel architecture: King's room is directly across from Victor's room, and they can look directly into the other's room. Once again, a big empty space separates the two rooms. King decides to sneak from his room into the other across the way with the intention of resolving his anxiety by seeing Victor's genitals. As he does so, hilarity ensues with a classic Edwards-style farce, physical comedy, and careful structured use of screen space and off-screen space.

All these scenes use set design to replicate such aspects of key psychoanalytic development as the primal scene, the mirror phase, and fetish formation. This is profound formal filmmaking, not psychoanalytic theory and certainly not "psycho-babble." In this book, we are trying to show how

Edwards works creatively in different media by telling his stories in a way that makes how the story is told a part of the story. He is a highly creative, inventive filmmaker, not a psychoanalyst (although Milton Wexler is), and not a theorist. The use of the mirror in the aftershock of an earthquake in *The Man Who Loved Women* is closer to genius than to babble. That is not to say that the film doesn't have such babble, but, rather, it should not be reduced to it.

The babble to which Ebert refers occurs around the issue of explaining or understanding David's womanizing and its relationship to Marianna, who goes from being his analyst to being his lover to being his apologist. Much of the dialogue around what causes womanizing, and the characterization of the female analyst, is often babble and, worse, tone-deaf and offensive in characterizing her. Again, Ebert perceptively describes this aspect of the film, dismissing the idea that David truly loves women by noting that, "nowhere in the movie do we really see him loving a woman," adding a simple reminder of the old truism that a man who loves all women loves no woman. In that sense, the film is nearly the opposite of *Julie*, which constantly depicts Edwards as being deeply in love with Julie Andrews.

Ebert's description of Marianna also hits the nail on the head:

When the analyst (played by Julie Andrews) makes her smarmy little speech about how he really and truly loved all of those women, each in her own way, she speaks like no woman I know. If she truly loved Reynolds and felt he truly loved her, and if she had half the brains you need to get out of Analysis 101, she would have (a) been a little hurt, (b) a little jealous and (c) deeply suspicious of the health of his motives.

We would add that she would also have insight into the deep psychological causes of such behavior beyond being "suspicious" of his motives, which are, of course, what he uses to fool himself into thinking that he really loves women. And what kind of female analyst would immediately be thrilled by his attentions and fall in love with him? And then must be reminded by her mentor of another thing she should know from Analysis 101, that she cannot be his analyst and his lover! She must choose one or the other. Ebert's use of the word "smarmy" is justified.

His conclusion is stunning: "This movie is a remake, by the way, of a little-seen 1977 Francois Truffaut film. In the Truffaut, the man was seen as something of a victim, suffering from an incurable disease. The tip-off to the phoniness of the Reynolds version is that the movie seems to be recommending the disease." This issue is particularly important because Edwards's exploration of womanizing men as the central character of his dark, late-period comedies always returns to this problem: he seems, on the one hand, to know that such men are desperately lost and in need of help while simultaneously clinging to the belief that they really love women. Indeed, an early example of this occurs in _The Pink Panther_, made in 1963, the beginning of his mature middle period. Sir Charles Litton (David Niven), a notorious womanizer, justifies his behavior in a dinner conversation with the Princess (Claudia Cardinale). She in turn describes him as pathetic, trying to prove something to himself that he never can – that he is a man!

During a rehearsal break of the Broadway production of _Victor/Victoria: The Musical_, Edwards told us that he was struggling with revising a scene to make clear that Marchand, another womanizer, really loves women. Yet, his womanizing is directly linked to homophobia! He "loves" Victoria only after he eradicates his intense fear and anxiety that, if she is a man, he is a homosexual. In fact, some psychiatrists recognize homophobia as one of the possible contributors to womanizing: the conquest of women "proves" to the womanizer that he is not gay. Edwards strives in his late comedies to make his womanizers sympathetic characters, thus justifying Ebert's claim that he is "spreading the disease."

That's Life! is the other late-period film Edwards made using his family members. The screenplay is credited to Milton Wexler (Edwards's analyst) and Blake Edwards, and it originally included Geoffrey Edwards, who left the project. The cast includes Julie Andrews, her daughter by a previous marriage, Emma Walton Hamilton, and Jennifer Edwards, all of whom appear in the documentary _Julie_. In this film the notion of family is extended by including Chris Lemmon, Jack Lemmon's son, and Felicia Farr, Jack Lemmon's wife. And Jack Lemmon, the film's star, was Blake Edwards's close friend dating back to his early period (see Chapter 2) as well as the star in two of his major mid-period films, _Days of Wine and Roses_ and _The Great Race_. Fittingly, the film's main set is Edwards's and Andrews's actual family home in Malibu.

The film is another semi-autobiographical film dealing with a creative figure, the architect Harvey Fairchild, who is having a late-period midlife crisis both creatively and sexually. He is depressed by the way he must compromise his vision to suit the demands of his wealthy clients (much like Edwards felt about compromises with the studios), and he has an affair with one of his clients. The film concludes at a family gathering for Harvey's 60th birthday. From one perspective it is a sequel to _"10"_ where the autobiographical figure is having an early-stage midlife crisis as he enters middle age. Harvey is having a late one as he enters old age. Edwards literally returned to _"10"_ with a late-period unproduced script _10½_ and another titled _10 (Again)_, which we discuss in Chapter 12.

That's Life! can also be described as a comedy with dramatic interruptions or as a drama with comic interruptions. The first two scenes in the film establish these jarring moods. It opens with coldly clinical images of Gillian Fairchild (Julie Andrews), a singer, undergoing a biopsy for possible throat cancer. The highly clinical images, including detailed sights and sounds of the diagnostic medical equipment, are cold and chilling. This is serious. That scene is directly followed by a scene of Harvey Fairchild arriving home in a van after a car breakdown. As he approaches his home, the automatic sprinkler system goes off, and, in a bit of wildly funny physical comedy, we see him trying to dodge and twist his way through the maze, all while carrying his brief case and having it and his suit drenched.

Once again, Roger Ebert's review is useful. After characterizing all the grim aspects of the plot, from Gillian's internal stress as she keeps her medical crisis to herself, having to wait over the weekend to get the results of her biopsy, while supporting her distracted, self-obsessed husband who is oblivious to her pain while being entirely focused on his career anxieties, his problems with his children, his fear of aging and death, Ebert declares: "What is remarkable is that Edwards makes this situation into a comedy."[7] This is a variation on his characterization of *The Man Who Loved Women* as a sad movie with a comedy trying to get out. He understands that these films are unusual in regard to the genre conventions of comedy and drama as two separate, almost opposing forms. Then Ebert further divides the movie:

He has two different comic approaches in the movie: One works but the other doesn't. The first approach is to observe his central characters very accurately, and with a certain irony ... Unfortunately, he has decided to introduce two characters who don't belong in this movie. Maybe they were left over from "S.O.B." One is a Catholic priest (Robert Loggia), who used to be Harvey's roommate at Notre Dame, and the other is a gypsy fortune-teller (Felicia Farr), who has a storefront on the Pacific Coast Highway. Both characters are written broadly and crudely, and most of the scenes with them don't work ... it is not all of a piece.... Tone is everything in a film like this. Unless you establish one, how can you get laughs by violating it? Edwards seems to switch at random from subtle social satire to broad physical comedy, and it's too distracting. If life in Los Angeles were like this movie, you'd go to sleep beside your pool and something would wake you up in three minutes.

Although we don't share Ebert's aesthetic judgment about how well this style works, he is very insightful about Edwards's blurring of traditional genre boundaries and his abandonment of the traditional value of generic unity.

This film is indeed "not all of a piece," nor does it establish a unified "tone." Throughout this section of the book on Edwards's so-called "serious films," we have identified moments and scenes of disruption and interruption. We used those terms precisely because they point to what is at times an almost jolting break from the "tone" of "the piece." It gets more pronounced in his late work, but he had been creating such ruptures in his early work. In an episode of the *Peter Gunn* television series, for example, Peter Gunn enters a restaurant and bar to interview someone. Suddenly, the episode cuts to a spatially ambiguous shot of a woman seductively approaching the camera. She may be a prostitute, but we never find out because we never see her interact with anyone, including Gunn. After that one shot, she disappears from the episode, and we never see a reaction shot from Gunn or anyone else evaluating her sexual promise. She contributes nothing to the plot or the tone of the episode. She interrupts the flow of the scene and the continuity of Gunn's goal of accomplishing his interview.

Edwards's late-period comedies foreground his long-term fascination with disrupting genre conventions. We have emphasized his non-comic films in this section of the book because they have usually been neglected and minimized, lost in the shadow cast by a filmmaker characterized as the greatest comic director of his generation. He was. But he was much more. We would also suggest a different hypothesis about what is going on in these films. Many artists pare down their style in their late-period work. Rather than fully developing something as they once did in their middle period, they refer to it in an abbreviated manner. It might be that Edwards had made so many farces dominated with physical comedy that he may have wanted to show audiences that he could still be as funny as he ever was but also that he now wants to hold back. Nearly all the films from this period include at least one full-throttled scene of hilarious physical comedy.

In *Skin Deep*, for example, after receiving an intense form of massage therapy including use of an electrical device, Zach, the John Ritter character, walks out of the office with his body spasming wildly out of control. In a remarkable long shot, we see him twisting and lurching his way down a long staircase only to encounter a blind man with his dog. He negotiates around them and continues lurching toward his car in the parking lot. A similar scene occurs in *That's Life!* when Harvey goes to a Catholic mass and is called by the priest to read from the gospels before the entire congregation. When he begins speaking, he suddenly loses control of his body, itching, twisting, and spasming for no reason that we understand. His loss of control recalls Zach's body in *Skin Deep*. Ebert dismisses the scene as follows: "Harvey writhes and squirms, but his reasons are not clear until much later – too much later to be funny." Remember that Ebert has already dismissed the character of the priest as having no place in the film. The extended scene is actually a hilarious eruption of physical comedy, and the fact that Edwards withholds the "reasons" foregrounds his interest in physical bodies out of control. We don't have to know why it is happening, which would in fact make it much less disruptive, perhaps even raising expectations. All Edwards needs is the priest and the church to set the gag up (yes, he needs the character of the priest!).

These chaotic bodies literalize the ways in which many of Edwards's male characters' lives are out of control. Zach, Ritter's character in *Skin Deep*, for example, is an alcoholic womanizer. Sometimes, as in the beginning of *That's Life!*, the chaos results from something as simple as a lawn sprinkler unexpectedly turning on or in *A Shot in the Dark* someone unexpectedly opening a door just as Clouseau rushes to break it down, sending him careening out of control across the room and falling out of an open window. In that film, the chaotic loss of control helps to set and maintain its prevailing farcical, physical comedy tone, whereas in *That's Life!* and *Skin Deep*, it is an abruptly disruptive element breaking the serious and often sad tone. Another such example occurs in *Skin Deep* in the infamous scene showing condoms glowing in the dark. There is nothing else like it in the film. It is a hilarious animated version of bodies out of control as two men who think they are about to make love to the same woman end up with dueling erections in the dark.

An unidentified IMDb user comment about *Skin Deep* notes: "The comedy was certainly up to par, but the movie makes you wait until [...] it is over half done to see it." Like Ebert, this commentator also senses that this movie seems like two different movies: one serious and the other funny. They also sense something unusual about the ending: "The ending also seemed left a little unfinished. Nothing really happens to end the movie." Throughout our work on Blake Edwards, we have stressed the way his films frequently have ambiguous and unresolved endings. Regardless of whether one loves or hates these strategies, it is important to recognize their place within Edwards's career-long creative engagement with both comedy and drama. Although he is commonly characterized as the greatest comic director of his generation, a careful examination of the documentary *Julie* and its connection with *The Man Who Loved Women* and *That's Life!* in which he is again working with his family demonstrates how pigeonholing Edwards has overshadowed the complex realities of his work.

Edwards made *Julie* in 1972 and directed his next film, *The Tamarind Seed*, in 1974. Although one is a low-budget made-for-television documentary and the other a gorgeous, widescreen theatrical film, there is a rich connection between the two. Near the beginning of *The Tamarind Seed*, we see Julie Andrews walking along the beach lost in introspective thought. Later, after she meets the Omar Sharif character, we see them walking along the beach in conversation. These shots recall those of Julie Andrews and Blake Edwards in *Julie*. In *Julie* the conversations Edwards and Andrews have deal with the potential difficulty in their relationship between her professional career development and their family life, and in *The Tamarind Seed* the conversations between the Andrews and Sharif characters deal with the conflict in their relationship caused by his being a Russian Marxist socialist and her being a British capitalist. The beauty of the nature settings in which these characters walk seeking peace and refuge stands in contrast to the potentially divisive realities of their lives. As diverse as Edwards's films are, they are rich with such connections.

NOTES

1. Richard Brody, "What to Stream: Blake Edwards's Masterwork Documentary of His Wife, Julie Andrews," March 26, 2020 (newyorker.com).
2. Our analysis of *Julie* is based on the version streaming on YouTube.com under the title "*Julie* directed by Blake Edwards." It is posted by the Julie Andrews Archive. Although it is a very low-definition print, at times blurry and difficult to see, it is the only print of which we are aware. Like Brody, we nevertheless highly recommend it.
3. The Columbia Film Language Glossary (https://filmglossary.ccnmtl.columbia.edu/term/cinema-verite).
4. Roger Ebert, Review of *The Man Who Loved Women*, December 20, 1983 (rogerebert.com).
5. Julie Andrews, *Home Work: A Memoir of My Hollywood Years*, with Emma Walton Hamilton (New York: Hachette Books, 2020).
6. For a detailed analysis of these films, including the set design in relation to key scenes within psychoanalytic theory, see William Luhr and Peter Lehman, *Returning to the Scene: Blake Edwards, Volume 2* (Athens: Ohio University Press, 1989). The title of our book is a pun referring not just to the scene of filmmaking and to our own second book-length engagement of Edwards's work, but also to psychoanalytic theory and the scene of the crime in detective fiction and movies.
7. Roger Ebert, Review of *That's Life!*, September 26, 1986 (rogerebert.com).

CHAPTER 10

The Tamarind Seed (1974)

Written and Directed by Blake Edwards

While we were visiting Edwards on the set of his 1988 film, *Sunset*, he told us that, as a way of sustaining his long creative career, "I've had to keep re-inventing myself." That perceptive comment provides an ideal approach to *The Tamarind Seed*, which not only reflects a major transition in Edwards's career but also presents central characters who are coping with fundamentally transitional points in their lives. Ken Wales, the film's producer, told us about the origins of the project. Edwards wanted to do an adaptation of *The Green Man* by Kingsley Amis but Sir Lew Grade had given Julie Andrews a copy of *The Tamarind Seed*, written by a woman, Evelyn Anthony: "So, Blake says, 'We can get that. As a matter of fact, Lew Grade really wants to do that and he wants Julie because he's always wanted to do a film with Julie.' Suddenly a new angel was appearing on the scene. Somebody that would fund the movie, Blake could direct it, Julie could star in it, and I'd produce it. So, I read it and I said, 'Well, that looks good.'" Ironically, the Julie Andrews character is seen reading an Amis novel in *The Tamarind Seed*.

At its deepest level, *The Tamarind Seed* is a film about remaking, on the part of its creators as well as the central characters who reconstruct their lives fully aware of the perils involved.[1] This was the first theatrical film that

Blake Edwards: Film Director as Multitalented Auteur, First Edition.
William Luhr and Peter Lehman.
© 2023 John Wiley & Sons Ltd. Published 2023 by John Wiley & Sons Ltd.

Edwards directed in the wake of the deeply distressing production problems that he encountered while making *Wild Rovers* (1971) and *The Carey Treatment* (1972), problems so personally erosive that they eventually led him to leave the United States and move to England. After a career making films in Hollywood with Hollywood production people, he made *The Tamarind Seed* in England using a mostly English production crew and cast. The film differs substantially in style and content from his earlier work and is from that perspective a declaration of independence, a move in new directions. Most obviously, it is not a comedy but a "serious" drama dealing with international espionage during the Cold War, a genre new to Edwards.

Edwards had previously made bold generic shifts in his career. By the early 1960s he had gained a reputation as a skilled director of Technicolor widescreen comedies, but following the comedies (which differ considerably among themselves) *Operation Petticoat* (1959), *High Time* (1960), and *Breakfast at Tiffany's* (1961), he shifted gears and made two black-and-white films in the 1.78:1 and 1.85:1 aspect ratio, *Experiment in Terror* (1962) and *Days of Wine and Roses* (1962). After receiving critical accolades for them, he shifted again to make the first two Inspector Clouseau comedies, *The Pink Panther* (1963) and *A Shot in the Dark* (1964), as well as the slapstick *The Great Race* (1965) and *What Did You Do in the War, Daddy?* (1966). In the late 1960s when the box-office returns for his films continued to falter with *Gunn* (1967), *The Party* (1968), and *Darling Lili* (1970), he moved on to the films cited above whose production problems led to his leaving Hollywood.

The Tamarind Seed is an international espionage thriller that does not echo the genre films and television shows on which Edwards had previously worked. Although it appeared in the wake of the enormous popularity of the James Bond films and featured credits by Maurice Binder and a musical score by John Barry, both of whom had worked on the Bond series, it does not focus on casual seduction, hi-tech gadgets, or pyrotechnical hand-to-hand fights. It does, however, show the influence of the work of Alfred Hitchcock and, unusual for Edwards, even contains a scene from one of Hitchcock's films, one that involves international intrigue and murder. At one point, we see the British agent, George MacLeod (Bryan Marshall), engrossed in watching a scene from Hitchcock's *Foreign Correspondent* (1940) on television. Intriguingly, and echoing Hitchcock's career-long interest in voyeurism, MacLeod finds this televised scene more compelling than the seduction gestures made by the woman who enters his room, sits on his bed, and presents her back to him so that he can unzip her dress, which he does while barely removing his eyes from the movie on the television. She then goes into the bathroom, finishes undressing, and climbs into bed with him. However, when she does, she is annoyed at his inattention and sharply tells him to turn the television off, which he reluctantly does. This unusual scene emphasizes the manner in which the central male characters are constantly engaged in watching and scrutinizing others, at times even at the expense of interacting with them within social norms.

Edwards and Andrews had first worked together on *Darling Lili* (1970), a film which had also encountered Hollywood production difficulties. *The Tamarind Seed*, made in England, was their first theatrical film made after their 1969 marriage and, over the next three decades, they would go on to make a number of theatrical films, a television documentary, several television specials, and a television series together. Here, she neither sings nor plays a popular stage performer as she had in many of her earlier films, including *Darling Lili*. Interestingly, *The Tamarind Seed* appeared around the time of two Andrews television specials that Edwards also directed, *Julie and Dick at Covent Garden* (1974) and *Julie: My Favorite Things* (1975). Andrews performed versions of her musical persona in each of these specials, which foregrounded her career as a popular performer.

The Tamarind Seed is manifestly a "serious" film, neither a musical nor a comedy. It does not have a single comic scene, verbal or physical. Although a great deal of it deals in wit, it is not the kind of wit calculated to induce laughter, rather the kind of verbal ripostes that underscore dialectical oppositions in discourse. The film tells the story of a romance between Judith Farrow (Julie Andrews), an assistant to a British minister in the Home Office, and Feodor Sverdlov (Omar Sharif), a Soviet attaché to Soviet General Golitsyn (Oskar Homolka) in Paris. The British suspect that Sverdlov is trying to recruit Farrow as a spy, and in fact Sverdlov tells Golitsyn that is his goal, although he also appears to be planning to defect. Much of the relationship between Farrow and Sverdlov underscores the differences in their backgrounds. They meet while on vacation in Barbados, which is neutral territory. Although both work in governmental positions, he was raised in communist Russia and she in capitalist England. Her background orientation includes optimism about the future and respect for religious traditions whereas his is materialistic, atheistic, and focused primarily on the present. In response to one of his comments she says, "God forbid," to which he instantly retorts, "How can he if he doesn't exist?" It produces a smile as the kind of wit that emphasizes a point in a debate. On the day before they plan to visit the plantation in which the legend of the tamarind tree originated and where Farrow hopes to find verification for her world view in locating a seed from that tree, he says, "What will you say if we don't find it?" to which she retorts, "What will you say if we do?"

The legend of the tamarind tree, the sacred tree of the Bambara traditions, involves the story of a slave from the colonial era who was unjustly hanged but whose spirit survives and is embodied in the seed of that tree, which resembles the man's head. Farrow finds sustenance in that story while Sverdlov mocks it as an unrealistic fairy tale. He declares that he is Russian and that Russians invented fairy tales. At first, he gently mocks her as an innocent sentimentalist who believes in innocent slaves and tamarind trees. She asks if that is wrong and, revealing another of his cultural prejudices, he replies, no, not in a woman. Later, he forcefully declares that the truth is that there is no tamarind tree, no innocent slave, no force outside this world that gives justice to the weak; that there are no standards, only expediencies, and the political winds are always changing. He says that ideology is like a weathervane, constantly spinning, and that survival is the only value. She replies that his perspective is just selfishness. However, in apparent contradiction to his surface posturing, he later locates a tamarind seed and gives it to Farrow as a gift, implying that miracles do happen. He does this as she is leaving Barbados to return to England and, as she departs, he returns to his hotel to watch her drive off. The camera shows him turn his head into profile, a movement which becomes a major motif. His gesture of giving her the tamarind seed underscores his ability to adapt and to change. He has not only demonstrated his respect for her point of view but, on a deeper level, is also in the process of contemplating coming over to her side and defecting to the West.

Farrow's and Sverdlov's relationship develops amid an environment of bold oppositions, many of which are explicitly raised in the dialogue as well as the visuals – reflecting world politics, gender differences, national and ideological differences, and complex and at times contradictory human interactions and behavior. They talk of their different perspectives on life since not only is he Russian and she English, but also each uses those differences at times to characterize the other. He quickly declares his desire to sleep with her and she as quickly tells him that she is not interested in having an affair. The motif of a car in a red saturated image driving off a cliff and hurtling downward establishes her grief over the loss of her husband as the underlying reason for her hesitancy to get involved with Sverdlov; it is personal and not about political ideology (Figure 10.1). Although she refuses his initial seduction attempts, they continue to talk, hence leaving open the possibility of an affair.

They discuss and reveal gender differences ("That is just like a woman") as well as differences between her capitalist world and his socialist one. Many of their discussions have a strong, witty, dialectical component. That structure appears in the many back-and-forth ripostes between them, about

FIGURE 10.1   *The Tamarind Seed*, © 1974 AVCO Embassy Pictures.

East versus West, seduction, religion, British optimism versus Russian materialism and cynicism, fairy tales, and capitalism versus socialism.

As they come to know one another, Sverdlov summarizes his sense of their dynamics. He tells Farrow that she came to Barbados running away from a bad love affair whereas he came there because he has nothing to run away from, saying that, although he has a good career, a successful young wife who is a famous medical specialist, and he is part of a rising socialist world, he is not happy. He doesn't love his wife and doesn't love the Soviet Union; the only thing that he wants to do is to spend time with Farrow.

Farrow wants to visit the Harwood plantation to validate the legend of the tamarind seed to him. Sverdlov says, "I am Russian. We invented fairy tales, like the existence of God." But he also says, "It's a good sign that we can have many dialectical arguments and can co-exist." Farrow replies that perhaps it's because they are on neutral territory. A revealing moment comes when Farrow tells Sverdlov that her previous lover, Richard Paterson (David Baron), was dull, that he seldom laughed. Sverdlov tells her that laughter is a serious business. This also applies to the wit in this film. Their discussions often touch on moral issues, as when Farrow tells Sverdlov that he knows when he has done something wrong. He replies that he knows when he has made a mistake, but that that's not the same thing.

Sir Lew Grade's ITC (Incorporated Television Company) produced *The Tamarind Seed* along with Blake Edwards's Jewel Productions. Although Edwards had frequently re-employed both actors and production personnel in his earlier films, forming at times his own informal "stock company," here, with few exceptions, he did not use either actors or production personnel with whom he had long been associated. The film also contains no references to Hollywood or even to the United States, and no scenes are set there. The music is not composed by Edwards's long-time collaborator, Henry Mancini, but by the prominent English composer John Barry, famous for the James Bond theme. The only major production person from Edwards's earlier work is the producer Ken Wales, who worked for the Blake Edwards company. Aside from Julie Andrews, the only featured actor returning from Edwards's earlier films is Dan O'Herlihy, who had played the sinister hospital head in *The Carey Treatment.*

The credits for *The Tamarind Seed*, designed by Maurice Binder, are like a silent film overture to this sound film full of conversations and dialogue that will follow. As such, the sequence points to the manner in which the visual style and motifs will supply the film's complexity around dialogue, which is frequently extremely simplified, with big issues reduced to one sentence. The dialogue is a direct statement embedded in a rich visual tapestry. The credit sequence is similar to an orchestral overture that introduces the musical motifs that will be developed in the following work; here, it is the visual motifs that are introduced and will be developed.

The sequence focuses almost exclusively on images of the film's stars, Julie Andrews and Omar Sharif, and is highly stylized, with slow, moody orchestral music playing throughout, giving a dreamlike sense to the images. The sequence opens with a rich blue tint as we see "A Blake Edwards Film" over a big close-up of an eye (Figure 10.2). The camera pulls slowly back, showing Andrews's face with her name appearing on the screen. The screen

FIGURE 10.2 *The Tamarind Seed*, © 1974 AVCO Embassy Pictures.

then splits, with the left half showing Sharif's face through a red tint against a black background (Figure 10.3). Where Andrews's face remains looking at the viewer, Sharif's turns to look in her direction as his name appears and Andrews's image fades (Figure 10.4). As mentioned above, this pattern of Sharif's head turning into profile will recur throughout the film. Sharif's head then blends into a shot of a deep red sunset and the film's title appears. We then see full-body silhouettes of Andrews and Sharif against a red backdrop. They move, fugue-like, past one another, sometimes scrutinizing the other as they move in different directions (Figure 10.5). Next, we see a close, rear-angle shot of Andrews over a shot of a falling car bursting into flames. We later learn that the image is a recurring nightmare of her husband's death in an auto accident. She at first looks right and then left, with flames and smoke in the background. The smoke blends into cigarette smoke from Sharif, who is looking at the camera as it moves in for a big close-up of him. This is followed by a deep red image of full-bodied silhouettes of both of them working at their desks, in separate abstract spaces. The camera then moves in on her and, in the same frame, we see a second silhouette of her walking toward the viewer. As she approaches the camera, the Sharif silhouette disappears as additional credits appear and then Sharif's silhouette emerges from behind her, coming in the same direction. As he approaches the camera, she moves off to the right and Sharif turns to look in her direction. Over a tinted rich red image, we then see the credit "Directed by Blake Edwards," first in the deep red tint which then fades into a shot of waves gently rolling in on a beach. The camera remains on the waves as the red tint disappears and we see naturalistic lighting. The camera then tilts up for a

FIGURE 10.3   *The Tamarind Seed,* © 1974 AVCO Embassy Pictures.

FIGURE 10.4 *The Tamarind Seed*, © 1974 AVCO Embassy Pictures.

FIGURE 10.5 *The Tamarind Seed*, © 1974 AVCO Embassy Pictures.

long shot showing Andrews in the far distance walking along the Barbados coastline toward the camera. The same music continues and, after two dissolves, she is close to the camera, still with a pensive, troubled look on her face. We then see again the image in red of the car hurtling over the cliff and bursting into flames.

The intense stylization of the credit sequence and its focus on interiority establishes central dynamics of the film. Most obviously it shows the two central characters in deep contemplation – they do not interact and seem immersed in serious and at times troubling reflection. They are each aware that they are facing fundamentally transitional points in their lives. We see no other characters, reinforcing the centrality of these two characters to the film. Clearly, this will not be a comedy.

In addition to the red versus blue opposition, the credit sequence sets up significant formal reference points that will be developed throughout the film – the emphasis on the eye and looking from the opening shot, the car in flames, the interiority of characters in contemplation, and the turning of their heads into profiles.

All of this is developed within multiple contexts. The largest one is historical. The film is not only set amid the political tensions of the Cold War, but it also references the larger convulsions of "History" itself. The highest-ranking Russian figure is General Golitsyn. When we see him in his office, we not only see a bust of Lenin as well as pictures of Lenin on the walls, indicating the Soviet era, but he also repeatedly stands before a huge tapestry representing a centuries-old cavalry battle – a brutal partisan conflict from a very different historical era that evokes the ongoing convulsions that have happened in diverse contexts throughout history.

Other contexts within which Edwards develops the central relationship between Farrow and Sverdlov are the binaries of Russia versus England, of capitalism versus communism, of private versus public life, and of male versus female. The boundaries of these binaries at first seem obvious and firm but, as the film proceeds, we see them become porous and fluid and eventually break down.

The first image we see of Farrow is of her eye in a blue-tinted image; the first image of Sverdlov is in a red-tinted image. The pattern is evident – blue versus red – she is "true blue" British, and he is a "red" Russian Communist. This opposition pervades the film, both in large-scale ways and in relatively small details, such as the fact that Fergus Stephenson (Dan O'Herlihy) generally wears a blue tie. When Sverdlov defects he first flies to Barbados, where he will turn the "Blue File," the documentation of Stephenson's betrayals, over to Jack Loder (Anthony Quayle) and hence secure his safety. In the first plane he takes the seats are all red, but, when he changes planes for the final lap of his trip, the seats are all blue. He is now in the British zone. However, as the film proceeds, the fixity of such oppositions becomes less certain and there is considerable crisscrossing and blending among them. Stephenson, who is secretly spying for the Russians, has the code name of "Blue," so even the "blue" character is simultaneously "red."

Following the credits, the film returns to Farrow on the beach, followed by two flashbacks from her point of view, both in sepia tone. In the initial flashback we hear the first dialogue in the film in which she requests an early vacation from her boss. In the second, we see her ending her affair with her married lover, the Air Attaché Richard Paterson. The film then switches to naturalistic color and we see Paterson and his wife Rachel (Celia Banner-man) preparing to attend a diplomatic party. Paterson goes into a different room and tries unsuccessfully to telephone Farrow. Rachel, while looking into a mirror and contemplating her pregnant abdomen, notices a tab on the phone light up, indicating that another line is in use. When she goes to check it, the light goes off. Her husband has tried unsuccessfully to call Farrow. At the end of this sequence, we see Farrow in her Barbados hotel room finishing a shower and walking onto her balcony in her robe, followed by a shot of Sverdlov standing on the ground outside and quietly looking up toward her, implying that, even though he will meet her for the first time on the follow-ing day, he has been following her for some time and hoping to engage her in his eventual plan to defect or perhaps to recruit her (Figure 10.6). It is not 100 percent clear at this point in the film. The main narrative has begun.

The car crash introduces the specter of devastating burn damage. When Sverdlov later approaches Farrow, she is lounging in the shade of a tree outside of her Barbados hotel. He warns her against sitting under that tree during rain because it can burn her skin. This friendly warning presages the time when, near the close of the film, the hotel suite that she shares with Sverdlov is firebombed and when, later, we see her convalescing in a sani-tarium after having suffered severe burns. The attack on the hotel is abrupt and brutal – making it appear as if no one could have possibly survived it. A minute earlier we saw the hotel sitting peacefully on a beautiful Barbados beach and the next minute we see all in flames. We also see the attackers quickly shot down by undercover British agents disguised as hotel employees. The presence of the agents as well as their ability to respond instantly and

FIGURE 10.6   *The Tamarind Seed*, © 1974 AVCO Embassy Pictures.

effectively indicates that the possibility of such an attack had been present all along while being invisible to casual observers. And then, as we see the devastating aftermath and Farrow rushed into an ambulance, we hear a radio news report describe the event, declaring that Sverdlov had been killed and Farrow severely injured, as the probable result of an electrical fire. Nothing is mentioned of the attack that we have just seen, so the cover-up, the almost instantaneous twisting of the events that we have just witnessed into a cover story useful to the British services, has begun. At the end, Farrow is shocked to learn that Sverdlov in fact survived the attack and the last shots of the film show her reuniting with him in Canada. She learns of Sverdlov's miraculous survival when Loder, the head of British Security, visits her and hands her an envelope from Sverdlov containing a tamarind seed, which the film has developed as a miraculous symbol.

And in fact Sverdlov escapes his government's hold on him by defecting to England, and he and Farrow seem poised to have a strong relationship in the neutral space of Canada. Hence, in the environment of omnipresent, oppressive surveillance conveying the sense of any possibility of privacy or a secure personal life being choked off by authoritarian forces, the film ends with an almost miraculous sense of escaping that surveillance, a happy ending. This is also signaled by a change in the color palate. Much of the film, as introduced in the credit sequence, has existed between the poles of red and blue, of Russia and England. Its closing, however, is set in the rich green hills of Canada, and green, with its traditional associations of hope, growth, and renewal, has largely been absent from the palate of the rest of the film.

The film establishes a pattern of the apparently calm surfaces of life covering over the possibility of unexpected and deadly violence that lurks just beneath. The threat of such disruptions also underscores apparently benign scenes of social interactions. Near the film's end we see the family of Fergus Stephenson gathered together for a holiday dinner. Except for Margaret, his wife (Sylvia Syms), they are unaware that he has been systematically subverting both his country and his marriage. At that moment he has placed events in motion that will result in the deaths of many characters, but he is unaware that, at the same time, events are also in motion that will result in his death. Earlier in the film, Margaret drops his cigarette lighter on a desktop and inadvertently discovers that it contains a recording device. When he returns home, she screams at him, "What else? What else am I going to learn about you?" She had already known that he is a closeted homosexual but had colluded in their public image of a successful marriage because she enjoys the lifestyle that his prestige has afforded them. But it had never occurred to her that he could also be spying for the Russians. The placid, socially success-ful face of their marriage covers a rat's nest of systematic and perilous decep-tion underneath.

Stephenson is a particularly intriguing character in that he systemati-cally causes destruction in both his private and public life while being, at the same time, from his point of view, perhaps the most politically altruistic character in the film. He is a high British official who has long been subvert-ing his own government by spying for the Russian government without rec-ompense because of what he considers altruistic motives, his devotion to communist social ideals. He is also a closeted homosexual masquerading as a happily married man.

Near the close of the film, Stephenson thinks that his subversive political actions have been successful and feels a level of security, unaware that he has been discovered and will soon be killed. The trajectory of his actions is the opposite of that of Sverdlov. Throughout the film, Sverdlov feels that things are closing in on him and that, as has just happened with his secretary, Igor Kalinin (Alexei Jawdokimov), he might be found out and sent back to Russia to be imprisoned or killed. In addition, he learns of another indication of his political disfavor, the fact that his wife has filed for divorce. Then, almost miraculously, he finds a way out. At the film's end, his own government thinks he has been killed on Barbados while in fact the British government has relocated him to a safe and secret haven in Canada. All of this occurs in an environment of intense surveillance, one that makes it seem to the viewer as if any independent activity is virtually impossible. The watchers are them-selves being watched and reported upon. Government officials, from Ste-phenson to Jack Loder, the head of British Intelligence, to General Golitsyn, the head of Russian Intelligence, are constantly poring over reports about the private and public activities of virtually everyone.

From the very beginning of Sverdlov's and Farrow's romantic relation-ship, the film's images indicate a developing personal relationship, but the soundtrack gives us an entirely different and troubling perspective. We hear various government officials discussing their private activities in great detail – what they are doing, where they have traveled together, how they are getting along, whether or not they have slept together. The surveillance is invisible and omnipresent and there seems to be no escaping it. The personal and the political are inextricable. Immediately after we see Sverdlov hand Farrow the tamarind seed, we see a scene of Stephenson and Paterson on a golf course. Stephenson informs Paterson that he is aware of his affair with Farrow and that Farrow has now become a security risk because of her relationship with Sverdlov. He tells Paterson that, if he doesn't end his relationship with

Farrow, he will be recalled. Paterson tells him that he and Farrow ended their relationship three weeks ago. Stephenson is pleased and mutters platitudes about disliking this aspect of their jobs. And this comes soon before his own wife discovers that he has been betraying his government in a much more extensive way by spying for the Russians.

In an apparently peaceful scene in Barbados, Farrow and Sverdlov leave their hotel for a sightseeing visit to a local plantation. But after the hotel concierge escorts them to their car, he immediately telephones to report on their activities – where they are going, how they are getting along, what activities they have been having, and whether or not he thinks they have slept together. We hear his report in voice-over as he returns to the hotel, as we see images conveying a sense of a casual day of recreation, but the words in voice-over make it all ominous and oppressively controlling (Figure 10.7).

Such a concern with oppressive and invisible surveillance has been evident in Edwards's work at least since *Experiment in Terror* over a decade earlier. In that film, the villain terrorizes the central character using the telephone and learns great amounts of detail about her daily activities by means of different forms of observation. At the same time, he is largely unaware that the FBI has begun surveilling him, and that that surveillance will eventually lead to his death. The generic presence of surveillance is also evident in Edwards's long association with detective stories, from the radio series, *Richard Diamond, Private Detective*, to his many television detective shows and series, most notably *Peter Gunn*.

When Loder at a diplomatic reception first hears that Sverdlov is vacationing in Barbados, he blurts out, "Barbados!" He feels that the Russians

FIGURE 10.7   *The Tamarind Seed*, © 1974 AVCO Embassy Pictures.

tend to stay close to home for their vacations and not venture to distant places like Barbados. The relative neutrality of the island does not fit with his oppositional sense of the world and triggers his suspicions.

In a brutally ironic comment on all of this, in one scene, Loder grimly confides to his superior that he has learned three things from life: "No one is to be trusted, nothing is to be believed, and anyone is capable of doing anything." And yet, in one of the film's many echoing ironies, the superior to whom he confides this is Stephenson, who at that moment is in fact betraying both Loder and his own government.

Nearly all of the romantic and interpersonal relationships in the film are corrupted and largely doomed. Although both Loder and Golitsyn keep close track of the intimate lives of those in their sphere, neither appears to have any visible private life; they are their jobs. The private lives of the other characters all exist within a political context. Stephenson's marriage is a sham with a placid surface, comparable to his political position. In addition, his wife is having an affair with Loder's subordinate, George MacLeod. When Loder learns of the affair, he orders MacLeod to end it, which MacLeod immediately does, although he is surprised to learn that Loder had discovered it. In addition, he breaks things off with Stephenson's wife just as she discovers her husband's treason, making her feel doubly betrayed. However, Loder later instructs MacLeod to resume the affair as a way of keeping tabs on Stephenson when he learns the extent of his betrayal. Farrow's previous lover, Paterson, had been cheating on his wife while falsely promising Farrow that his marriage was ending. Sverdlov has a superficially happy marriage but he admits to Farrow that it is hollow and he feels no loyalty to it; we eventually learn that he is planning to leave both his marriage and his political job behind. At around the same time, he learns that his wife has filed for divorce, which implies that he is also in political danger. The only hints of supportive relationships are on the periphery, as with Sverdlov's former colleague Dimitri Memenov (Constantine Gregory) and his British girlfriend, Sandy Mitchell (Sharon Duce). When Dimitri learns that Sverdlov is to be arrested if he returns to Moscow, he sends Sandy to tell Judith at her London apartment to warn Sverdlov to abort his trip. Farrow travels to Paris to do so and this awareness triggers Sverdlov's final steps to defection. Hence, in this whirlpool of erosive relationships, the success of the central one seems miraculous.

Sverdlov is supremely skilled at navigating under tremendous pressure. In one sequence, he descends into the bowels of the Russian embassy to secure the "Blue File," the top secret file that reveals the identity of the top-level British official who is working for the Russians (i.e., Stephenson). This is the bargaining chip with which he will be able to secure British support for his defection and lifetime security. The basement resembles a prison, with menacing, grim corridors. He descends into it via a caged elevator that itself looks like a prison. As he goes in and out, the music underscores the tension and menace of the situation. If at any moment he is discovered, he is likely to be imprisoned and his life will be over. He extracts the file, conceals it under his jacket, maintains a serene surface demeanor, reenters the caged elevator, and ascends.

Later in the film, in an intense sequence, we see him changing planes on his route to defect. The entire sequence is dramatically edited relying solely upon visuals and music to build suspense. Harkening back to the credit sequence, it is like a short silent film, notably without dialogue in a film full of dialogue and voice-over. A Russian agent follows him. But we also see MacLeod, who works directly under Loder, following the agent. At a security checkpoint, MacLeod appears to accidentally bump into the agent and utters a word of apology as he slips a toy pistol into the agent's pocket. That word highlights the absence of all other dialogue. When the pistol triggers airport surveillance, the agent is detained by security. He quickly realizes that MacLeod has outwitted him. Here the surveillance is not invisible but effective nevertheless and, again, the watcher has found himself being watched, perilously so.

But the film has another, later intense scene with no dialogue, the fire-bombing of Farrow and Sverdlov's resort suite in Barbados which does not even have one spoken word. We see the approaching ship, the preparations for the attack, the disguised agents on the lookout, and Farrow oblivious of it all until the terrible explosion. Edwards develops the entire scene around composition (including off-screen space), editing, and music. Both of these non-dialogue scenes build an extraordinary, edge-of-your-seat excitement. Such intense action sequences, which also include the sequence of Sverdlov stealing the "Blue File," much of which is also "silent" in the midst of such a "talky" film, are reminiscent of the comic disruptions in some of his other serious films, such as the one in which a character watches an old, silent film comedy in *Experiment in Terror*. The different tones of these scenes stand in stark contrast to the constant talk about such things as capitalism and socialism, the history of the tamarind seed mythology, and the constant voice-over narrations where we hear off-screen characters talking about the characters we see.

The Tamarind Seed was to be one of the last non-comic films that Edwards would make. Nearly all of his subsequent films would either be comedies, many with shockingly dramatic scenes, or "serious" dramatic films with eruptive comic bursts in them. It is often hard to tell: Are they comedies with drama or dramas with comedy? In the next chapter, we conclude our analyses of the so-called "serious" films with *Sunset*, an extreme example of Edwards's bold genre mixes that points to the close connection in his mind between comedy and drama. Whichever you think it is, the other is usually not far behind.

NOTE

1. This pattern includes Cory in *Mister Cory* and Carey in *The Carey Treatment*. Cory escapes from the working-class, immigrant Chicago neighborhood in which he grew up. He remakes himself as a wealthy businessman and returns to Chicago. In a milder variation, Dr. Carey leaves free-spirited California of the 1970s to join a prestigious East Coast hospital in Brahmin Boston, a major cultural shift.

CHAPTER 11

Sunset (1988)

Written and Directed by Blake Edwards

Sunset appeared at a time of intense creativity in Edwards's career but also a time in which his work received little critical acclaim or box-office success. Although a rich and complex film, it is difficult to categorize since it moves in so many different generic directions. Its elasticity embodies the declaration by the movie director in *S.O.B.* (1981): "Every time I think I know where 'it's at,' it's always somewhere else." When we visited the set of *Sunset*, Lindsey Jones, the film's publicist, told us that he was frustrated because he didn't know what genre to call the film in its promotion and asked us what we thought. We didn't know either. IMDb describes the film's genre as "Crime, Mystery, Thriller, Western." And, it *does* include that genre mix and more, such as films about Hollywood and filmmaking.

The Western component of *Sunset* recalls the beginnings of Edwards's film career since his first two films as writer and producer in the late 1940s were Westerns. Furthermore, in 1971 he had returned to the genre with *Wild Rovers*. But *Sunset* is clearly not a Western in the classical sense since it is set in 1929 Los Angeles, long after the era of the Wild West had passed. It is also a film about Hollywood and the industrial dynamics and politics of filmmaking. This links it with such major Edwards's mid-career comedies as *The*

Blake Edwards: Film Director as Multitalented Auteur, First Edition.
William Luhr and Peter Lehman.
© 2023 John Wiley & Sons Ltd. Published 2023 by John Wiley & Sons Ltd.

Party and *S.O.B.* All three films include a character threatening another with what for Edwards had become a tagline for the arrogance of some of Hollywood's most powerful people: "You'll never work in this town again!"[1] Significantly, *Sunset* climaxes at the industry's very first Academy Awards dinner. But it is also a detective film with murder and mystery, linking all the way back to the beginning of Edwards's work in radio with *Richard Diamond, Private Detective* and in television with *Peter Gunn.* The manner in which *Sunset*'s two central characters become amateur detectives parallels the manner in which Doctor Carey becomes an amateur detective in *The Carey Treatment.* And we will see that it has some direct links to the detective film *Gunn.*

At the same time *Sunset* is Edwards's only film to center on identifiable historical characters, in this case Wyatt Earp (James Garner) and Tom Mix (Bruce Willis), who both lived in Los Angeles in the 1920s and who were friends, although the film presents them as roughly twenty years younger than their ages at that time. When Earp died in January of 1929, Mix served as a pallbearer at his funeral. Edwards, however, has an unusually explicit acknowledgment at the end of this film: "'*Sunset*' is not a true story, nor is it based on fact. Although some of the characters bear the names and physical characteristics of celebrities, the events, dialogue and other characters are fictitious, and no similarity to real people is intended or should be inferred." This is an extreme departure from the common claim that many historical films make that some of the characters and events in the film are added for dramatic purposes. This is an imaginary history, more extreme than the assertions of his characters who joke that their stories are real, "give or take a lie or two." As is typical of Edwards, he departs from genre norms in unusual ways, creating a strange tension between entirely fabricated scenes and events and actual historical ones. Although the first Academy Awards celebration, for example, did take place in L.A. in 1929, Edwards does not attempt to factually recreate it;[2] instead, he employs the event as a symbolic springboard for the concerns of the film.

This has some relation to his semi-autobiographical films, including "*10*" and *That's Life!*, into which he incorporated events from his own life. In *That's Life!* he pushed things to an extreme, since he shot it in his own home and used members of his own family as well as friends in the cast. Most obviously, Julie Andrews plays the wife of the central character, who is played by longtime Edwards's collaborator and friend, Jack Lemmon, and his character's behavior draws upon often unflattering personal characteristics that Edwards has discussed publicly. He is clearly not trying to present a glorified version of himself. But even though the film draws upon numerous aspects of his life, it is not in a traditional sense an autobiographical film. Furthermore, it is not unusual for creative artists to draw upon events in their lives in their works. But this is very different from the employment of widely identifiable historical events and characters in a work. Traditionally, since such a work deals with the public record, the creator feels some obligation to the historical "truth," even though it is often merely window dressing, since the audience is likely to have its own sense of that "truth." But Edwards approaches this in an entirely different and original way.

Sunset also draws upon Edwards's own past in yet another way, since he was born in 1922 and spent most of his youth in Los Angeles around the film industry. His stepfather, Jack McEdward, was active in Hollywood as an assistant director among other roles and his step-grandfather, J. Gordon Edwards, was a successful director of big-budget films at the Fox Film Corporation, particularly of grand historical epics like *Cleopatra* (1917) and *The Queen of Sheba* (1921).

Since *Sunset* is set at the end of the silent era when the movie industry was destabilized by the imminent transition to sound, the casting is revealing. Both Garner and Willis had dealt with industry convulsions of a different sort following the rise of television in the 1950s. Each had gained fame as television actors – Garner in the 1950s and 1960s and Willis in the 1980s – and made the difficult transition to films. On the set of the film, Willis told us about his gratitude to Edwards for taking the perilous gamble of casting him in this film, defying strong industry prejudices holding that television actors were unlikely to be able to successfully transition to films.

For Edwards, casting Willis was a major compromise. He told us he had originally written the script with Robert Duvall, born in 1931, in mind for playing Tom Mix. James Garner was born in 1928. In the original screenplay, Mix and Earp would have essentially been the same age. When Edwards could not get funding, he rewrote the script to accommodate Willis, who also produced the film, which Edwards said further affected the production. But that ironically aligns *Sunset* with *Mister Cory*, Edwards's first drama, and with *Wild Rovers*, his mid-period dramatic Western. All three films deal centrally with male bonding between an older and a younger man and in all three the young men are played by attractive leading men: Tony Curtis, Ryan O'Neal, and Bruce Willis, respectively. The older characters were played by leading men from earlier eras, namely, Charles Bickford, William Holden, and James Garner. All three films mark the relationships as between a young man and a father figure and all three mark the young men as strikingly heterosexual, although the films center strongly on the male bonding. Like *Sunset* they relegate their romantic and sexual relationships to the margins, something which the endings foreground and to which we will return.

Then, what is *Sunset*? An unusual Western? A detective murder mystery, a dark imaginary history? A reflection on changing times, on ways in which actual events, people, and filmmaking patterns are continually recast and distorted by publicity and changing cultural imperatives, on changing modes of masculinity and femininity, on the fluidity of identity, on the continuity of corruption at the centers of wealth and power?

What are we to make of this almost bewildering array of "hooks" for this film? One clue comes from an insight we received nearly twenty years later during the production of Edwards's Broadway musical, *Victor/Victoria*. Tony Roberts, one of the lead actors, was concerned that the show deviated from the dominant model for Broadway plays. He compared that model to a railroad train steadily crossing the stage, with the audience seeing only one of its cars at a time. When that car moved on, the audience would see a new railroad car (or the following scene), with the implicit meaning being that each scene should have a single meaning that was readily comprehensible to the audience. When we discussed this with another of the lead actors, Michael Nouri, he laughed and said that he felt that Edwards's model was not a train sequentially moving its cars in an orderly fashion across the stage but, rather, a train wreck, with multiple components impacting simultaneously. This description has analogies with the many generic associations that *Sunset* evokes and with the structure of individual scenes, as we demonstrate below with one of the most complex such scenes in his career.

Sunset opens with an immediately recognizable genre scene, a stagecoach robbery in the Old West. A lone coach riding across the prairie is attacked by half a dozen robbers who shoot both the driver and the shotgun guard. A terrified young woman is inside. A lone rider on a hilltop observes this and rides down to the rescue, shooting the robbers and rescuing the damsel in distress. However, when she throws her arms around him in gratitude, we see something discordant for the genre in this era. His hand slides down her back and begins to caress her buttocks. This is followed by something even more disorienting. Someone shouts "Cut!" and the camera pulls back to show that all of this is part of a movie being made, not a nineteenth-century action scene but rather a twentieth-century entertainment. Hence, we have begun thinking that we are immersed in one kind of generic reality, only to find something discordant in it, and then we see the entire "reality" reframed into something utterly different. This jostling of our perceptions occurs repeatedly in the film and is a cue to what it is about.

Such abrupt perceptual reorientations appear repeatedly in Edwards's work. A signal instance occurs in his 1982 film, *Victor/Victoria*, when, as the climax to her stage act, Victoria dramatically removes her wig to reveal herself as not a woman but rather as a male performer. The audience is stunned. This is doubly intriguing since, for the audience within the film, it shows the performer as not a woman but a man. The viewing audience knows all along that Victoria is a woman enacting multiple gender masquerades.

The overall structure of *Sunset* follows the historical Wyatt Earp arriving at a Hollywood movie studio in 1929 to serve as technical advisor for a film about his life, which is to be called *Lawman* and feature the popular star Tom Mix. Earp finds himself engulfed in studio politics and briefly reunites with a former lover who is now married to the studio head. His dealings with the studio head lead to the exposure of a complex mix of tyranny, perversion, and murder.

When Mix first learns of the project, he is resistant, saying that up to this point he has only played fictional characters suited to his screen image. However, after being pressured by the producer, he agrees. When he meets Earp, the two intuitively bond, and share an understanding of the world of publicity and hype. Soon after this, Earp, uncomfortable with the media frenzy at the hotel in which the studio plans to house him, asks Mix to take him to someplace more comfortable. Mix drives him to the modest bungalow colony in which he lived when he first came to town. When Earp asks if he can get him in, Mix tells him that he owns the place, saying, "Mi casa, su casa." Earp asks if he learned Spanish when he was fighting with the Rough Riders in Cuba. Mix asks where he learned that about him and Earp replies that he read about it in a rotogravure magazine article. Mix is silent. Then Earp asks about Mix's participation in the Boer War, something that he read about in *Liberty* Magazine. Mix asks if any photographs accompanied the article and Earp replies, no, just drawings and engravings. Mix muses, "Engravings, that's the way they make funny money, isn't it?" He knows the stories are false but accepts such hyperbole as part of his image. Earp, whose popular image has undergone similar exaggerations and reformulations, quickly understands.

A central trope is the fluid stability and constant reframing of the significance of what we see. Soon after this, Earp watches as Mix portrays him in a filmed recreation of the O.K. Corral gunfight, while simultaneously, in slow motion, recalling his own quite different participation in the actual event nearly half a century earlier. Afterward, Mix asks if that was the way it really was and Earp replies, "Absolutely..., well, give or take a lie or two." This tagline is used throughout the film and the closing credits declare: "And that's the way it really happened ... Give or take a lie or two." It applies to minor situations as well as to central ones. Earp later watches Mix filming a barroom brawl, after which Mix asks him how he liked it. Earp replies that it was thrilling, but that he'd never been in a fight like that in all his life. Mix tells him, "Yeah, and I'll bet Buffalo Bill didn't kill all them Injuns either." Earp replies, "Well, you'd win your bet. Buffalo Bill Cody was a good man but he wasn't nearly as good as his publicity." Mix, referring to himself, says, "Sounds like a movie star cowboy I know."

Both men are comfortable with the world of fluid appearances that surrounds them. Parallel with these diverse variations on popular images is the impaction of radically different but adjacent worlds upon one another. This can come from actual events, like the fact that Earp recognizes one of the patrons of The Candy Store as Dutch Kieffer (Joe Dallesandro), a Chicago gangster who initially seems out of place, since Hollywood and Prohibition-era Chicago seem like entirely different worlds. Cheryl King (Mariel Hemingway), who works at The Candy Store, a popular brothel which is run by her mother, Candace Girard, is surprised that he even knows about the 1920s Chicago underworld and Earp simply tells her, "East or west, a crook is a crook." Kieffer accompanies Victoria Alperin (Jennifer Edwards), the sister of the studio head, Alfie Alperin (Malcolm McDowell). Cheryl tells Earp that Victoria is a lesbian and that Kieffer is a voyeur who enjoys watching her sexual activities. Cheryl has relatively short hair arranged in what was for the time a masculine cut and wears a tuxedo, implying that, like Victoria, she also is a lesbian. However, she tells Earp that her mother orchestrated the illusion in order that Cheryl would not have to "entertain" the heterosexual clients. And soon, when she is traumatized by her mother's murder, she asks Earp to sleep with her, and they maintain a relationship for the remainder of the film. At the outset of their relationship, the issue of Earp's age comes up, as it does repeatedly in the film in different contexts. He tells her that he is old enough to be her father and, unperturbed, she smiles and replies that he is old enough to be her grandfather.

We also see the impaction of different genres within the film world. As Earp and Mix walk back to Mix's dressing room after the barroom brawl scene, they pass two adjacent studio stages on which different films are being shot, films that evoke radically different genres and perspectives on reality. The first is a lavish "Cleopatra"-type historical epic and the second is a frenzied Keystone Kops-type custard pie-throwing scene. The two men simply chuckle at them.

In these instances, the pattern of reframing actuality is relatively minor and quickly understandable, but its significance expands when both Earp and Mix go to The Candy Store, in which the prostitutes are made up and dressed to look like doubles for famous actresses like Greta Garbo, Pola Negri, the Gish sisters, Janet Gaynor, and Mae West. The Candy Store has important parallels with The Ark, the floating brothel in *Gunn*. When they enter, we see Mix and Earp walking toward us (Figure 11.1) when suddenly a mirror slides away, instantly reorienting us to the fact that we have been seeing their mirror image. To compound this shock, a woman dressed as a man walks through the opened mirror door into their space (Figure 11.2). Both the mirror image and the woman dressed as a man show that everyone has more than one fixed identity, linking to mirror images and identity in *Gunn*. And the prostitutes looking like famous movie stars also recall the prostitutes in The Ark, all of whom appear to be twins. In The Candy Store the prostitutes' real identities are hidden behind those of the celebrities they impersonate and in The Ark we see each prostitute doubled in her twin.

FIGURE 11.1   *Sunset*, © 1988 Tri-Star Pictures.

FIGURE 11.2   *Sunset*, © 1988 Tri-Star Pictures.

In each of these cases, the doubling is not intended to deceive since it is obvious to everyone that the disguises are closer to riffs on the initial image than genuine disguises. Both the observer and the impersonator are aware of this. This makes the act of impersonation very different from, for example, the way in which the villain in _Experiment in Terror_, Red Lynch, disguises himself as an old woman to deceive and intimidate the central character. Lynch uses the disguise to lie and threaten, not to riff, and he certainly doesn't use it to playfully engage the central character who, at first, is entirely unaware of the deception.

Much of the appeal of The Candy Store lies in the attraction for clients of having sex with a copy of a famous star and this is complexly related to Mix playing a movie version of Earp, while Earp watches. Later in the film, when Earp is threatened by both Dutch Kieffer and the armed L.A.P.D. Captain Blackworth (Richard Bradford), Mix suddenly turns up pointing what appears to be a double-barreled shotgun at them. Blackworth reluctantly drops his pistol and, as Earp, Mix, and Cheryl back away, Mix smugly says, "In an actor's world, things are seldom what they seem. A pauper is a prince, or a shotgun is a mop." What had appeared to be a shotgun is in fact a mop handle and he drops it to the floor, but the illusion had its desired effect. In addition, when Captain Blackworth later confronts Earp at Candace Girard's funeral, Earp menacingly challenges him to draw his gun. When Blackworth warns him that his men will cut him to ribbons, Earp replies, "Not before I shoot out your eyes." Blackworth backs down. Immediately after, Cheryl asks if Earp would have killed him and Earp replies, "No." When Cheryl asks why, Earp replies that he is not packing a gun. So, like Mix's bluff with a mop handle, Earp has also backed down the sinister Blackworth by creating an illusion.

Toward the end of the film, Mix learns that Dutch Kieffer's henchmen are planning to kidnap his girlfriend, Nancy Shoemaker (Kathleen Quinlan), who is in hiding at Tom's ranch. Mix and Earp race to her rescue, hoping to arrive before the henchmen, who are driving. Earp and Mix first take an airplane, during which Earp is terrified since it is his first airplane ride and Mix claims that he has never even piloted one, and then they continue on horseback. When Earp falls from his horse, Mix picks him up and they ride together on Mix's horse, echoing the "buddy" poster image of William Holden and Ryan O'Neal together on horseback in _Wild Rovers_. When they arrive at Mix's ranch, they confront the four gangsters. Earp and Mix, wearing Western garb, stand resolutely side by side and are photographed frontally with the prairie and skyline behind them to resemble one side of a traditional Western confrontation, whereas, in the reverse-angle shots, the gangsters are chaotically clustered around their automobile as they try to flee with Nancy. Where Earp was out of place in the plane, now Mix is concerned since he has never participated in an actual gunfight. The mix of genre cues is jarring – first a plane racing an automobile, then horseback riders on the open range, then a confrontation that, on one side, looks like an Old West gunfight but, on the other side, looks closer to a Chicago street fight with frenzied men in suits clustered around an automobile.

Although most of the film's main characters undergo significant changes in their appearance, Earp is the only one who looks the same throughout, even, curiously, in his memory of himself nearly half a century earlier in the O.K. Corral gunfight. In this the Earp of 1929 recalls the Earp of 1881. Other characters, however, comment frequently on his age, in some cases insultingly calling him "Grandpa," but his appearance remains resolutely unchanged. Mix assumes a variety of appearances, most in service of his flamboyant image of himself as a cowboy movie star with theatrical cowboy outfits and driving in ostentatious cars, with one sporting a huge set of antlers over its radiator. The studio head, Alfie Alperin, dresses mainly in business attire of the era except for the sequence near the end in which he dons his "Happy Hobo" character costume. We first see Cheryl dressed in a tuxedo at The Candy Store but later in more traditional female attire. Most of the supporting characters, however, maintain the same appearance, including Alfie's sister, Victoria, who generally wears 1920s-style dresses and jewelry, Captain Blackworth, who always appears in his police uniform, and the head of the studio police, Marvin Dibner (M. Emmet Walsh). The significance of all of this gets darker as we see how everyone is drawn into Alfie's malignant world.

The film's murder plot begins at The Candy Store. Early on, its Madame, Candace Girard, is brutally murdered and Alfie's drunken son, Michael (Dermot Mulroney), appears guilty, although neither Earp, Mix, nor Girard's daughter, Cheryl, believe it. They think he has been set up. Furthermore, Michael's mother is Christina Alperin (Patricia Hodge), with whom Earp had been romantically involved some years earlier. At the time of his marriage to Christina, Alfie had learned that he was not Michael's biological father. Although he had assured Christina that he accepted that fact and would raise Michael as his own, he had grown increasingly resentful of the boy over the years, triggering Michael's alcoholism and erratic behavior. Eventually, Alfie will murder Candace and implicate Michael; he will also beat Christina to death.

Michael is deeply troubled and chaotic from the outset. When we first see him, he is drunk at midday. When he is introduced to Earp, he hardly believes it is the actual Earp and swaggeringly declares, "Well, I'm Billy the

Kid!" He is also drunk on the night Candace is murdered and so disoriented that he moronically claims that he did it. When Earp and Mix try to keep him in hiding until they can solve the crime, he stupidly escapes without his pants. Only at the very end, after Alfie's death, does he seem to have stabilized.

Alfie's relationship with his sister, Victoria, is perverse and intriguing. She is blindly loyal to him even though we see little reciprocation from him. She walks with a limp but its origin is never established. Near the end, she complains to Alfie about how Mix barged into her place and wrecked it during his fight with her houseman and demands, "Well, are you going to take care of Mix, or do I have to tell Dutch?" Alfie abruptly spins her chair around and menacingly tells her, "You're not going to tell Dutch anything!" She is suddenly terrified as he grabs her legs and squeezes them painfully. He sadistically continues, "Or else you're going to have two gimpy legs, little sister." He then menacingly wraps her long pearl necklace around her neck and prepares to beat her brutally, telling her that, once he has done so, she should call the police and tell them that Mix gave her the bruises, and then raped her. Regardless of this treatment, when she and Alfie are seated together at the Academy Awards dinner near the end of the film, she is enthusiastic about the way in which the Academy honors him even though he barely responds to her. When she is dying, she tells Earp that her blind loyalty to Alfie comes from her understanding of the fact that they both are bad people and they only have one another in life. Then, in a deeply mysterious manner with perverse overtones, she utters her dying words, "Daddy, Daddy." Since her father has not been a character in the film and since we hear nothing about him, we can only imagine what it was that he did to his children to make them such "bad people." Her dying invocation of her father also directly parallels that of the younger brother in *Wild Rovers* when he ominously calls out to his dead father as he perversely mauls William Holden's body after having shot him to death.

Alfie stands at the opposite end of the spectrum from Earp and Mix. They accept distortions of actuality as a part of modern life and the attendant publicity that accompanies fame. When, for example, a studio employee disappointedly tells Wyatt Earp that he does not look like Wyatt Earp but rather like a Texas oilman, he takes it in stride. Alfie, however, is less an embodiment of the modern world of publicity than of the Victorian model of Dr. Jekyll and Mr. Hyde. He had achieved fame as a slapstick film star in the mode of Charlie Chaplin and had built upon that success to become the head of the studio. Where many see Earp in light of his frontier lawman image, many see Alfie in light of his past "Happy Hobo" image. But Alfie has long lived a double life, appearing genial and businesslike in public, while being savagely sadistic in his private life. He takes pride in his athletic prowess as a former slapstick star and continually demonstrates it with bizarre and largely unfunny little theatrical tricks, but his physicality repeatedly leads to savage outbursts, harming his wives, his sister, his chauffeur, and others. He knows the power of publicity and skillfully manipulates it. He uses his connections with the L.A.P.D. as well as the studio police to conceal his crimes. He murdered his first wife and ultimately murders Christina. He brutalizes his loyal but embittered sister and manipulates her into ugly, self-destructive situations. He also brutalizes his chauffeur, Arthur (Andreas Katsulas), holding the fact of his criminal past over him and threatening to have him sent back to Folsom Prison. Everyone near him suffers, while also systematically protecting him. Even Christina, after having been fatally beaten by Alfie, tries to cover for him. When Earp visits her in the hospital, she unconvincingly mutters, "So silly, falling over like that," implying that her fatal injuries resulted not from a beating but from a simple accident.

Sunset is set in Hollywood in 1929, a date that marks the end of the silent era as well as of the heyday of slapstick comedy, a form of comedy that would soon be marginalized in sound films but which Edwards prominently revived in A-level productions beginning with *The Pink Panther* (1963) and continuing throughout his career, with his last film being *Son of the Pink Panther* in 1993. Slapstick thrives on instantaneous changes in the meaning of what we see, often a puncturing of pretensions. An elegant, dignified person slipping on a banana peel and falling chaotically or being hit with a pie in the face is immediately transformed into a comic spectacle.[3]

The flip side of slapstick humor can be shock and horror since it revels in brutal situations. Generally, regardless of the extreme violence often experienced by Chaplin or Keaton or the Keystone Kops, they seldom REALLY get hurt. They simply brush themselves off and move on, almost like animated characters. But Andrew Sarris once observed that Edwards gets laughs from situations that are often too brutal for horror movies.

The use of slapstick in *Sunset* is minimal and strange, marking the film's departure from what critics and the public had seen as a main component defining Edwards. When Earp and Mix briefly pass the studio stage mentioned above in which a Keystone Kops-type pie-throwing scene is being shot, the comic routine is never presented for the pleasure of the film's spectators. Edwards, however, invokes a classic slapstick routine in the fight scene in Victoria's house when Mix takes on her houseman and, as they fight, they also attempt to protect a valuable, fragile vase. The gag structure is simple and brief. It begins when Mix crashes into a wall, inadvertently causing the vase to fall from a shelf above, which he somehow miraculously

FIGURE 11.3 *Sunset,* © 1988 Tri-Star Pictures.

FIGURE 11.4 *Sunset,* © 1988 Tri-Star Pictures.

catches (Figure 11.3). Edwards then tops that when Mix, instead of safely putting the vase aside before continuing to fight, tosses it to the houseman who, in a reflex response, catches it as Mix rushes at him and the fight continues (Figure 11.4). Moments after that, Edwards tops the topper when Mix punches the vase directly as the houseman holds it in front of himself (Figure 11.5). The punch shatters the vase and sends the houseman reeling backward, shattering the glass French doors through which he crashes (Figure 11.6). This appropriation of a slapstick structure does not create Edwards's usual laugh-out-loud structure for the delight of the film's spectators for several reasons. Most simply, it is very brief without the usual elaborate development of topping the topper topper. But more significantly, it is

FIGURE 11.5   *Sunset*, © 1988 Tri-Star Pictures.

FIGURE 11.6   *Sunset*, © 1988 Tri-Star Pictures.

dark from the very beginning when Victoria sadistically tells her houseman to "Hurt him. REALLY hurt him!" Such slapstick fight scenes as the barroom brawl in *Wild Rovers* are normally lighthearted exactly because they invoke the opposite slapstick response where we know that, as in cartoons, however brutal the action is, the characters will not be "hurt." No matter what side they are on, the drunken cowboys are having a good time. The lighthearted aspect of slapstick in *Sunset* is also undermined by the motif of shattering glass, which also has a three-part topping the topper structure. First, Victoria crashes through her glass coffee table (Figure 11.7), then Mix shatters the vase, and then the houseman shatters the glass doors. But again, there is nothing laugh-out-loud funny about this since the broken glass fits ominously with the "hurt him" tone of the scene. Unlike a drunken cowboy, the houseman really wants to hurt Mix badly.

FIGURE 11.7 *Sunset,* © 1988 Tri-Star Pictures.

A similar structure is at work in *Sunset*'s other main scene invoking slapstick comedy, the celebration of Alfie Alperin's "Happy Hobo" screen character at the Academy Awards dinner for the delight of the 1929 audience within the film. The film's spectators, however, know that Alfie is the center of evil who corrupts all about him: his family – he kills both his wife and ex-wife, drives his son into alcoholism, and gets his loyal sister to conceal his crimes – as well as the Los Angeles Police Department (Captain Blackworth is on his payroll), the corrupt studio police chief, Marvin Dibner, his chauffeur Arthur, and he has links with Dutch Kieffer, a Chicago mobster. All systematically cover for his crimes. He is received with enthusiastic applause when he reprises his slapstick routine at the first Academy Awards dinner, although we see the performance knowing he is literally in the midst of a murderous rage. Soon after, in the film's climactic final fight scene with Mix, he employs the very same slapstick acrobatics, not for laughs this time but in a serious and sadistic effort to murder Mix. Edwards here creates a single stunning image that shows how the usual lighthearted fun and pleasure of slapstick where no one gets hurt is replaced in *Sunset* with true horror where nearly everyone gets hurt. In *A Shot in the Dark*, for example, when Clouseau gets knocked out of a second-story window, we see a cartoon-like image of him lying flattened on the ground. Yet, the next time we see him, he is untouched by it. With the brief exception of the studio Keystone Kops-type scene, there is no such "innocent" scene of slapstick anyplace in *Sunset*.

Not only does the film contain multiple diverse impacting components, but also some of its scenes are amazingly complex, so much so that on a first viewing it can be difficult to follow their choreography. The narrative and choreographic complexity of the sequence in the lobby of the Hollywood

Roosevelt Hotel while the first Academy Awards ceremony occurs in an adjacent ballroom exemplifies this. No sooner does one event happen than another impinges on it, and then another, at times bewildering the characters and likely the audience itself.

At the Awards dinner, Alfie has just reprised his slapstick routine, with his trademark top hat and pasted-on mustache. As he holds his top hat up, the audience cheers, especially his sister Victoria. However, he sees that Earp and Mix have entered the room and knows that they are aware of his perfidy. Victoria sees this also. Alfie affectionately tells the cheering audience, "Thank you for remembering." He removes his mustache and congratulates everyone present, but then says that he must leave because "My dearest wife, Christina, is seriously ill in the hospital." Earp watches as Alfie receives a standing ovation and departs. Earp follows him and he in turn is followed by Victoria.

As Alfie walks through the lobby, Earp comes up behind him holding a pistol and saying that he is making a citizen's arrest. He shows him an eyewitness document from Candy Girard testifying to the fact that Alfie murdered his first wife. But then Victoria, also holding a pistol, comes up behind Earp and tells Alfie to flee, which he does. She orders Earp to walk up a staircase with her, reinforcing her threat by telling him that she killed Candy and now has nothing to lose. Earp tells her that she couldn't have beaten Candy so savagely but, upon reflection, concludes that she came upon Candy after Alfie had beaten her and finished her off with an icepick. She admits that she killed Candy because Candy was going to reveal how Alfie killed his first wife, and that she "loved every minute of it" (her murder of Candy). But as they approach the stairway, they encounter Captain Blackworth and Chief Dibner descending it. Blackworth, whose nose is covered with a large, ridiculous-looking bandage, the result of an earlier encounter with Earp and Mix, points his pistol at Earp. He says that he received a report from the Santa Robles police that Earp and Mix shot four men at Mix's ranch and is arresting Earp for murder. He tells Victoria to stand away from Earp and orders Dibner to take Earp's gun. Dibner is utterly confused throughout. Considering Victoria's direct threat to him, Earp eagerly agrees to the arrest, saying, "Let's go." But then Victoria points her pistol at Blackworth, saying, "No!" Blackworth, now confused, asks, "What's going on?" She says, "He can hurt Alfie and I'm not gonna let him." Blackworth tells her not to do it this way, that there are too many witnesses here, and assures her that he will "take care" of Earp. She angrily retorts that Alfie has paid him a fortune and tells him to just continue down the stairs. Dibner, hoping to intervene, walks toward her. In the heat of this intense situation, she shoots him and he tumbles down the stairs. Earlier in the scene we had seen Dibner's head swiveling from side to

FIGURE 11.8 *Sunset*, © 1988 Tri-Star Pictures.

FIGURE 11.9 *Sunset*, © 1988 Tri-Star Pictures.

side in confusion while Blackworth was forcefully focused on Victoria. Throughout the film, Dibner has been largely clueless as to what is going on in most situations (Figure 11.8) while Blackworth has been rigorously and often malignantly focused (Figures 11.9). Now, we see Blackworth's head swivel from side to side in utter confusion, resembling Dibner's, and providing an image echoing the mechanics of the entire scene.

To further complicate things, Dutch now enters the lobby and calls to Victoria, who replies, "No, Dutch, it's gone too far. Go away." And then Mix enters and Victoria yells, "You son of a b..." and shoots at Mix but hits a lamp behind him. At this point, Blackworth shoots but hits her. She falls, then Dutch shoots and hits Blackworth, who falls. Earp catches Victoria, who is dying, and Mix and Dutch look on. Earp tells Mix to take the gun from Dutch and pursue Alfie. As Mix races off, the camera moves in on the dying Victoria. When Earp asks, "Why did you kill Candy?" she, half deliriously, replies, "It hurts.... She [Candy] was going to tell about what happened on the boat [Alfie's murder of his first wife], uh, to protect Alfie. You don't understand, do you? Sometimes bad people like me and Alfie only have each other...." As she dies, ominously uttering "Daddy, Daddy," we hear applause from another room. In a high-angle shot, we see Cheryl (now in a dress) and Nancy enter the lobby.

The scene is bewildering in its complexity. Only two scenes follow, both comparatively straightforward in their structure. In the first, Alfie flees the Awards dinner and orders Arthur to drive him to his yacht in order that he can make his escape. However, he is unaware that Arthur has reached the end of his rope under his domination. At the dock, Arthur does not stop the car at Alfie's yacht as ordered but instead drives directly off the pier, presumably committing suicide and murder rather than continue under Alfie's long-term domination. But then Mix dives in and rescues Arthur, leaving Alfie to drown and, once he has done so, tells Arthur to flee and find a new life for himself.

After this, Alfie suddenly and unexpectedly emerges from the water, looking like a sea monster. He and Mix fight and, as mentioned above, at the fight's climax, Alfie employs some of the same acrobatic moves that he had used to comic effect at the Awards dinner, but this time not for humor but in a serious attempt to kill Mix. He aims a pistol directly at Mix and smiles as he sadistically waves "Bye-bye." However, at the last moment and uncharacteristically wearing a large, dramatic white scarf over his standard suit and tie, Earp suddenly appears and shoots Alfie. Earlier, after Chief Dibner had organized a failed attempt to have Mix and Earp attacked at a nightclub, Mix had berated him. Then Earp followed and simply told Dibner that, if he did anything like that again, he'd kill him. Mix jokingly told Earp that he was upset that Earp had upstaged him. Now, at the close, Mix tells him, "You know, partner, you're developing a real knack for upstaging me," and both smile.

The final scene occurs at the Pasadena railroad station as Mix sees Earp off (Figure 11.10). Earp bids farewell to Cheryl and then tells Michael, as he had told his mother years earlier, that he should contact him if he ever needs him. Once on the train, he smiles as he sees Mix riding alongside, doing equestrian tricks and waving. The scene has complex gender dynamics recalling the end of *Mister Cory*, Edwards's first drama. In classic Hollywood bookend fashion, it mirrors the earlier scene near the beginning

FIGURE 11.10 *Sunset*, © 1988 Tri-Star Pictures.

FIGURE 11.11 *Sunset*, © 1988 Tri-Star Pictures.

of the film when Mix arrived at the train station to greet Earp who is arriving (Figure 11.11). The two men quickly develop a close bond that becomes the center of the film, marginalizing their relationships with women who, however, mark them as heterosexuals. Instead of uniting a man with a woman as many films do at their conclusion, this film steeps itself in the emotional, elaborate send-off between two men. Earp's mentioning that he may be back for Cheryl echoes Tony Curtis's claim to the woman in his life at the airport at the end of *Mister Cory*. But unlike Cory, the idea that Earp would return to a woman young enough to be his granddaughter rings hollow. Even more interesting are the final shots of the film where we first see Earp alone and lost in thought as the train pulls away

FIGURE 11.12   *Sunset*, © 1988 Tri-Star Pictures.

FIGURE 11.13   *Sunset*, © 1988 Tri-Star Pictures.

(Figure 11.12). Then, unexpectedly, we suddenly see Mix appear from off-screen as he rides by (Figure 11.13), performing tricks for Earp. That moment reuniting them and the brief acknowledgment of it as their glances meet (Figures 11.14, 11.15) is the true ending at the emotional core of the film and is followed by the last shot of the train heading into the sunset, both of the film's ending and of the end of the relationship between Earp and Mix.

Sunset is the most complex genre mix in Edwards's long career of such mixes, which also accounts for why it is the strangest film he ever made and why it may be his most experimental one. This section of the book, beginning with *Mister Cory* in Chapter 3 and ending here with *Sunset* in Chapter 11,

FIGURE 11.14 *Sunset,* © 1988 Tri-Star Pictures.

FIGURE 11.15 *Sunset,* © 1988 Tri-Star Pictures.

has been organized around an exploration of genre in Edwards's oeuvre. Our primary goal has been to carefully analyze all the non-comic feature films Edwards directed (dramas and so-called "serious" films) with the hopes of shedding light on how he worked creatively and to understand the relationships between the comedies for which he is best known and these films as well as their relationship to his work in radio and television.

The "imaginary history" sub genre to which *Sunset* belongs offers a particularly profound insight. As noted earlier, when we asked Edwards on the set of a film he was directing whether he enjoyed working in radio, television, or film the most, he answered radio (although he has noted in later interviews that the answer would be different at different times). But his reason for saying radio was profound. When he created and wrote for radio, the writing was the most central component of the finished work, some sound effects and music being the only other things the listeners heard. They had to fill in everything else with their imaginations since they never saw the characters, the setting, or the action. He valued that crucial role of the listener's imagination. Jack Lemmon rightfully observed that Edwards's use of off-screen space, which we have detailed extensively, is so brilliant precisely because of what it leaves to the viewer's imagination. Edwards took his love of imagination to the fullest level in *Sunset*, freeing himself of the common claim of showing what "really" happened historically (as many films about the O.K. Corral gunfight naively claim). *Sunset* with its bewildering variety of film genres exists only in an imaginary world of film representation. What may well have attracted him to this film, which he also wrote, may precisely have been the temptation to take two legendary figures in American history who actually met and then make up everything that happens between them. This strategy celebrates the imagination over reality, even reveling in the recreation of the first Academy Awards ceremony that departs from everything that is known about that much-documented event.

The genre mix in *Sunset* carries this kind of imagination further than that in Edwards's other films by creating tones that are jarring rather than unifying. It is hard to identify what the dominant tone of this film is, and which are the disruptions. Contrast this with such dramas as *Days of Wine and Roses*, *Experiment in Terror*, and with such comedies as *S.O.B.* and *The Great Race*.[4] In *Days of Wine and Roses* and *Experiment in Terror*, the dominant tone of dark drama and noir terror are disrupted by abrupt scenes of slapstick comedy (in the former, by Jack Lemmon's character drunkenly walking into a large picture window and abruptly becoming shocked and horrified and, soon after, an elevator door closing behind him and chopping the blooms off the flowers he holds; and in the latter, a jarring cut to a slapstick silent film comedy filling the entire screen before the film cuts back to reveal a minor character watching that film). In *S.O.B.*, which is a comedy, the situation is reversed when laughter is shockingly replaced with the slow-motion shooting death of the film's main character. *The Great Race* is of special interest here because, like *Sunset*, it contains a wide variety of genres but there is a profound strategic difference between the films. In that comedy the main characters compete in an automobile race around the world which Edwards represents as them racing from one genre into another. When they race into the American frontier town of Boracho, for example, the film turns into a Western, with barroom brawls and lynch mobs, but when they later arrive at the mythical European kingdom of Carpania, the film becomes a

Prisoner of Zenda parody, a Ruritanian romance with swashbuckling duelists, castles, and a wacky crown prince. Although the film is modernist in its foregrounding of its construction and in never claiming to represent reality, it is not jarring, shocking, or even confusing because it has a unified comic narrative about this ridiculous car race.[5]

Sunset, however, is experimental in how it jars, confuses, and bewilders spectators who never have a unified genre position in the film. There is no connective thread. It does not move the spectator through multiple physical locations. Instead, set in Hollywood, it evokes multiple cinematic worlds, starting at the very beginning when it appears to be showing us a Wild West scene but almost immediately reframes that and transitions into a scene about 1920s filmmaking, and then continues the abrupt reframing process throughout the film. Just when we think we have some grasp of all the various genre tones in the film, other ones appear. Earp and Mix seem to be part of a film about Hollywood studio politics, then in an ugly domestic melodrama and murder mystery, then suddenly an action-adventure film with an airplane racing a car only to then appear in a Western gunfight, and on and on.

One aspect of *Sunset* bears comparison to *The Party*, which opens with a scene from what appears to be a *Gunga Din*-type historical action-adventure film. Then we suddenly hear "Cut!" and Edwards cuts to reveal a film set and we now know we have been watching a film being made. But unlike *Sunset*, we are then anchored in a slapstick comedy about Hollywood. When the director in *Sunset* yells "Cut!" and we recognize that we have been watching a Western film being made, we continue in a film in which we never know where we are or where we will be next. Trying to give a unified reading of *Sunset* is a little like trying to view a cubist painting from a fixed Renaissance perspective or trying to find a representation of a real object in a totally abstract painting. *Sunset* exists solely in the imaginary space of a jarring variety of film genres that never really come together. There is no "Cut!" which returns us to a stable, fixed reality.

NOTES

1. *The Party*, which was heavily improvised, is also relevant here not only in how it was made but also in how it incorporates Edwards's lifelong love of silent film comedy, which on the surface seems to contradict his love of radio, since radio is entirely reliant on the spoken word and sound effects and silent slapstick had no spoken dialogue at all and is primarily reliant on visually depicted

physical movement and editing. The centerpiece of *The Party* is a long slapstick dinner scene during which we hear almost nothing but a din of conversation where we can only occasionally discern a word or two. That scene was in fact scripted for an earlier, unproduced film, *Pie Face*, starring Soupy Sales and written by Tom and Frank Waldman as an entirely silent film. Edwards, thus, lifted a scene from a planned silent film and used it in a sound film. But *The Party* was a silent film only in regard to the absence of spoken dialogue in the film. It has a rich, complex soundtrack including the formal use of such sound effects as we might hear on radio – dishes crashing, running water, and so on. Thus, much like Edwards loved mixing genres in his films, he also mixed much of what he had learned from one media like radio with another like film.

2. This aspect of *Sunset* is an early example of a small subgenre of films dealing with imaginary histories of famous people. Some examples include Nicholas Roeg's *Insignificance* (1985), which is based on an imaginary meeting between Albert Einstein, Marilyn Monroe, Joe DiMaggio, and Senator Joseph McCarthy; Steven Shainberg's *Fur: An Imaginary History of Diane Arbus* (2006), dealing with an imaginary relationship between the photographer and a man whose body is excessively covered with hair; and Regina King's *One Night in Miami* (2020), which deals with an imaginary meeting between Muhammad Ali, Malcolm X, Sam Cooke, and Jim Brown. Unlike these films, however, *Sunset* mixes such an imaginary history with many other genres.

3. One form of continuity for the slapstick tradition in the sound era was in animated cartoons, and it is revealing that the credit sequences for Edwards's Pink Panther films as well as a number of others such as *The Great Race* used animated characters. In addition, the Pink Panther character became the basis for a successful television cartoon series on its own.

4. Edwards's use of mixing jarring genre tones into his films may account for one of, if not *the*, biggest mistake of his career – casting Mickey Rooney as Mr. Yunioshi, a perverse Asian photographer who lives in the apartment above Holly Golightly in *Breakfast at Tiffany's*. Many critics have rightfully highlighted the racism of casting a white man and comically stereotyping the character's masculinity, both physically (grotesque buck teeth, thick glasses, speaking in an exaggerated accent, and bumbling and stumbling around) and sexually (he gets perverse, lascivious sexual pleasure in trying to get Holly to agree to pose for him). This subplot is crude and totally out of place with most of the rest of the romantic comedy style in the film in its use of slapstick and physical comedy (Yunioshi, for example, awakens from sleeping and abruptly sits up, banging his head into a circular, low-hanging paper

lantern). Edwards always maintained that he added that character and the comic subplot to the film. That fully conforms with his style of mixing genres and also accounts for his adding a party scene choreographed entirely around slapstick physical comedy. That in no way excuses the deplorable racism of the Yunioshi subplot but it may well explain why Edwards introduced it into the film, disrupting its dominant tone. At one point, we asked Edwards if he considered the Yunioshi subplot racist and he replied, "I certainly hope not. I have two adopted Vietnamese daughters." His love of genre disruption may well have clouded his judgment at the time. By the end of his life, he had come to regret using Rooney in that manner in *Breakfast at Tiffany's.*

5. In this it echoes an enormously popular film of nine years earlier, *Around the World in Eighty Days* (1956), which was based upon the 1873 Jules Verne novel and concerns a man making a round-the-world trip to win a bet. It uses dozens of cameo roles by famous movie stars, unusual for the time and widely commented upon. The cameo appearances are so systematic, however, that they quickly become part of the film's attraction and not a deviation. Set in the late nineteenth century, the main narrative foregrounds a sense of wonder at the impaction of multiple diverse civilizations and modes of existence in the world, suddenly made accessible by modern transportation technologies like hot air balloons, railroads, and steamboats. Although it patronizingly presents many of the diverse civilizations as highly exotic, it also associates them with film genres such as the Western or the British colonial empire film. Most of this is presented straightforwardly to induce a sense of wonder at the diversity of the emerging modern world. *The Great Race*, however, employs this global diversity in the service of crazed comedy, and in fact it contains an epic custard pie-throwing scene, a classic slapstick routine. In both films the viewer is clearly grounded with a sense of generic stability; they know the rules of what they are experiencing.

CHAPTER 12

The Late Period: Play It Again, Blake

Blake Edwards directed his last film, *Son of the Pink Panther*, in 1993. The film got bad reviews and did poorly at the box office except for Italy, where Roberto Benigni, the film's Italian star, was very popular. From a traditional auteur perspective that would mark the end of his career. But for Blake Edwards as a multi-hyphenate, multimedia creator and for us as scholars embracing that approach to his total career, it marked the beginning of an extremely productive and unusual final phase in his late period. Within two years he would be back as the writer-director-producer of *Victor/Victoria: The Musical* (1995) on Broadway, an adaptation of the film *Victor/Victoria* which he wrote and directed in 1982. He then followed this with an out-of-town tryout production of a new musical he wrote, produced, and directed, *Big Rosemary*, another musical adaptation, this time of the second film he had written and directed, *He Laughed Last* (1956). He stayed highly active as a screenwriter and playwright of unproduced works until his death in 2010. During those years, he also placed a new emphasis on the public exhibition of his works as a painter and sculptor.

It is not uncommon for serious filmmakers in their late period to reflect upon aspects of their mid-period career. Such accomplished filmmakers as

Blake Edwards: Film Director as Multitalented Auteur, First Edition.
William Luhr and Peter Lehman.
© 2023 John Wiley & Sons Ltd. Published 2023 by John Wiley & Sons Ltd.

John Ford and Clint Eastwood, for example, took a revisionist approach, reconsidering their representations of such things as race, gender, and sexuality. Our primary purpose here, however, is not to make a case for Edwards's status as such an auteur but, rather, to continue our effort to analyze how he engaged creatively with various media and art forms wearing his various creative hats. As we might expect, there are some highly unusual, perhaps unique aspects to his final works. For us, the unproduced screenplays and theatrical plays are not unfinished projects, but, rather, his final works as a writer, an important component of his multi-hyphenate creative output. Edwards began his career primarily as a writer and ended his career primarily as a writer. Perhaps tellingly, he wrote all of these unproduced scripts and screenplays by himself whereas in his film career he frequently cowrote his scripts, sometimes with another writer working on his story. Since these scripts are not currently available to the public, we will not give detailed analyses of movies that were never made and plays that the public can no longer see and scripts and screenplays they cannot even read. But we hope to shed some creative light in the at times startling way Edwards creatively engaged with his material.

During the world premiere production of *Victor/Victoria: The Musical* in Minneapolis, we asked Edwards if he was intimidated by the challenges of a totally new form. He quickly replied that he wasn't. When we brought up the substantial differences between film and theater, he minimized them, saying that he had always approached filmmaking by composing his shots with the proscenium arch in mind. But in the theater the proscenium arch is fixed, as is the spectator's relationship to the space it frames, depending upon their seating in the auditorium. In a movie, with cutting and camera movement, the proscenium arch (or the frame) is constantly being reconfigured but every spectator's relationship to the represented space is essentially the same regardless of where they are sitting.

As we watched Edwards blocking out the play in Minneapolis, we were struck by the profound differences that he was struggling to master. We were able to move around the theater at will, sitting close or moving to the rear, watching from one side or the other, and so on. Why would this matter? Edwards was working in a manner closely related to one of his favorite visual techniques in filmmaking in which he stages multiple actions taking place simultaneously, often placing one thing in the foreground of the frame and another in the rear. This can get quite complex, as it does in a film such as *The Party* (1968). Sophisticated film viewers used to scrutinizing the image, regardless of where they are sitting in the movie theater, can easily follow such multiple planes of action. In the theater, however, it was difficult and at times even impossible for us (and we are familiar with his style) to spot and follow some of the gags because theatrical space is configured and perceived so differently. Furthermore, as we moved around, we noticed that things we could follow from one area of the auditorium were almost certain to be lost in another because of changing sightlines and distances from the stage. For many gags, some people would simply be too close or too far away or too far to the left or the right.

Tony Roberts, a featured actor in the musical, told us that Edwards hadn't yet understood the linear nature of theatrical staging. He compared that linearity to a train pulling boxcars across the stage, with each boxcar representing a dramatic moment conveying a single meaning on which the audience could focus. Then the next one would follow. He felt that only one event could dominate the stage at any one time and that attempting to do more, such as giving multiple focal points to a scene, would confuse the audience. We suspect that Edwards understood that just as he understood the dominant Hollywood style, which he had challenged regularly throughout his career. When we discussed Roberts's linear train analogy with his co-star, Michael Nouri, Nouri agreed that that analogy worked for much of traditional theater but said that, for Edwards, the more appropriate analogy was not one of a train moving in a linear fashion across the stage but, rather, one of a train wreck, in light of Edwards's interest in developing the impact of a number of things happening simultaneously.

But Roberts placed his observation within another relevant context. Edwards could do as he pleased in this production because he was the writer-producer-director. Referring to his own extensive theatrical experience, Roberts indicated that all of his earlier plays, no matter how famous the playwright or director, had involved group conferences involving the writer, the producer, and the director to work out difficulties and disagreements. In this production, however, everything periodically ground to a halt while Edwards contemplated his next move, something which we regularly witnessed on the sets of his films.

Edwards brought his strong *auteur* tradition of total control from filmmaking to the Broadway stage where it was virtually unknown and where there was little precedent for it in relation to the tradition of adapting films for the theater. He fought for total control of his films, and he wanted total control of the play. Tony Roberts was quite perceptive in linking the aesthetic style of the production, regardless of whether one sees it as experimental and creative or naive and uninformed, to the production circumstances. The only way to fully understand this unusual production is within the context of Blake Edwards, the writer-producer-auteur film director, bringing that vision to a highly personal project on Broadway.[1]

Edwards himself may have sensed the difficulties because he was in a very dark mood throughout the week in Minneapolis during which we attended rehearsals and watched the evening performances. Throughout the 1980s he was typically a quiet, moody director who kept his thoughts to himself. During our set visit to *A Fine Mess* (1986), for example, Ted Danson, one of the leads, asked us what Blake thought of his performance. He was so puzzled by Edwards's silence that he felt insecure. On our set visit to *Son of the Pink Panther*, Herbert Lom, who had played Chief Inspector Dreyfus throughout the series, complained bitterly about how grim the set was in comparison to the jovial, collegial sets he recalled from the earlier Pink Panther films. When we asked Edwards about these things, he responded that, for a man of his age, it was inappropriate for him to interact with the mostly much younger stars such as Danson, Howie Mandel, and Bruce Willis. He had gone from being a peer to being a father figure. This is a valid point, and many academics go through a similar shift with their graduate students as they move from young assistant professors to tenured senior faculty. But something different was going on in the set in Minneapolis. He had gone from being a taciturn, somewhat distanced director to being a sullen, at times threatening authority figure. One report compared him to looking like Dante striding across the inner circles of hell. This atypically angered Blake, who told us he had been betrayed after giving access to the journalist with the understanding that he would only focus upon an aspect of the production they had agreed he would cover. We mention these anecdotes as evidence that he was in a very intense, difficult mood during the out-of-town tryout. Even the friendly exchanges we had with him throughout our previous film set visits were gone. On the set of *Sunset*, for example, he invited us to watch dailies with him and Julie Andrews. On the set of *Son of the Pink Panther*, he invited us to lunch with his daughter, Jennifer.

However dark the mood on the set frequently was, Edwards succeeded in creating an entertaining and original piece of musical theater which fully reimagined his hit film while remaining true to its spirit of boldly challenging gender and sexuality norms. The set design and Edwards's use of stage space were impressive and totally departed from that in the film.[2]

Some of the characterization in the play that had been done through action and dialogue in the film is done through song, such as with "King's Dilemma," a song, new to the play, that develops King's gender confusion. Although Julie Andrews starred in both film and play, her performance style is very different in each. In the movie, she acts in a highly "dramatic" manner – grand gestures, dramatic poses, full oratorical voice – whenever she is on stage as the title character performing before audiences. Andrews employs a more muted, intimate manner when interacting with other actors in private moments when no audience is present. In the play, the difference in acting style between her "performance" life and "private" life is much less than that in the film. Even her "private" moments appear highly performative in the play because she is always performing before the live audience in the theater, including those seated in the back rows.

The play has a great deal of physical comedy and some hilarious bedroom farce which involves dividing up the space in the elaborate sets (Figure 12.1), but the kind of complex cutting in the film is impossible. The film's hallway scene using off-screen space has no parallel in the play but could conceivably have been adapted because it involves a single-audience perspective. Other scenes, such as the cockroach in the restaurant or King sneaking into Victoria's bathroom to see her naked (again without parallel in the play), rely on different camera perspectives and movement and would have had to be entirely reconceived. Some scenes in the play without parallel in the movie, however, like Victoria's tango with Norma, are well suited to the traditional strengths (single-audience perspective, music, carefully choreographed dance and movement, dramatic production values) of the musical stage.

As has happened several times in Edwards's career, long after both the movie and the play, Kenji Fujishima published a major 2021 article, "*Victor/ Victoria*: The Better Drag Comedy of 1982?" making a case for a strong

FIGURE 12.1   *Victor/Victoria: The Original Broadway Cast Production,* © 1995 Victor/ Victoria Company.

reevaluation of both of Edwards's works. Of special interest to us here is that he published it on Theatermania.com, a website devoted to New York City theater news.[3] Due to the suspension of live theater during the COVID-19 pandemic, Fujishima suggested that readers should watch and reevaluate Edwards's 1982 film, *Victor/Victoria*. He argues that, despite some good reviews and award nominations, the film has been vastly underestimated. He goes on to note:

> And *Victor/Victoria* was eventually turned into a hit Broadway musical, also starring Julie Andrews, that opened in 1995 and ran for 734 performances – though it is perhaps best remembered now for Andrews' refusal to accept her Tony Award nomination in order to stand with "egregiously overlooked" members of the production. But in this critic's estimation, not only is *Victor/Victoria* more progressive in its views of gender roles than *Tootsie*, it has stood the test of time better, despite *Tootsie*'s continued reputation as a classic.

He implies that the way the play is now mostly remembered for Julie Andrews declining her Tony Award is related to the way the film was similarly underestimated.

He argues that *Tootsie*, also made in 1982, was hailed as an important achievement while *Victor/Victoria* was lost in the shuffle. He structures his gender analysis around the fact that both films feature drag, Dustin Hoffman as a woman and Julie Andrews as a man pretending to be a woman but also, in the film's conclusion, Robert Preston performing in drag as a woman: "But *Victor/Victoria*'s queerness isn't just relegated to that one character and co-star Julie Andrews's transvestism. Edwards's film also plays as a pointed deconstruction of gender norms. In contrast to Toddy's flamboyant homosexuality, there's the equally flamboyant heterosexuality of King Marchand ... All the characters are challenged to step outside their comfort zones in *Victor/Victoria*." We made similar arguments in *Returning to the Scene: Blake Edwards, Volume 2*. Instead of *Tootsie*, we contrasted Edwards's representation of gay culture with that in *La Cage aux Folles*. Instead of making fun of gay men for the pleasure of a mainstream audience, Edwards's King Marchand and his macho, heterosexual posturing is the butt of much of the film's humor.

Fujishima's excellent reevaluation appearing within the context of important developments in Broadway theater is a major intervention and his conclusion also relates to our analysis of Edwards's work throughout this book: "Befitting Edwards's wide-ranging view of life, *Victor/Victoria* is similarly expansive in its range of styles and emotions, with musical numbers coexisting with silent-movie-like slapstick sequences and intimate dramatic confrontations, and euphoria mixed in with heartbreak. There's a sense of freedom to this film, as if anything and everything could happen. Even now, there are very few films, musical or otherwise, like it." We hope to have demonstrated that a similar wide range of styles and emotions and narratives that affirm that "anything and everything could happen" are in fact hallmarks of his films, whether they celebrate freedom or brood about entrapment.

Victor/Victoria: The Musical defines some of the major aspects of the final phase of Edwards's late period. First and foremost, he goes back to a previous work of his and in some manner creatively reengages with it, here adapting his film as a play. But the film itself was a remake of an earlier German film, *Viktor und Viktoria* (1933), which had already been remade as *First a Girl* (1935). Edwards told us twice that he had no awareness of and interest in *Viktor und Viktoria* and that someone had brought the film to his attention. He contrasted this with his remake of François Truffaut's *The Man Who Loved Women* since he knew Truffaut's work and held it in high regard. But the fact that he remade a German film and a French film points to his larger interest in going back to previous works and creative reengaging with them.

While *Victor/Victoria: The Musical* was still on Broadway, Edwards premiered an out-of-town tryout for *Big Rosemary*, which was a theatrical adaptation of the second film he had written and directed, *He Laughed Last* (1956). His next project was *The Pink Panther Musical*, which returned to the first film in that highly successful series, and he also adapted *A Shot in the Dark*, which ironically had been based on a play of the same name. He similarly returned to his hit *"10"* with two entirely different screenplays: *10 (Again)* and *10½*. We know of no other filmmaker whose late period included such a direct reengagement with their earlier work. And near the end of his life, he was working on a proposal for a television series, *Peter Gunn* again!

Luckily, Edwards gave us scripts for all these projects and more, and we turn now to a brief consideration of these scripts and screenplays that complete his oeuvre as a writer and highlight how he engaged creatively with musical theater as well as comic and dramatic theater and writing screenplays that now stand alone from films that he never made, though others of course might one day still make.

We attended afternoon rehearsals for *Big Rosemary* and the first evening public performance of it at the Helen Hayes Theater in Nyack, New York. Although Julie Andrews had no onstage role in the play, she attended most rehearsals and wrote detailed production notes. At a rehearsal, Blake made a highly unusual request of us. He said he knew we would recognize it as an adaptation of *He Laughed Last*, his second film, but he asked that we not say anything to the media about that. He had never asked us not to speak about anything, nor had he ever criticized anything we had ever written about his work. We were, of course, happy to comply with his request, which we found revealing. During the 1980s critics commonly and dismissively characterized his films as being yet another sex comedy about a privileged, upper-middle-class, whining, white male's midlife sexual crisis, as if he had run out of fresh ideas and was self-indulgently repeating himself instead. This had also followed increasingly bad reviews of all his post–Peter Sellers Pink Panther films, implying he was again simply repeating himself by wringing every last drop of blood out of a dead series. In short, he was perceived as an artist who had run out of creative ideas, falling back on simply repeating himself.

But Blake's request to us pointed to another aspect of *Big Rosemary. He Laughed Last* was such an obscure, forgotten movie made forty years earlier that it was unlikely that most critics would even know about it. And this strikes us as the most important aspect of what would be Edwards's last project directing anything that he had written. Why did he choose such an unlikely project? And why would he most actively pursue doing a fully mounted theatrical production of it to the end of his life? In 1956 he was still under contract to Columbia for a series of B films starring Frankie Laine. The films were mostly written by Richard Quine and Edwards and had been directed by Quine until the studio elevated Quine to the status of a director of A films. When this happened, the studio moved Edwards up to direct the two remaining low-budget B films, which were to star Frankie Laine. Edwards is credited as the screenwriter based on a story by Edwards and Quine in *He Laughed Last*. Predictably, no one paid major attention to these films either at the time they were released or even after Edwards became a rising young director with such films as *Operation Petticoat*, *Days of Wine and Roses*, and *Breakfast at Tiffany's*. From a traditional auteur perspective, Edwards's first important writing-directing experience was *Mister Cory* at Universal. The point is not about the different statures of the two respected studios, but rather about Edwards going from a B series where he was limited not only by a small budget, but even more so by having to make films starring Frankie Laine.

We always thought these films were of interest, especially *He Laughed Last*, with its explicit questioning of gender norms of the times. We wrote our first book on Edwards before he even began making such films as *"10," S.O.B.*, and *Victor/Victoria* which dealt with a new level of explicit sex and gender issues. But of course, in its own way and in its own time, *He Laughed Last* was as explicitly about gender issues as his 1950s wartime comedies were. The thought of women in the military and on submarines during wartime was not so far removed from that of women running the mob.

There is a profound point in understanding this context. Blake Edwards did not approach writing and directing a B series featuring a popular singer as what John Ford used to call "a job of work." It was a meaningful creative enterprise for him, or he would not have thought back to it in his late period. He took the title *Big Rosemary* directly from the poster advertising *He Laughed Last*. The poster declares in increasingly large blue letters, "LITTLE CAESAR!, SCARFACE!, DILLINGER! and now... [in red letters] BIG ROSE-MARY!" Frankie Laine, the film's titular star, is simply described as her bodyguard, "AND WHAT A BODY TO GUARD!" More on that in a moment. The most important aspect of Edwards's adaptation is that he eliminates Frankie Laine's character. Since his play is a musical, he could easily have written the part for a current musical star. This choice tells us much about how Edwards engaged with the original film that had to star Laine and with the theatrical adaptation of it. He found a way to work Laine into his movie about a woman becoming the head of the mob without in any way making him central to that plot. Although he is boldly declared the star in the poster, under his name he is more accurately described as "Booming out the songs," while Lucy Marlow, who plays Rosemary, is described as "Zooming along to stardom!"

But the poster also points to ideologically contradictory aspects of the representation of the lead female character. Directly under Marlow's name she is described by her height, weight, and measurements: 36–24–25, as in WHAT A BODY TO GUARD. It would be easy to ascribe this excessive dwelling on the erotic details of Rosemary's body to sexism in the publicity department unrelated to Edwards's film. But, as we shall see, unfortunately just this kind of description of a "leading lady" including giving her measure-ments characterizes many of Edwards's unproduced scripts and screenplays. While he remained wildly creative, he seemed hopelessly trapped in the dated notion that a woman's body was the primary feature of her character. And he always details their beauty within the 1950s norm of a curvaceous body like that of a *Playboy* centerfold or a star such as Marilyn Monroe. He is so fixated on one type of attractive body that his works assume that all men will desire and fantasize about such a woman. While he progressively under-mines many old-fashioned gender and sexuality norms, he continually reaf-firms the sexist cataloguing of a woman's measurements and dwells on her beautiful body as the primary reason that his central male character is inter-ested in her in the first place. Even if he may want to critique such a view of women, he affirms it. His scripts are dominated by womanizers who are fetishists, frequently focusing on legs, and they fall in "love" with a woman by merely looking at her from a distance without any sense of who she is or what she is like as a person. These men frequently insist that they "truly love women" and Edwards develops the characters as if they truly did. The way this objectification of women's bodies is deeply embedded in his work may help explain why his late-period work seems so dated and repetitious to many and why he had trouble getting these projects produced. Nearly all the lead female characters are first and foremost described as being strikingly beautiful.

After the tryouts for *Big Rosemary*, Edwards put that project aside for further development and created *The Pink Panther Musical* with the following credits on the first page: "Book by Blake Edwards, music by Henry Mancini, Lyrics by Leslie Bricusse, directed by Blake Edwards." Once again, he returns to a film that marks a key moment in his career, this time the beginning of his middle period where he fully developed his signature style of physical comedy and bedroom farce. This project must have originated earlier since Mancini died before he could finish his score for *Victor/Victoria: The Musical*. Edwards told us in detail how he went to Mancini's home every day to work with him on the script and songs while Mancini was terminally ill.

As the credits indicate, *The Pink Panther Musical* is intended as a lavish production with elaborate sets, musical numbers for all the main characters, and a chorus. It is an excellent hilarious script with inventive set design and extensive use of various kinds of off-stage space. The play begins with a framing device of a play within the play. The audience sees scaffolding and workers coming and going before Dreyfus enters and addresses the audience, declaring, "I am your host," and then claims that the play they are about to see is "for your edification and entertainment, the unexpurgated and uncensored tale of romance, intrigue, and sheer stupidity that has become known as modern times' Greatest Jewel Robbery." This is the exact opposite approach to that in *Big Rosemary* where Edwards tried to keep *He Laughed Last* a secret. Here he introduces the play as designed for an audience who not only knows the story of *The Pink Panther* film but is also familiar with the major characters. Even in his introductory direct address to the audience, Dreyfus twitches at the mere mention of Clouseau's name. He ends with, "Let the play begin," and the stage directions are, "Dreyfus giggles, exits." He will of course shortly reappear as a character in the play that he now hosts. There are thus two versions of Dreyfus, the host about whom Edwards writes, "Something is definitely not kosher in the Dreyfus psyche," and the play will show him undergoing the trials and tribulations of working with Clouseau which drive him crazy. The first scene includes a startling use of off-stage space when the "Phantom makes a death defying slide down the wires, over the audience and into the Jewel Room."

Despite the excellent script with top collaborators, Edwards had trouble getting funding for the production. Edwards told us that Kevin Spacey loved the Pink Panther movies and wanted to play Clouseau in the musical. Spacey enthusiastically enacted a one-man version of the film for Edwards, playing all the parts by heart. Gene Schwam, Edwards's publicist, told us that, at one point around 2003, they explored opening the play in Las Vegas before taking it to Broadway. Schwam set up a meeting with MGM executives at the MGM Grand to discuss a proposal for a one-year residency at the hotel. The meeting went extremely well and was heading toward a deal when Edwards suddenly went into a negative rant about the plans for a new Pink Panther film starring Steve Martin as Clouseau. Edwards had sold the film rights for the series to MGM while retaining all other rights for himself including theatrical productions. According to Schwam, Edwards's insults to MGM executives sank the project. Much as, despite his notorious battles with the studios, Edwards continued to make Hollywood films, despite his problems with Broadway he apparently felt that opening the play in Las Vegas would be settling for second best.

Edwards also adapted *A Shot in the Dark* for the theater and once again approached the material in an entirely different way than that in *The Pink Panther*. This production is not a musical and is thus not as elaborate. The first page is a simple epigraph: "The secret of Clouseau's success.... To know him is to underestimate him." It is worth recalling that Edwards's film was itself an adaptation of a stage play with the same title, but he entirely rewrote it making the major characters Clouseau, Cato, Dreyfus, and Hercule, all of whom are again the center of the play. The plot closely follows that of the film, although some scenes such as that in the nudist camp are omitted. And he once again adapts many of the same scenes of physical comedy and bedroom farce restructured for the stage. For example, while the film begins with Clouseau arriving at the scene of the crime and stepping out of his car and falling into a pool with a fountain, in the play we hear an off-screen crash before Clouseau enters soaking wet and we quickly learn Clouseau has also killed all of Ballon's valuable rare goldfish collection and destroyed a valuable Degas statue as well. And once again, as he examines the room, he gets knocked out of the window. Others rush over to look down. Whereas in the film we see a shot of Clouseau flattened against the ground like a cartoon character, here Edwards leaves that to our imagination and Clouseau eventually climbs his way back into the room.

In these two plays, Edwards once again revisits the Pink Panther-Inspector Clouseau films for which he is most famous. He initiated a new phase in his career with *"10,"* which we have argued in our previous books marks a shift in his work with the emergence from what had been elaborately structured sexual subtexts into what now would become the overt subjects and themes of the films. Not surprisingly therefore, he also wrote two plays with direct reference to that film: *10½* and *10 (Again)*. *10½* establishes its relationship to *"10"* in the opening "SERIES OF SHOTS of ANGELIQUE CASSIDY, TEN magazine's choice of the world's most perfect female – a 10½." That is the main direct connection to the previous film, where Edwards made rating women a "perfect 10" a household word. The title, of course, also refers to Federico Fellini's *8½* and at one point a character blurts out, "Oh My God. It's Fellini." As the credits begin, we learn from a television host that "Angelique's vital statistics are 36, 26, 34," another instance of Edwards's nearly compulsive repetition of describing the beautiful women in his films as conforming fully to the old 1950s and 1960s statuesque norm for female beauty. As if to level the playing field, shortly after that Edwards includes a long repartee between two characters about penis size. Brewster calls Dudley (the central male character) a "little prick," to which Jennifer, the main female character, quickly replies, "Not so little," to which Brewster replies, "That supposed to impugn my manhood?", to which she responds, "Yeah." And on it goes. Although this is a highly creative and frequently very funny screenplay including bedroom farce, such overused clichés as describing beautiful women by their measurements and affirming or questioning masculinity with penis size jokes unfortunately dates the project and makes it sound at times more like a run-of-the-mill teen comedy than a sophisticated Edwards film.

Perhaps most significantly in terms of Edwards's declining critical and commercial reputation, Dudley is another of Edwards's leading men who is a womanizer. While being lawyers on opposite sides of a trial involving the mob, Dudley and Jennifer are a separated married couple, presumably due to Dudley's womanizing. In one of the few scenes that link this film to *"10"* Dudley has a "large telescope" in his home. Whereas in *"10"* he was spying on his neighbor, here the telescope is focused on a nearby nudist beach. Edwards elaborately develops the use of the scope and of Dudley being a voyeur in a hilarious version of his topping the topper topper gag structure which becomes intertwined with other motifs and is only finally topped at the film's climax. Many critics of Edwards's 1980s comedies bemoaned the, for them, tiresome repetition of his dwelling on the sexual problems of privileged upper-class white male characters and in fact most of his unproduced scripts continue that pattern. *10½* includes such other Edwards staples as Dudley having an episode of impotence.

As the title *10 (Again)* indicates, this film bears a much closer relationship to its predecessor but the opening shot marks a major distinction: the film is set in New York during the winter. Once again, the central character is named George Webber and once again he is a composer who works with a gay lyricist named Hugh, and this brings the script close to being a remake of the original film. George passes a limo with a beautiful bride on her way to her wedding and he instantly becomes obsessed. George follows her to the synagogue (it is a church in the original film) where he hides behind flowers to watch the ceremony when a powerful sneeze knocks the flowers over, revealing him fleeing the scene. And as in the original, he returns to the synagogue to meet with the rabbi who officiated at the wedding, hoping to learn the name of the bride and where she went for her honeymoon. As George sits listening to the rabbi play a song for him, Edwards describes the scene which virtually repeats one from *"10"* as follows: "Asleep on the sofa, a standard poodle opens one eye as MRS. KISSEL, ancient housekeeper appears in the doorway carrying tea. The poodle watches as she moves across the room like an arthritic sloth. When George rises to help her, she stops him with a sound that resembles a cross between a fog horn and a death rattle." Even the name Mrs. Kissel is the same! And the entire gag structure is repeated. George tries to stop Mrs. Kissel from walking into the fireplace and the scene ends when Mrs. Kissel "farts" again, the poodle dashes out of the room, and the rabbi explains: "For Mrs. Kissel's sake, when she breaks wind, we beat the dog."

Many other elements from the original film reappear in this script: George has a telescope he uses to spy on his neighbor, he uses his bartender as a therapist, he is impotent, "Bolero" is heard, and so on. But once again, the screenplay is inventive and funny and, while it reengages with the earlier one, it is in no sense a repeat of it. It is more along the lines of a theme and variations, a common musical structure. Of special interest for this overview of Edwards's unproduced late-period scripts, Kevin Spacey appears in a lengthy speaking cameo at the film's conclusion. As mentioned above, Edwards and Spacey were in talks for Spacey to play Clouseau in *The Pink Panther Musical*. Edwards always surrounded himself with an unofficial "company" of actors and talent who worked with him repeatedly. For example, he wrote *Scapegoat* with John Ritter in mind as the male lead. Ritter had starred in his 1989 film, *Skin Deep*.

Before turning to that and the final group of unproduced scripts, we want to draw some conclusions about these projects which return to *Victor/Victoria*, *He Laughed Last*, *The Pink Panther*, *A Shot in the Dark*, and *"10."*

The critics notwithstanding, we do not believe that Edwards's late period suggests someone who has run out of ideas. Something much more complex and even unique is happening here. In addition to all the above titles, recall that the last film he ever made was *Son of the Pink Panther* (1993). That was his third effort revisiting the Pink Panther series after Peter Sellers, who had played Clouseau in the first five films in the series, had died. At the time that Edwards died he was once again working on a new version of his *Peter Gunn* series. What is going on here?

It is commonplace in traditional auteurism, and even prior to that, to recognize that some filmmakers rework their favorite themes, characters, and narrative structures, sometimes even making trilogies. Jean Renoir once remarked that filmmakers make the same movie over and over. Furthermore, it is commonly recognized that filmmakers go through periods, with the early work introducing their subjects and style, the middle-period work developing and complicating those preoccupations, and the late period paring down the works with filmmakers no longer fully developing what they have already done, instead simply referring to it. Such late periods also may offer a revisionist approach to the early work.

It is also well known that some filmmakers like Alfred Hitchcock and John Ford remade earlier films, but always with a different format such as remaking a silent film with sound or a black-and-white film in color. But these were also rare and usually singular occurrences rather than career patterns. As with so much of his career, none of these useful methodologies explain what Edwards is doing. To the best of our knowledge, he is the first major filmmaker to systemically return to his early and middle-period works to in some way remake them, either by going from one form to another such as film to theater (*Victor/Victoria* and *Victor/Victoria: The Musical*; *He Laughed Last/Big Rosemary*, *The Pink Panther/The Pink Panther Musical*, *A Shot in the Dark/A Shot in the Dark*), or by reimagining a film not as a traditional remake or series or one tied to any new technologies but, rather, as a continuing creative enterprise such as *"10," 10½*, and *10 (Again)*. Then consider that all this was bookended with *Son of the Pink Panther*, which concludes with the promise of a whole new series with a female version of Inspector Clouseau, and with his planned fourth version of *Peter Gunn* re-envisioning it once again as a series.

In Chapter 1 we placed Edwards within a very specific historical context: he began his career under the old studio system and then successfully transitioned to the new era when that system collapsed. And from the beginning he also worked in radio and television when radio was in its final phase of being an important series storytelling medium and when television was a comparatively new medium replacing radio and evolving as the main form of media storytelling. His career as a filmmaker ended just when the entertainment and technology industries converged around new digital technologies. Furthermore, many of the creative people he worked with in his early period, such as Dick Powell and Richard Quine, were themselves multi-hyphenate, multimedia artists and he would later become a model for many talented young filmmakers in the digital era, including J. J. Abrams and Judd Apatow.

As we have seen, Edwards's work in radio and television was almost exclusively in the series format, including shows that he created such as *Richard Diamond* on radio and *Peter Gunn* on television, but also many successful radio shows to which he contributed as a writer, such as *The Line Up* and *Yours Truly, Johnny Dollar*. This form of storytelling was strongly tied to returning to well-known characters and narrative settings. But he also witnessed the creative move of many radio shows to television, including his own *Richard Diamond* with which he was not involved, and an unproduced 1962, 30-minute pilot for *Yours Truly, Johnny Dollar*, which he wrote, directed, and executive produced. Edwards honed his craft during an era where creativity not only included series storytelling but also adapting radio shows to television and even movies. These enterprises were not perceived as indicating that the creators were "out of ideas" but, rather, were creatively engaged with adapting from one medium to another. Even his main introduction to filmmaking included a variation on the traditional series format since he was Richard Quine's writing partner on a series of B films under contract. The last two films in the series became the first films that Edwards directed. And when he became an A-list film director in the early 1960s, such successful series as the James Bond films were taking off and Edwards's Pink Panther films would soon become part of that genre of film storytelling.

But Edwards's interest in and involvement with the other arts may have also played a role. As we will discuss below, he was a painter and sculptor in an art world where many of the greatest artists constantly repeated their stylistic explorations of the same visual motifs and subject matter. No one complained that Monet must have been out of ideas when he returned to painting water lilies or that Cézanne suffered the same fate when he repeatedly painted views of Mont Sainte-Victoire. Nor would admirers complain that most episodes of the *Richard Diamond* radio show and the *Peter Gunn* television series would begin with the detectives getting phone calls interrupting their personal pursuits. And although he was not a musician, Edwards was also a self-taught jazz aficionado, a form that valued theme and variation and improvisation as highly creative activities. In many ways, it is precisely such theme and variations that drove his creativity. There were countless ways he could develop the theme of the lead detectives being interrupted by a phone call or being interrupted during a phone call with their girlfriends.

Although we consider his late period to be misunderstood and undervalued, our primary goal here is not to make a case for how good or bad Edwards's late-period work may be, but to try to understand how he creatively engaged in his projects, including the unproduced scripts. Within the historical context of his career as a multi-hyphenate, multimedia creator, going back to a comprehensive reengagement with his earlier works regardless of how he succeeded or failed might well be for him the ultimate creative challenge. Even his family background may have played a role. He proudly called himself a third-generation filmmaker since his step-grandfather had been a silent director and his stepfather had been an assistant director. In an age of cinema's rapid technological developments, he was always returning to his beloved Laurel and Hardy and silent film comedy. For Edwards, looking back was a highly creative enterprise.

In addition to these direct reengagements, Edwards finished three other late-period scripts which revisit the preoccupations of his earlier work: the theater piece *Scapegoat*, and the screenplays *It Never Rains* and *Alter Ego*. In our final conversations with him, he placed a special emphasis on *Scapegoat*. He was in talks with John Ritter to play the lead and Ritter told us with great enthusiasm that he thought it was an excellent play. The premise of the play is that the devil, Nick, seeks psychiatric help from Sarah Moss, an attractive psychiatrist at the Preminger Clinic, named after the famed psychiatrist Karl Preminger. Although they think that Nick is a deluded man in serious need of medical attention, he maintains that he really is the devil. The play brings together Edwards's preoccupations with psychiatric treatment and, surprisingly in his late period, with God and the devil. We asked Edwards in 2005 if he was an atheist, which he had suggested to us years earlier, and his answer was hilarious: "Almost"!

Several of his late films such as *"10"* and *That's Life!* include clergy in minor roles that do not involve issues of faith, agnosticism, or atheism. Others, like the made-for-television *Justin Case* (1988), engage themes often related to explorations of the supernatural and religious belief, such as reincarnation and crossovers from the afterlife into this one, but use them primarily as plot devices. In this film, the title character is found murdered at the beginning and returns from the dead to help a woman, who is the only person able to see him, to solve his murder. *Switch* has no clergy but God him-/herself and the devil are characters. The film begins when the main character, a womanizer, is killed by three former lovers. When he goes to heaven, God, speaking in alternating male and female voices, denies him entry based on how poorly he has treated women. He is ordered to go back to earth to find one woman who loves him, or he will be sent to hell. But the devil convinces God that Steve should be sent back as a woman so that he may learn what it is like to be treated by men like him. The premise is obviously entirely in the service of a gender and sex comedy which all can enjoy regardless of their religious beliefs or lack thereof. There is no exploration of religion or of the real existence of God or the devil – they are simply comic devices.

Edwards will use the same device in his screenplay, *It Never Rains*. That screenplay combines elements of *S.O.B.* with *Switch*. The central male character is a film writer-director with writer's block who is also a womanizer. He eventually breaks his writer's block with a script about God coming to destroy Hollywood. "One of the angels asks God, 'If I find fifty honest people, will you spare Hollywood?' And God says, 'Yep' ... How about forty, then thirty, then finally ten, and God agrees, if they only find ten honest people he'll spare Hollywood." Once again, Edwards creatively uses a variation of the premise of a previous film. And once again it is a variation on another previous film with its dark vision of Hollywood, and once again it has a central privileged white male semi-autobiographical artist with a midlife creative and sexual crisis. Exactly what the critics had been complaining about. But once again it is a hilarious, creative screenplay.

Edwards did not date most of his late-period scripts, but the copy of *Alter Ego* he gave us is dated January 14, 1993, the beginning of this late phase of his career but an interesting place for us to conclude our survey of these screenplays. It revisits the primary focus of *Mister Cory*, which tells the story of two gamblers who work closely together and the women who come between them. Edwards's critical reputation began with that film, which he wrote and directed at Universal where his new freedom allowed him to originate his own project. The opening scene of *Alter Ego* distills the relationship at its core: "TONY CARR Handsome number one at the box-office, sits at the far end of the pool watching the attractive, blonde, JAN-ICE, swim towards him. CAMERA RISES to reveal STEVE SOMMERS watching from his room over the garage. Steve is about the same size as Tony, but much stronger ... [he] would have made the Olympic team except for a last-minute knee injury."

Steve, Tony's stunt double and driver, is his alter ego and Janice is the first woman to come between them. The two men practically live together with power and class distinctions: Tony is not only a box-office star but also the producer of their current film and, while he lives in a Hollywood mansion, Steve lives in a room above the garage. Rumor has it that they are so close that any woman who wants to get Tony has to first get Steve's approval, something that Janice accomplishes by having oral sex with him while he is driving.

In a remarkable scene the subtextual issues are explicitly brought to the surface. Tony explains the history of his relationship with Steve to Susan, an actress with whom he is having an affair. She remarks, "And you still live together?" Tony asks, "What are you getting at?" Susan replies, "I don't think either one of you understands the kind of relationship you really do have." Tony asks, "You mean gay? Because that's been common gossip for ten years. Or bisexual because it's hard to explain the women." Susan then asks, "Does Steve have a lot of women ... I just have the impression he doesn't really like women." Tony counters, "Steve dates women but he doesn't trust them! Does that make him gay or bi – or even a latent homosexual?" To which Susan replies, "Maybe latent."

This astonishing conversation addresses a host of sexual issues at the core of Edwards's work from an early period where, as in *Mister Cory*, it was all subtextual through a transitional period (*"10,"* *S.O.B.*, and *Victor/Victoria*) where we see the subtext become the text and finally to this extreme textual articulation of the entire issue. It is perhaps significant that during an interview Edwards himself broached the issue with us of the rumors of him being gay. He brought it up, not us. Although this book is not a biography and we have avoided biographical readings of Edwards's work, what he said directly relates to this screenplay. As he has repeatedly done, he denied being gay and said that, if he were, he would be the first to be open about it. He also not only denied being bisexual but went so far as to say that he did not think bisexuality even existed. He had never known one and he even asked us if we knew any bisexuals. We mentioned a couple students who had self-identified as being bisexual but only as a phase to help them determine if they were lesbians or heterosexuals.

Blake was never self-defensive with us during any of our interviews, regardless of the questions we asked or the issues we touched on, including those about gender and sexuality about which we had extensively written. He answered the questions as well as he could. But we never asked these questions about his being gay, bisexual, or latently homosexual; our focus was on textual analysis of his films. On a few occasions he was very critical about reviewers who had fundamentally misunderstood his films or on one occasion about a journalist who had betrayed an advance agreement they had before he was granted access to the set. After talking with Blake about this, we did write an article, "What Business Does a Critic Have Asking If Blake Edwards

Is Gay? Rumor, Scandal, Biography, and Textual Analysis."[4] That essay explores these biographical issues but our point here is that Edwards was uncharacteristically open with us in how he brought up and talked about the issues. Clearly, he wanted to set the record straight. We did not argue with him then and we are not judging the validity of his points here. But we are documenting that he struggled with these issues in his life. The rumors to which he referred at that time circulated around his close relationship with Tony Adams, his producer, and how in some ways their lives mirrored each other; they were alter egos and like the relationship between Tony and Steve in *Alter Ego*, the rumors swirled around them.

Alter Ego is one of Edwards's late-period comedies with dark drama, perhaps the darkest, most violently shocking in his career. In that regard it also recalls *S.O.B.*, another Hollywood comedy which turns instantly deadly when the main character is graphically shot and killed in slow motion. It also recalls *Gunn* in which a cross-dresser is brutally and graphically killed. And like *The Man Who Loved Women* and *S.O.B.*, it ends with a funeral but in this variation also a wedding. The final sequences of the film include Steve violently attacking two women in his and Tony's lives: Janice and then Susan. In a scene late in the film, when Janice opens the door to her apartment and smiles, "Steve punches her in the mouth. Janice is literally knocked off her feet. She lands in a heap." Steve then attacks her date and leaves him helpless on the floor with two broken knees: "Janice is groaning, coming around. Steve grabs her by the hair, pulls her head back. Her nose and lips are bleeding." The scene ends when Steve calls her a "cunt" and threatens, "Open your mouth again and I'll fuckin' kill you." In the next scene Steve goes to Susan's apartment where he confronts her, accusing her of being "a hooker" who has hidden her true self away from Steve. Susan admits to having "slept around a lot" and to having had a baby who suffocated in her crib while she passed out from drinking. She tells Steve she will tell Tony before they get married. Steve then also asks if she will tell him about "The rich guy in Chicago." When she says she'll tell him everything, Steve says, "You think he'll believe you?" Susan goes to call Tony to prove it when Steve says, "Get away from the phone" and grabs her: "With enormous force he flings her aside. There is a sickening CRASH as she goes through the plate glass door. She screams once as she falls backwards over the balcony and hurtles to the courtyard below." She ends up in a critical condition in a coma with multiple fractures and serious brain trauma.

The broken glass door recalls the broken glass in *Gunn*'s violent conclusion and the fight scene in Victoria's home in *Sunset* where Tom Mix punches her servant through a glass French door. The two scenes of violence against women in *Alter Ego* are all carried out by Steve believing he has discovered the disgusting truth behind both women and his violent reactions are also linked to the pain meds he takes. These two violent scenes against women who are supposedly hiding their true selves not only formally recall the violence in *Gunn*, but also have another connection in that, in *Gunn*, Daisy Jane is punished for being a lying woman, who is really George Gethers. In other words, none of these brutally punished women are who they appear to be; they are all, like Susan, actresses. The utterly depraved hatred of women in *Alter Ego* also surfaces in the language when Steve calls Janice "a cunt." It is almost unimaginable to hear that word spoken in a Blake Edwards film. Steve may be the alter ego, but he also mirrors the ego.

Edwards manages to concoct a closing scene with a funeral and a wedding, thus explicitly acknowledging his dark destruction of genre conventions in which comedies end with weddings and tragedies with funerals. The screenplay involves several scenes with Tony and Susan filming love scenes in the film they are making. *Alter Ego*'s climax occurs immediately after the above-described scenes when Steve, Tony's stunt double, attempts a planned death-defying stunt by crashing through a window and falling to the ground 35 floors below. In a suicidal frame of mind, Steve insists on filming the scene without the proper safety precautions and the planned presence of cast and crew. There is no safety net and he plunges to his death in slow motion, recalling the deaths in *S.O.B.* and *Wild Rovers*. All the major characters are present at Steve's funeral and, after Susan recovers from her injuries, the film ends with a freeze frame of Tony and Susan at the helm of their boat as "it heads into the setting sun." This is one of the strongest heterosexual couple endings in Edwards's career but it comes at the expense of Steve's life. He commits a form of suicide to get out of the way and enable Tony and Susan to unite. We do not actually see the wedding but it is implicitly clear that they will marry or may even already be married.[5]

During this late period in which Edwards was unable to get funding for his various film and theater projects, he highlighted another extensive part of his creative career, being a painter and sculptor. We begin our brief survey of his art exhibitions with an anecdote about his interest in art which he told us about on the set of one of his films. As a young man, he encountered a Jackson Pollock painting for the first time in his life while visiting a museum. He hated it with unusual intensity. He soon became obsessed with wanting to know why he had such a virulent response to the painting. He returned to the museum again and, after studying the painting carefully, he fell in love with it and Pollock's abstract expressionism. This anecdote reveals much about Edwards as a man who not only took art very seriously but was also deeply contemplative about it, even to the point of entirely changing his mind about the meaning and value of a particular piece. In a review of *The Great Race* in 1965, Andrew Sarris would perceptively point out that a stunning pie fight scene was filmed like an action expressionist painting. The widescreen frame is filled with the pies whizzing by as a character dressed all in white walks through the maze, immaculately emerging without a spot on himself. On the one hand, this is a rare instance of Edwards's filmmaking style being directly influenced by his interest in art while, on the other hand, in *The Man Who Loved Women* (1983), he made an entire film about a sculptor, using his own (Edwards's) sculptures in the film.

The relationship between Edwards's art and his films is complex and not primarily about the connection between the two but, rather, about the differences between them. Most of Edwards's artwork is abstract and entirely non-narrative. All his work in radio, television, film, and theater were about storytelling. But the most profound difference lies in the creative process: all his work in radio, television, film, and theater involved highly collaborative productions including with studios and networks who among other things controlled the budgets. And his ability to continue working in these forms depended upon the box-office success or the ratings his work received. Much of his multi-hyphenate career was spent in adversarial relationships with studio and network executives as he fought for total control of the creative process, from writing through editing in what in film is termed "the final cut." Edwards made entire films about the agonies of that process, including *S.O.B.* about the film industry and *That's Life!* about architecture with an architect who struggles with a client to fulfill his creative vision for the house he is designing. The manner in which he must please the client and work within her budget is analogous to the manner in which a filmmaker must please their studio and audience.

Edwards's studio art, on the other hand, gave him total creative control. He was in that sense an "amateur" painter and he did not need to please art critics or museum curators since he neither intended his work for public exhibition, nor was he primarily concerned with selling his work or soliciting commissions to create a certain kind of work to please the commissioner. When late in his career he finally went public with his work, it had already been created without the conflict surrounding his "professional" work. He may in that sense have been an amateur, but his work was not that of the commonly described amateur "Sunday painter" who takes an easel out into a park or nature setting to relax and peacefully capture the setting. As the Pollock anecdote indicates, he was a very serious, self-taught student of art history who engaged with it in his work. He credited Henry Moore with being a major influence on his sculpture and told us with great delight about the time he was invited by Moore to come to his home and view his backyard sculpture garden. Edwards was overjoyed with seeing the work arranged by the sculptor in that manner. The last time we visited Edwards in his home in Brentwood, he told us that, due to space issues and ease of access, he switched from acrylics to pastels, what he called "crayons." As with his writing, he was painting to the end of his life.

Edwards had three exhibitions of his work between 1988 and 2011. "The Premiere Exhibit of Paintings and Sculpture by Blake Edwards" took place at the Feingarten Galleries in Los Angeles from September 28 to December 31, 1988. Much of the gallery space was devoted to his work, including acrylic canvasses and sculpture. The next exhibition, "The Art of Blake Edwards: A Retrospective of Sculpture and Paintings 1969–2002," took place at the Pacific Design Center in Los Angeles, January 9–30, 2009. The opening night reception hosted by Julie Andrews took place on January 8, 6–8:30pm. This is by far the most major exhibition of his work to date, beautifully curated and filling a large space. The opening night reception was revealing in several ways. It attracted a wide variety of successful creative and executive people in the entertainment industry, including the prominent producer-writers James Hirsch and Robert Papazian from Papazian and Hirsch productions. Much of their best-known work was done for television, including at that time the highly popular cable TV series, *Rome*. They told us they both held Edwards's artwork and his multi-hyphenate, multimedia work in high regard; they were impressed with the exhibition. Film director Peter Bogdanovich was absorbed in intense, careful contemplation of the exhibition, seemingly oblivious of the celebrity crowd around him. These people were not there to be seen but rather to honor Blake Edwards and to see his artwork. Edwards did not make any opening remarks to the group, preferring to speak to the guests who approached one on one.

Unfortunately, Edwards's artwork is currently unavailable to the public. The most important exception is the book *The Art of Blake Edwards*, which was published to accompany the Pacific Design Center Exhibition.[6] The book includes a short critical essay on Edwards's work and over 100 pages of beautiful color plates with examples of all periods of his work, including acrylics, watercolors, and sculpture.

The last exhibition of Edwards's "Lenses" took place at the Leslie Sacks Fine Art Gallery in Los Angeles from June 8 to June 26, 2010 with a VIP Reception for the Artist hosted by Julie Andrews and Leslie Sacks, 4–7pm, June 5, 2010. It was scaled back from the previous one but, once again, the invited guests at the opening reception demonstrated the serious regard many hold for Blake Edwards as an artist. When Peter Lehman was introduced to Frank Gehry, he told him about the time he and Bill Luhr interviewed Milton Wexler, Edwards's psychologist. Edwards had requested that we do the interview and, after it was over, we commented upon a stunning, unusual chair in the office. Wexler told us Frank Gehry had designed it. Edwards moved in privileged circles but he always remained humble about it and the only times we learned about some of these relationships were when he referred to someone to illustrate a point. For example, during a casual conversation with him on a set visit, we commented upon how funny we thought the airport sequence in *Curse of the Pink Panther* was and he told us that André Previn considered it the funniest thing he had ever done. The only way we learned about his relationships with such people as Henry Moore, André Previn, and Frank Gehry was through such references and introductions which he made for us. These three men were part of the world of art, architecture, and music, worlds which intersected with Edwards's extensive and varied career.

During his late period, Edwards was often honored with awards in a manner he seldom had been during his most active years. Although his 2003 Academy of Motion Picture Arts and Sciences Lifetime Achievement Award for writing, producing, and directing was televised and garnered much major media attention, he received several equally prestigious awards from various professional guilds and associations. The Academy Award also highlighted the manner in which Edwards, like such other genre directors as Howard Hawks and Alfred Hitchcock, had never won a Best Director Academy Award. The flurry of awards from this period in general appeared as efforts to make up for long neglect.

The most prestigious of these was the 1993 Preston Sturges Lifetime Achievement Award from the Writers Guild of America West and the Directors Guild of America "in recognition of a career in achievement in filmmaking." Edwards was only the third honoree to receive this award as a writer-director. We were invited to contribute to the event with two publications.[7] Capping a week of screenings and events, Edwards was honored at a gala evening ceremony with guest speakers including Billy Wilder, one of the writer-directors he greatly admired. Yet, Wilder said he was originally not a fan of Edwards's early slapstick hit, *The Pink Panther*, but that Edwards eventually won him over. Geoffrey and Jennifer Edwards, who were introduced as "the keepers of the flame," spoke personally about their father. It was all the more touching to us, therefore, that, after the ceremony when we approached Edwards to congratulate him, he greeted us by saying, "Here come the true keepers of the flame." Earlier in the week, when we were entering the auditorium to see Blake being interviewed, Julie Andrews stopped us to say that she thought our books had played an important role in bringing critical attention to Blake's achievements leading to awards like this. Those comments from Blake and Julie along with our invitations to write the critical analyses of his work accompanying the award were especially meaningful to us since it is commonplace to view academic film studies as part of "the Ivory Tower," separate from the supposed real world of Hollywood. Without ever commenting directly on our work, Blake always implicitly made it clear that he considered our work far more important to him than most of the reviews and media attention he was getting.

In March 2002, Edwards received the Writers Guild of America West Laurel Award recognizing his "more than 50-year screenwriting career." Edwards always considered himself a writer and his success as a director never minimized that. Attending such events often helped us connect with people in Blake's inner circle and it was here that we met and talked with John Ritter, who had starred in *Skin Deep* and was in talks with Blake to star in the theater piece, *Scapegoat*. He asked us if we had seen the script, saying that, if not, we should ask Blake for copies. He thought it was brilliant in a manner that highlighted Blake's work as a writer. Awards like this and conversations with an actor like Ritter made clear that we should devote a portion of this chapter to an overview of Blake's unproduced screenplays and theater scripts. For anyone interested in Edwards's career, they are worth reading.

We first asked Blake Edwards if he would be interested in receiving an honorary degree on the set of *Switch* during a summer visit in 1990. Without missing a beat he quipped, "Well, Julie has one so I think I should have one too." The film *Switch* was released in 1991 and on September 23, 2005, Blake Edwards received an honorary degree, Doctor of Humane Letters, from Arizona State University during a School of Music concert, "A Musical Tribute to Blake Edwards."

The concert featured the University Symphony Orchestra with Monica Mancini, soprano, Michael Dixon, narrator, with narration written by Peter Lehman and William Luhr, and Timothy Russell, conductor. In addition to a musical selection from many of Edwards's most well-known films and television shows, beginning with the theme from *Peter Gunn*, Monica Mancini, Henry Mancini's daughter, sang versions of the most famous songs that her father had written for the films, including, of course, "Moon River." The musical numbers were interspersed with rare video clips of highlights from Edwards's career. After the intermission, Edwards was presented with the honorary degree by President Michael Crow and Peter Lehman. Waiting in the wings as Monica Mancini finished singing a song followed by a video clip of Mancini playing a newly composed theme song which Blake was hearing for the first time, Edwards teared up. He recovered, however, in time for a classic Blake Edwards entry on stage. The presentation was announced as Crow and Lehman stood center stage and the orchestra started playing the music for his entrance. Suddenly, as if in a gag from one of his films, Edwards came shooting out from the wings on a seemingly out of control motor scooter, careening across the stage and finally crashing into the orchestra, causing a cacophony of sound as everyone on the stage looked over in disbelief. Crow and Lehman then walked over to Edwards, lifted him up, smiling, from the midst of the chaotic crash, and escorted him to center stage where he was formally hooded.

The gag meant so much to Edwards that two deans grew nervous during the afternoon rehearsal since the auditorium was rented by the hour. Having watched Edwards develop so many gags during our visits to his sets, we had to explain that he needed some time to quietly structure his idea for his entry during the ceremony. He always improvised those things on the set. The deans then agreed he should be allowed the time he needed and it paid off when the concert audience howled with laughter at the unexpected gag, which even caught Julie Andrews, who was sitting front row center, totally by surprise.

Days before Edwards was to receive the degree, his longtime producer and close friend, Tony Adams, died unexpectedly. At a private memorial honoring Adams in Los Angeles, Peter Lehman had the opportunity to talk with Blake privately before he joined the guests. As he approached Edwards and said, "Hi Blake," without missing a beat the reply came, "Dr. Edwards to you." He said it with a big smile, but it showed not just how much the degree meant to him, but also that he recalled when he told us on the set of *A Fine Mess*, "Call me Blake." Always the formalist and always topping the topper topper. As with his onstage entry at the honorary degree, he always found the humor no matter what the occasion.

That was the last time we both saw Blake Edwards together. On March 29, 2011 we both attended "Blake Edwards: A Celebration," a private memorial in Los Angeles hosted by the Academy of Motion Pictures Arts and Sciences, the Directors Guild of America, and the Writers Guild of America. We stayed afterward to say hello to Julie, whom we had gotten to know on a number of occasions through our work on Blake. She had always shown us the greatest respect and generosity. When we first met her on the set of *A Fine Mess*, she said, "It's a pleasure to meet you. I learned things that I did not know about Blake from your books." As mentioned above, at the Preston

Sturges Lifetime Achievement Award she said she thought that our books contributed to Blake's recognition as a major filmmaker. But she also treated us both as very special. A couple of examples. When we said goodbye on our last day, Peter gave her a slip of paper, asking for her autograph for his daughter for her birthday. She said, "Please give me her address so I can send her something." A large autographed photograph arrived days later. Bill was an honored guest at the ASU Blake Edwards Tribute events. At the dinner before the Honorary Degree ceremony, Peter was seated with President Crow and Blake and Julie while Bill was seated at another table across the room. As soon as Julie saw Bill, she enthusiastically shouted his name and waved at him across the room. This was more than a polite greeting. Whenever either or both of us attended a performance of *Victor/Victoria: The Musical* or *Putting It Together: Musical Revue by Stephen Sondheim*, she greeted us backstage afterward, happy to see us and to chat. We always felt that the movies she made with Blake and her roles in those films were overshadowed by her early films, *Mary Poppins* and *The Sound of Music*, as well as by her Broadway plays. But *Darling Lili, The Tamarind Seed, "10," S.O.B., Victor/Victoria, The Man Who Loved Women*, and *That's Life!* are all major Blake Edwards films and Julie's roles both in them and in bringing them about are central. We can think of no better way to end this book than to acknowledge the privilege we have had in spending so much time watching artists of this caliber work and of getting to know them personally. It is also a reminder of work still to be done. An entire book could be devoted to Blake's work with Julie, including the television work such as the 1992 TV series *Julie*, and the many other TV specials they made together in addition to the documentary *Julie*.

NOTES

1. For a detailed discussion of the place of *Victor/Victoria: The Musical* within the changing history of Broadway film adaptations of Hollywood films, see our essay, *"Victor/Victoria de Blake Edwards: un auteur hollywoodien à Broadway," Alternatives théâtrales*, No. 101 (2009), pp. 74–77. *Victor/Victoria: The Original Broadway Cast Production* is a filmed-for-television Image Entertainment DVD, 1995.

2. For a detailed chapter analysis of the film *Victor/Victoria*, including the extraordinary set design, see William Luhr and Peter Lehman, *Returning to the Scene: Blake Edwards, Volume 2* (Athens: Ohio University Press, 1989), pp. 44–68. For a comparison of the film and play, see Peter Lehman and William

Luhr, *Thinking About Movies: Watching, Questioning, Enjoying, Fourth Edition* (Hoboken, New Jersey: Wiley Blackwell, 2018), pp. 228–229.

3. Kenji Fujishima, "*Victor/Victoria*: The Better Drag Comedy of 1982?", Theatermania.com, March 30, 2021.

4. Peter Lehman and William Luhr, "What Business Does a Critic Have Asking If Blake Edwards Is Gay? Rumor, Scandal, Biography, and Textual Analysis," in *Headline Hollywood: A Century of Film Scandal*, edited by Adrienne McClean and David Cook (New Brunswick: Rutgers University Press, 2001), pp. 253–272.

5. The closing shots in *Alter Ego* recall those in *The Tamarind Seed* with Omar Sharif and Julie Andrews united in Canada and walking hand in hand away from the camera. Once again, even though we do not see a wedding, it is implicit that there will be one.

6. *The Art of Blake Edwards: A Retrospective: Sculpture and Paintings 1969–2002*, curated by Gail Feingarten Oppenheimer, Feingarten Galleries (Beverly Hills: Feingarten Galleries, 2009), including an essay by Peter Clothier, "Blake Edwards: The Artist," pp. 9–19.

7. The 1993 Preston Sturges Lifetime Achievement Award Monograph was written by Peter Lehman and William Luhr and included two articles, "The Survivor: Blake Edwards Writer/Director" and "Laughing Until It Hurts and Laughing Because It Hurts," as well as "Capsule Reviews of Blake Edwards' Films." We were also invited to contribute two articles to a special issue of *DGA News*: "Blake Edwards: Back in the Pink": "Blake Edwards: An Enigma Unto Himself," by William Luhr and Peter Lehman and "In the Pink: On the Set," by Peter Lehman and William Luhr, *DGA News*, Vol. 18, No. 4 (August–September, 1993).

Appendix 1

BOOKS ON BLAKE EDWARDS

Peter Lehman and William Luhr, *Blake Edwards* (Athens: Ohio University Press, 1981).

———, *Blake Edwards* (Los Angeles: Directors Guild of America, 1993). Monograph consisting of two articles and nineteen capsule film reviews on the occasion of Blake Edwards receiving the Preston Sturges Lifetime Achievement Award.

William Luhr and Peter Lehman, *Returning to the Scene: Blake Edwards Volume 2* (Athens: Ohio University Press, 1989).

Gabriella Oldham, editor, *Blake Edwards Interviews* (Jackson: University Press of Mississippi, 2018).

Gail Feingarten Oppenheimer, curator, *The Art of Blake Edwards* (Beverly Hills: Feingarten Galleries, 2009).

Sam Wasson, *A Splurch in the Kisser: The Movies of Blake Edwards* (Middletown, CT: Wesleyan University Press, 2009).

———, *Fifth Avenue, 5 A.M.: Audrey Hepburn, Breakfast at Tiffany's, and the Dawn of the Modern Woman* (New York: HarperCollins, 2011).

BOOKS INCLUDING BLAKE EDWARDS

Julie Andrews, *Home Work: A Memoir of My Hollywood Years, with Emma Walton Hamilton* (New York: Hachette Books, 2019).

Martin Jurow, *Seein' Stars: A Show Biz Odyssey* (Dallas: Southern Methodist Press, 2001).

Blake Edwards: Film Director as Multitalented Auteur, First Edition.
William Luhr and Peter Lehman.
© 2023 John Wiley & Sons Ltd. Published 2023 by John Wiley & Sons Ltd.

Henry Mancini, *Did They Mention the Music? The Autobiography of Henry Mancini* (New York: Cooper Square Press, 2001).

Miriam Nelson, *My Life Dancing With The Stars* (Albany, Georgia: BearManor Media, 2015).

Steven Ribyn, *Playful Frames: Styles of Widescreen Cinema* (New Brunswick: Rutgers University Press, 2023).

BOOK CHAPTERS ON BLAKE EDWARDS

Peter Clothier, "Blake Edwards: The Artist," in *The Art of Blake Edwards,* curated by Gail Feingarten Oppenheimer (Beverly Hills: Feingarten Galleries, 2009), pp. 9–17.

Peter Lehman and William Luhr, "'I Love New York!': *Breakfast at Tiffany's,*" in *New York: City That Never Sleeps,* edited by Murray Pomerance (New Brunswick: Rutgers University Press, 2007), pp. 23–32.

———, "What Business Does a Critic Have Asking If Blake Edwards Is Gay? Rumor, Scandal, Biography, and Textual Analysis," in *Headline Hollywood: A Century of Film Scandal,* edited by Adrienne McClean and David Cook (New Brunswick: Rutgers University Press, 2001), pp. 253–272.

———, "Dreaming and Thinking: *S.O.B.* and Its Relationship to Blake Edwards's Genre Films," in *The Kingdom of Dreams*, edited by Douglas Fowler (Tallahassee: Florida State University Press, 1986), pp. 21–39.

William Luhr and Peter Lehman, "Experiment in Terror: Dystopian Modernism, Film Noir, and the Space of Anxiety," in *Cinema and Modernity*, edited by Murray Pomerance (New Brunswick: Rutgers University Press, 2006), pp. 175–194.

———, "Writing a Biography of Blake Edwards," in *Biography and Source Studies,* edited by Frederick R. Karl (New York: AMS Press, 1998), pp. 71–86.

Appendix 2: The Interviews

Tony Adams, 1989
Julie Andrews, August 7, 1992
Ellen Barkin, June 8, 1990
Roberto Benigni, August, 1992
Max Bercutt, 1989
Owen Crump, December 14, 1987
Ted Danson, 1985
Joe Dunne, May 30, 1991
Jennifer Edwards, August 4, 1992
James Garner, 1987
Lindsey Jones, 1987
Michael Kidd, 1994
Burt Kwouk, August, 1992
John Larroquette, June, 1989
Jack Lemmon, July, 1986
Alan Levine, June 6, 1990
Herbert Lom, August 7, 1992
Henry Mancini, November 6, 1987
Rodger Maus, July 3, 1990
Elton McPherson, June 7, 1990
Peter Mullins, August 8, 1992
Miriam Nelson, November 6, 1987
Michael Nouri, June 15, 2011
Richard Quine, June 21, 1984
John Ritter, 1993
Tony Roberts, June, 1995
Gene Schwam, June 8, 2011
Alexis Smith, December 13, 1987

Blake Edwards: Film Director as Multitalented Auteur, First Edition.
William Luhr and Peter Lehman.
© 2023 John Wiley & Sons Ltd. Published 2023 by John Wiley & Sons Ltd.

Jimmy Smits, June 7, 1990
Graham Stark, August 5, 1992
Craig Stevens, December 6, 1987
Peter Strauss, March 22, 2023
Francine Taylor, August 7, 1992
Robert Wagner, January 28, 2019
Ken Wales, June 23, June 30, and July 8, 2011
Milton Wexler, 1988
Richard Williams, October 15, 2003
Bruce Willis, 1987

Our Published Interviews with Blake Edwards

Peter Lehman and William Luhr, "'Too Much to Do, Not Enough Time to Do It': An Interview with Blake Edwards," *Wide Angle*, Vol. 3, No. 3 (1979), pp. 48–56.

Peter Lehman and William Luhr, "'I Write on What I Know': Interview with Blake Edwards," in *Blake Edwards Interviews*, edited by Gabriella Oldham (Jackson: University Press of Mississippi, 2018), pp. 69–88.

Index

Page numbers: Figures given in *italics*.

Blake Edwards: Film Director as Multitalented Auteur, First Edition.
William Luhr and Peter Lehman.
© 2023 John Wiley & Sons Ltd. Published 2023 by John Wiley & Sons Ltd.